THE CONSTITUTION

DEMANDS IT

P9-DFR-978

RON FEIN · JOHN BONIFAZ
BEN CLEMENTS

★ ★ ★ ★ ★ ★ THE ★ ★ ★ ★ ★ ★

CONSTITUTION
DEMANDS IT

THE CASE FOR
THE IMPEACHMENT OF
DONALD TRUMP

"Read this book to learn how best to protect
our democracy." —**Tom Steyer**

Foreword by JOHN NICHOLS

★ ★ ★ ★ ★ ★ ★ ★ ★ ★ ★ ★ ★ ★ ★

🏠 MELVILLE HOUSE
BROOKLYN · LONDON

THE CONSTITUTION DEMANDS IT

First Melville House Printing: August 2018

Melville House Publishing   Suite 2000
46 John Street   and   16/18 Woodford Road
Brooklyn, NY 11201   London E7 0HA

mhpbooks.com
@melvillehouse

ISBN: 978-1-61219-763-0
ISBN: 978-1-61219-764-7 (eBook)

Designed by Fritz Metsch

Printed in the United States of America
1 3 5 7 9 10 8 6 4 2

A catalog record for this book is available
from the Library of Congress

The President, Vice President and all civil Officers of the United States, shall be removed from Office on Impeachment for, and Conviction of, Treason, Bribery, or other high Crimes and Misdemeanors.

—UNITED STATES CONSTITUTION
(ARTICLE II, SECTION 4)

CONTENTS

FOREWORD

"My faith in the Constitution is whole; it is complete; it is total. And I am not going to sit here and be an idle spectator to the diminution, the subversion, the destruction, of the Constitution."

Texas Congresswoman Barbara Jordan,
Statement on the Articles of Impeachment
(July 25, 1974)

Impeachment is *not* a constitutional crisis.

Impeachment is the cure for a constitutional crisis.

Like any antidote, it must be employed judiciously. When the crisis arises, however, patriots cannot be cautious about utilizing the strong medicine that was conjured in the summer of 1787 by the authors of a constitution that was written with an eye toward averting the elected despotism of a president who might conspire to make himself "a king for four years."

The wisest of the delegates who gathered in Philadelphia, just four years after their rebellion had seen off the rule of King George III, were well aware that their imprecise efforts might forge not just a new nation but a new approach to governing. They well recognized the vulnerabilities of a project that experimented, however tentatively, with the revolutionary prospect of democracy. They worried, as Lincoln would decades later, about "whether that nation, or any nation so conceived, and so dedicated, can long endure." Above all, they recognized that their project of replacing the rule of man with the rule of law would be threatened by what George Mason described as the "easy step to hereditary Monarchy." To avert it, Mason warned, "No point is of more importance than that the right of impeachment should be continued."

It would, Mason suggested, provide an eternal answer to questions that plagued the convention as it pondered the presidency: "Shall any man be above Justice? Above all shall that man be above it, who can commit the most extensive injustice?"

Mason placed his faith in a rigorous system of checks and balances that was enforced, ultimately and definitively, by the power of the U.S. House of Representatives to impeach a president whose continued tenure threatened the republic, and of the United States Senate to remove the offending officeholder.

Impeachment was never meant to be about crimes and punishments. It was intended at the founding of the American experiment, and should be so understood today, as a remedy for the monarchical tendencies of men who answer Mason's questions differently than did the Virginian and his compatriots.

Donald Trump is such a man.

In the spring of 2018, as the 45th president of the United States and his legal minions scrambled to limit the scope of questioning of the commander-in-chief by special counsel Robert Mueller, Trump revealed himself. He insisted that the deputizing of a veteran lawman as an investigator of monumental concerns regarding manipulation of the electoral and governing processes by foreign powers was "totally UNCONSTITUTIONAL!" Trump claimed that he cooperated with the inquiry not out of respect for the laws of the land but because he chose to do so as one who claimed to "have done nothing wrong." At the same time, Trump asserted that he retained an "absolute right" to pardon himself should the heat of official scrutiny grow too intense.

These were not the words of a Democrat or a Republican. They were monarchical words, uttered by a man whose tenure had strained even the most liberal interpretations of executive authority. Now, this man was asserting that he was above justice. And, yes, he was doing so as the man who, by

virtue of his position, could commit the most extensive injustice.

These are the rough outlines of the constitutional crisis that
the founders feared. Our contemporary media and political
elites recognize its contours. They know the sickness is upon
us. Yet, they choose, out of quivering fear and overwhelming
incomprehension, to reject the constitutional remedy. After
too many years of making too many apologies for an imperial presidency, too many of those who define our discourse
have lost any real sense of the anti-royalist "spirit of '76" that
Jefferson asserted in his final letter should forever serve as
"the Signal of arousing men to burst the chains, under which
monkish ignorance and superstition had persuaded them to
bind themselves, and to assume the blessings and security of
self-government."

The author of the Declaration of Independence was a flawed
man who can be criticized for missteps and misdeeds—as can
all of the founders. Yet Jefferson, a man of the world who had
traveled more broadly than his revolutionary co-conspirators,
was surely right to assert that ignorance could bind not just
human beings but nations. If we do not recognize the threat
posed by a president who imagines himself to be above the
law, or by those who suggest that this man's tenure may not be
interrupted by the subpoenas and the investigations and legal
requirements that demand the respect of all other Americans,
then surely we have abandoned the most basic premises of the
American experiment.

The authors of this vital text refuse to accept so perilous a
surrender. They seek to burst the chains of our contemporary
superstitions regarding impeachment and to restore a proper
understanding of its role in maintaining the right balance of
American governance. Misguided people who imagine that
liberty and justice for all can long survive in a circumstance
where a president places himself above the law fret about the
political consequences of addressing a constitutional crisis with

a constitutional remedy. They foolishly imagine that it is better to wait a lawless presidency out, with faint hope for better results on some distant election day. They refuse to recognize that each failure to demand necessary accountability invites greater abuse and diminishes the prospect that accountability will ever be achieved. When human beings who are ailing receive prescriptions for curing medications and then refuse to take those medications, we are horrified because we know that these choices may lead to their deaths. What we must understand is that republics are similarly vulnerable. They, too, can die for lack of proper treatment in moments of emergency.

Ron Fein, John Bonifaz, and Ben Clements recognize our predicament, and they call out for us to address it with the courage of a nation that seeks to heal itself. They do not do this for purposes of politics—indeed, politicians for the most part fear impeachment. Nor do they do this for purposes of achieving power—as these authors are dissenters who have frequently sacrificed gain in order to assert constitutional certainties that they know to be true.

The authors of this book have been about the business of defending the Constitution for many decades now. They know of what they speak, especially in matters of presidential accountability. They choose their words deliberately, with an understanding of the social and political demands that attend any call for an impeachment process—and of the particular demands that attend a call for an impeachment process that would hold to account so unprecedented and so reckless a figure as Donald Trump. They are precise in their assessment of the high crimes and misdemeanors that might form the basis for this process. And they are equally precise in their explanation of its urgency.

Just as George Mason answered his essential questions of 1787 with an argument that the power of impeachment must be outlined in the Constitution, so Fein, Bonifaz, and Clements answer the essential questions of 2018 and 2019 about the application of that power. They recognize and respect legal inquiries into alleged wrongdoing by the president and his associates. Yet, they remind us that impeachment is a political process—not a legal one—and that it must play out in the Congress as opposed to the courts. They assert, correctly, that the Congress does not need wait for Robert Mueller to finish a report, or for Donald Trump to pardon those who might be implicated—up to and including himself. Sufficient evidence of wrongdoing has already been assembled to justify—indeed, to demand—the opening of a congressional investigation into whether this president shall be impeached.

As the evidence is sufficient—and no reasonable observer would deny that it is—then why not simply pen the articles of impeachment and do the deed immediately? It is in the answering of this question that Fein, Bonifaz, and Clements display their genius, and the genius of this book.

Impeachment is best understood, they remind us, as a process with many moving pieces. It is not the work of one man or woman, not the project of a moment. Rather, it is an expansive undertaking that works best when it draws many voices into a serious conversation about wrongdoing and accountability.

There is nothing wrong with individual members of the House proposing articles of impeachment. Some of the most honorable members in the long history of the chamber—Father Robert Drinan of Massachusetts, Pete McCloskey of California, Bella Abzug of New York, Henry B. González of Texas—have done just that. Some of the most honorable members of the 115th Congress (including Steve Cohen, the Tennessee Democrat who serves as the ranking member of the House Judiciary Subcommittee on the Constitution and Civil Justice) have done the same. The current initiatives serve a purpose; they outline appropriate objections and remind Americans that at least some members of Congress are fully prepared to honor their oaths to "support and defend the Constitution of the United States against all enemies, foreign and domestic." But it is unlikely that the articles already proposed will form a final congressional indictment against Donald J. Trump.

The articles that might accomplish this necessary work are most likely to emanate from the House Judiciary Committee. There is a reason for this, and it is not just a matter of following the traditions and utilizing the infrastructure of the Congress.

Because impeachment is a political process, it must develop in the political context of a Congress made up of members who are not always courageous, who are invariably calculating and who are easily distracted in even the most urgent of circumstances. Three presidents have been seriously targeted for impeachment by the House. Two were impeached, and then acquitted by the Senate. One was at the brink of impeachment—following the decision of the House Judiciary Committee to support three indicting articles—and chose to remove himself before trial. There are those who argue that the resignation of Richard Nixon upended the impeachment process, but anyone who understands the point of a system of checks and balances will recognize the absurdity of this claim.

Nixon was threatened with impeachment and removed himself—thus ending his abuses of power and restoring the proper functioning of the office of the presidency. By any reasonable measure, that was a successful application of the constitutional remedy. Keep in mind that the point of impeachment has always been to address the abuses of executive authority that might see a president assume the mantle of an "elected despot." Whether a president is impeached and convicted or simply resigns in order to avoid inevitable impeachment and conviction, the constitutional crisis has been cured.

Thus, the American who can most justifiably be said to have continued the right of impeachment as George Mason and his compatriots intended is Peter Rodino, the former chairman of the House Judiciary Committee who, upon his death at age

ninety-five, was recalled by *The New York Times* as "an obscure
congressman from the streets of Newark who impressed the
nation by the dignity, fairness and firmness he showed as
chairman of the impeachment hearings that induced Richard
M. Nixon to resign as president."

Rodino was a Democrat and Nixon was a Republican.
Rodino's Democrats had majorities in the House and Senate
in 1974. Yet, the savvy veteran of the rough-and-tumble politics of New Jersey's Essex County well understood that, in
order to hold Nixon to account, he was going to need cautious
House Democrats and skeptical House Republicans to accept
the necessity of impeachment. This wasn't about building
a narrow coalition in order to clear the constitutional hur-
dles of a simple majority vote in the House and a two-thirds
supermajority in the Senate. This was about building a case
that was convincing to the American people. The case that
Rodino and his Judiciary Committee colleagues crafted over
many months, with hearings that entertained a wide range
of offenses but finally focused on a few of the most egregious
wrongs, was sufficiently compelling to secure Republican
support for three articles of impeachment and to send Nixon
packing.

These are different times. There are plenty of pundits and
politicians who now assert that our partisanships have become so great that even a Peter Rodino could not make an
impeachment process work. If that is the case, then the United
States has not continued the right of impeachment as a whole
instrument of the Constitution. The licensing words may remain in the document, but they are merely assertions of an
ideal—not a practical tool for making real the founding promise of accountability for errant executives.

If we have reached such a point of compromise, then the
American experiment is finished. Donald Trump may be
voted out of office after one term. Or he may retire after two.
Better presidents may come. Or worse. But the vision that

ours would be a government of laws, not men, will be finished. We will, like the monarchies of old, be able to hope for no more than a "good king." We will be more akin to the monarchies of old, which might have produced a "Bad King John" or a "Good King Richard," but that always had kings. And those kinds ruled by "divine right," rejecting the rule of law in favor of rule by fiat—just as Donald Trump does when he suggests he cooperates with inquiries not out of respect for the rule of law but because it occurs to him that he has "done nothing wrong."

This new America with its diminished system of checks and balances, where impeachment is never an option, will not be a formal monarchy. Jurists may still prattle on about statutory requirements, and those requirements will undoubtedly be applied to citizens. But those requirements will no longer be applied to the executive branch, which will go from bad to worse; on a downward spiral of imperial presidents where good commanders-in-chief are the exceptions that prove the rule. The failure of Congress to hold Ronald Reagan and George H. W. Bush to account for their Iran-Contra transgressions cleared the way for George W. Bush and Dick Cheney to engage in far more destructive transgressions in Iraq. A failure to hold Donald Trump to account for his lawlessness all but guarantees that a more lawless president will eventually occupy the Oval Office. To think otherwise is to engage in the cruelest of fantasies.

This book rejects fantasy. It chooses the realism of long-settled history over the conjecture of a chaotic present. Taking the long view is rarely rewarded in these times of "instant analysis." But it is the only view that provides us with the hope of righting the ship of state for more than a passing moment. This book outlines a serious vision for renewing the system of checks and balances, not merely to hold Donald Trump to account but to restore the basic premises of accountability

that were embedded in the Constitution by the founders—
and that have been preserved by true patriots in even the most
daunting of times.

The patriots who have contributed to these pages propose
nothing more radical than a reconnection with the deepest
understandings from the summer of 1787, and from the summer of 1974. They recognize the necessity of wielding the
awesome power of impeachment with the "solemnness" that
Congresswoman Barbara Jordan described on July 25, 1974.

An African-American lawyer and legislator born and raised
in the segregated Texas of "Jim Crow" times, she was serving
her initial term in the U.S. House of Representatives as the first
African-American woman ever elected from the Deep South.
Now, Jordan sat on the Judiciary Committee as "an inquisitor"
charged with determining the fate of a president who had only
recently been reelected with 61 percent of the vote and a 520–17
Electoral College landslide.

"Earlier today, we heard the beginning of the Preamble to
the Constitution of the United States: 'We, the people.' It's a
very eloquent beginning," she told her colleagues. "But when
that document was completed on the seventeenth of September in 1787, I was not included in that 'We, the people.' I felt
somehow for many years that George Washington and Alexander Hamilton just left me out by mistake. But through the
process of amendment, interpretation, and court decision, I
have finally been included in 'We, the people.'"

There was perfection in the language that Barbara Jordan chose on that historic day. She took hold of the right of
impeachment and made it what it should always have been:
the possession of every American. Every American. And she
declared that this right must have meaning, not merely in history but in the present.

"James Madison, again at the Constitutional Convention,
[said]: 'A President is impeachable if he attempts to subvert the

Constitution.' The Constitution charges the President with the task of taking care that the laws be faithfully executed," she explained, "and yet the President has counseled his aides to commit perjury, willfully disregard the secrecy of grand jury proceedings, conceal surreptitious entry, attempt to compromise a federal judge, while publicly displaying his cooperation with the processes of criminal justice."

Jordan repeated Madison's words: "A President is impeachable if he attempts to subvert the Constitution." Wearing the armor of history, she explained why the standard would need to be applied to Richard Nixon's sins against the republic. "If the impeachment provision in the Constitution of the United States will not reach the offenses charged here," said Jordan, "then perhaps that 18th-century Constitution should be abandoned to a 20th-century paper shredder!"

Those are words as wise as any handed down from George Mason or James Madison or Thomas Jefferson. They form an impression of the impeachment power as we today must recognize it. So, too, does Jordan's willingness in so charged a moment to maintain the right of impeachment.

"Has the President committed offenses, and planned, and directed, and acquiesced in a course of conduct which the Constitution will not tolerate? That's the question," explained the congresswoman. "We know that. We know the question. We should now forthwith proceed to answer the question. It is reason, and not passion, which must guide our deliberations, guide our debate, and guide our decision."

The authors of this book speak a historic language when they demand that Congress ask again: "Has the President committed offenses, and planned, and directed, and acquiesced in a course of conduct which the Constitution will not tolerate?" This is a book that extends from the founding moment of 1787 through the accountability moment of 1974 to the urgent moment of today. It demands more of us than many of our ancestors were willing to provide the republic. But not more than George Mason demanded. Not more than Barbara Jordan demanded. Not more than solemn and sincere patriotism has always demanded of us.

We do know the question that extends from the right of impeachment. And if the Constitution is to remain full in its meaning and its promise, then we should now forthwith proceed to answer the question.

JOHN NICHOLS
June 8, 2018

John Nichols, the national affairs correspondent for *The Nation*, has covered impeachments and impeachment movements for decades. He is the author of the 2006 book *The Genius of Impeachment: The Founders' Cure for Royalism,* for which author Gore Vidal wrote the introduction. In 2007, he appeared on the historic *Bill Moyers Journal* broadcast "Tough Talk on Impeachment with Bruce Fein and John Nichols."

PREFACE

President Donald Trump has been violating the Constitution since the moment he took the oath of office—and since then, the corruption, abuse of power, and abuse of public trust have only gotten worse. The purpose of this book is to provide the factual and legal basis for why Congress should begin impeachment hearings to protect our constitutional democracy— and to show what you can do to help.

We begin by summarizing the basic constitutional and legal principles of impeachment—the purpose, the standard, and the process. But the heart of the book is the discussion of the major grounds for impeachment hearings. After a review of the publicly available facts and the legal principles underlying impeachment, we have identified eight categories where Trump has already crossed the line into impeachable territory. These eight grounds are:

1. Accepting unconstitutional foreign and domestic government emoluments;
2. Conspiring to solicit and then conceal illegal foreign assistance for his presidential campaign;
3. Obstructing justice;
4. Directing law enforcement to investigate and prosecute political adversaries and critics for improper purposes;
5. Abusing the pardon power;
6. Advocating illegal violence and undermining equal protection of the laws;

7. Reckless endangerment by threatening nuclear war; and
8. Undermining the freedom of the press.

Several of these eight grounds overlap with criminal offenses
(e.g., obstruction of justice), others involve violations of specific
but noncriminal prohibitions (e.g., receiving unconstitutional
emoluments), and still others do not violate any specific textual prohibition at all, but involve abuses of presidential power
(e.g., abuse of law enforcement power to harass adversaries).
The factual summaries of the grounds for impeachment are
based on publicly reported facts, including statements made
by Trump himself, and testimony to Congress, as of the date
of this writing.

The U.S. House of Representatives nearly always chooses to
investigate impeachment charges as the first step. For some of
the eight grounds that we have listed, there is already a "prima
facie" case—evidence sufficient to prove the case unless and
until contradicted—but the committee might benefit from
calling fact witnesses and subpoenaing documents to round
out the factual record. For others, the central facts are already
known, and the question for these hearings will be: Why is
this an impeachable offense? While that is ultimately for Congress to decide, this book lays the legal case for why each of
these eight grounds constitutes an impeachable offense, based
on the text, structure, and history of the Constitution and federal law, as well as precedent. We also discuss potential emerging new grounds based on currently known facts. (Of course,
even more may emerge with time.)

Finally, we summarize next steps: why Congress does not
need to wait for pending civil or criminal cases to play out to
their conclusion, but rather can and should start impeachment
hearings now, and how citizens can help make that happen.

As we will show, Donald Trump was in violation of the
Constitution from the moment he swore the oath of office.
But Members of Congress also swear an oath of office—not

to Trump, nor to the leaders of their caucuses, but to support and defend the Constitution. And for a president as dangerous as Trump, the Constitution demands impeachment hearings.

RON FEIN,
Legal Director, Free Speech For People

JOHN BONIFAZ,
President, Free Speech For People

BEN CLEMENTS,
Chair, Board of Directors, Free Speech For People

June 2018

Free Speech For People is a nonpartisan, nonprofit organization, founded in 2010, dedicated to reclaiming democracy and the Constitution.

To join our impeachment campaign, please visit the site www.impeachmentproject.org. To learn more about Free Speech For People's other work, please visit www.freespeech forpeople.org.

INTRODUCTION

In 1970, Representative (later President) Gerald Ford quipped that "an impeachable offense is whatever a majority of the House of Representatives considers it to be at a given moment in history."[1] That might be an accurate empirical description of how Congress operates. But fidelity to the Constitution requires more.

The Constitution provides that "[t]he President, Vice President and all civil Officers of the United States, shall be removed from Office on Impeachment for, and Conviction of, Treason, Bribery, or other high Crimes and Misdemeanors."[2] Treason and bribery are clear enough. But what are "high Crimes and Misdemeanors"?

The framers of the Constitution settled on this language after first considering and rejecting various alternatives, including a narrower alternative that would have only allowed impeachment for treason and bribery, and a broader alternative that would have allowed impeachment for mere "maladministration."[3] The phrase "high Crimes and Misdemeanors" is a term of art that the framers understood from English history. Unfortunately, it did not come with a precise definition.[4] Yet the general contours are well established.

Part of the answer comes from founding-era sources, such as the debates at the Constitutional Convention in Philadelphia in 1787; the Federalist Papers, a collection of essays written by leading founders to persuade skeptics in the states to ratify the new Constitution; debates in state ratifying conventions; and contemporaneous writings. For example, in the Federalist Papers,

Alexander Hamilton described impeachable offenses as arising from "the misconduct of public men, or in other words from the abuse or violation of some public trust."[5] They are, Hamilton explained, "of a nature which may with peculiar propriety be denominated POLITICAL, as they relate chiefly to injuries done immediately to the society itself."[6] Other parts of the answer come from the structure of our constitutional government, and Congress's own findings and precedent in various impeachment proceedings over more than two centuries of history.

Putting all these together, constitutional law scholars have provided slightly different explanations of the phrase "high Crimes and Misdemeanors," but their definitions share several themes: "offenses (1) which are extremely serious, (2) which in some way corrupt or subvert the political and governmental process, and (3) which are plainly wrong in themselves to a person of honor, or to a good citizen, regardless of words on the statute books";[7] or "illegal acts of a serious kind and magnitude and also acts that, whether or not technically illegal, amount to an egregious abuse of office";[8] or offenses that "involve corruption, betrayal, or an abuse of power that subverts core tenets of the US governmental system."[9] Similarly, in 1974, the House Judiciary Committee's impeachment inquiry staff produced a highly regarded report on *Constitutional Grounds for Presidential Impeachment*. This report, examining past congressional impeachments, divided the themes of the offenses into "three broad categories: (1) exceeding the constitutional bounds of the powers of the office, in derogation of the powers of another branch of government; (2) behaving in a manner grossly incompatible with the proper function and purpose of the office; and (3) employing the power of the office for an improper purpose or for personal gain."[10] For our purposes, any of these formulations will do; the differences between the abstractions tend to melt away when confronting specific grounds.

Contrary to a common misunderstanding, "high Crimes and Misdemeanors" need not be criminal offenses.[11] While this point may surprise some readers, it is well supported in the constitutional record and by congressional precedent since the founding, and it is broadly accepted among constitutional scholars.[12] As the renowned early-nineteenth-century commentator and U.S. Supreme Court justice Joseph Story explained:

> The offences, to which the power of impeachment has been, and is ordinarily applied, as a remedy, are of a political character. Not but that crimes of a strictly legal character fall within the scope of the power, (for, as we shall presently see, treason, bribery, and other high crimes and misdemeanors are expressly within it;) but that it has a more enlarged operation, and reaches, what are aptly termed, political offences, growing out of personal misconduct, or gross neglect, or usurpation, or habitual disregard of the public interests, in the discharge of the duties of political office.[13]

On the eve of impeachment proceedings against President Richard Nixon, Professor Charles Black observed that "the limitation of impeachable offenses to those offenses made generally criminal by statute is unwarranted—even absurd."[14] And during the impeachment proceedings against President Bill Clinton, Professor Laurence Tribe agreed that it was "all but universally agreed that an offense need not be a violation of criminal law at all in order for it to be impeachable as a high crime or misdemeanor."[15]

The types of presidential conduct that would violate no criminal law but nonetheless be grounds for impeachment are not precisely defined, but they fall into several rough categories. An often-repeated hypothetical is deliberate and complete neglect of duty—not mere "maladministration," but rather gross neglect, such as a president "who completely neglects his duties by showing up at work intoxicated every day, or by lounging on the beach rather than signing bills."[16] More importantly, *gross misuse of official power* may be impeachable. This is a category in which the president uses a legitimate presidential power in a grossly inappropriate way. For example, the president has the power to pardon crimes, but, in Professor Black's classic example, it would be impeachable for a president to "announce and follow a policy of granting full pardons, in advance of indictment or trial, to all federal agents or police who killed anybody in line of duty, in the District of Columbia, whatever the circumstances and however unnecessary the killing."[17]

An important part of the distinction between ordinary crimes and "high Crimes and Misdemeanors" is that the purpose of impeachment is not to *punish*, but to *protect* the body politic. We remove a lawless president to prevent him from further harming the country via the *"prospective* tainting of the presidency."[18] Even for the specifically enumerated impeachable offenses of treason and bribery, "[s]o far as *punishment* goes, we could punish a traitorous or corrupt president after his term expired; we *remove* him principally because we fear he will do it again, or because a traitor or the taker of a bribe is not thinkable as a national leader."[19] In Justice Story's words, impeachment "is not so much designed to punish an offender, as to *secure the state* against gross official misdemeanors."[20]

Another reason that "high Crimes and Misdemeanors" do not correspond precisely to ordinary crimes is that the president has unique powers that give rise to unique opportunities for abuse. Even if Congress thought it was a worthwhile use of time to pass a lengthy set of criminal statutes that only apply to the president, it could never anticipate all the possibilities for abuse of the office. As Justice Story observed, impeachable offenses "are so various in their character, and so indefinable in their actual involutions, that it is almost impossible to provide systematically for them by positive law."[21]

This understanding is supported by over two centuries of congressional practice from impeachment proceedings against three presidents and dozens of federal judges.[22] Many past impeachments have included conduct that does not violate *any* criminal statute. As Congress itself has explained, "[t]he House and Senate have both interpreted the phrase broadly, finding that impeachable offenses need not be limited to criminal conduct. Congress has repeatedly defined 'other high Crimes and Misdemeanors' to be serious violation of the public trust, not necessarily indictable offenses under criminal laws."[23] Indeed, "[m]any of the impeachments approved by the House of Representatives have included conduct that did not involve criminal activity. Less than a third have specifically invoked a criminal statute or used the term 'crime.'"[24]

By the same token, not all crimes meet the threshold of "high Crimes and Misdemeanors." For example, a president who takes a car out for a spin with an expired license and causes an accident would probably not be subject to impeachment. The 1974 Nixon impeachment inquiry's report on *Constitutional Grounds for Presidential Impeachment* concluded that impeachable conduct must meet a "substantiality" requirement: "conduct seriously incompatible with either the constitutional form and principles of our government or the proper performance of constitutional duties of the presidential office."[25]

Since not all impeachable offenses violate criminal laws, and not all criminal offenses are impeachable, we can visualize the relationship something like this:

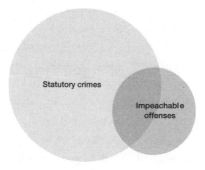

This diagram will be helpful to keep in mind while reading the grounds presented here. Some of the grounds, such as obstruction of justice, correspond to specific criminal violations. For those grounds, the text of criminal statutes, and judicial precedent that has arisen from past criminal cases, can be a helpful guide in understanding what criminal jeopardy the president may face. Yet the impeachable offense of "obstruction of justice" is not *quite* identical to the federal crimes under the "obstruction of justice" heading. The questions that Congress must ask in an impeachment proceeding are different from those that a prosecutor must ask.

In other cases, grounds for impeachment hearings arise from a specific textual provision of law, such as the Constitution's Foreign Emoluments Clause, and the violation is an impeachable offense, but not a *criminal* offense. And in still other cases, grounds for impeachment hearings arise from abuse of presidential power or public trust, such as abuse of the pardon power, that does not neatly correspond to any specific textual prohibition. Yet in all of these cases, "the crucial factor is not the intrinsic quality of behavior but the significance of its effect upon our constitutional system or the functioning of our government."[26]

The distinction between *violations of the criminal code* that can lead to criminal indictments, prosecution, and conviction, and the *high crimes and misdemeanors* that can lead to impeachment and removal from office, is especially important when, as now, a criminal investigation is underway. In President Trump's case, Special Counsel Robert Mueller or other prosecutors may uncover evidence pertinent to an impeachment inquiry, but much of the evidence is already available. And under the Constitution, the House's power and decision to impeach is entirely separate from prosecutorial authority. The House may approve articles of impeachment even without an indictable criminal offense. Indeed, in 1989, Judge Alcee Hastings was impeached and convicted by the Senate

for obstruction of justice and conspiracy to accept bribes—
*even though a federal jury had already acquitted him of some of
those same offenses.*[27] The impeachment inquiry and prosecutors' investigations are bound by different rules—in the
words of leading framer (and later Supreme Court justice)
James Wilson, they are "founded on different principles, are
governed by different maxims, and are directed to different
objects"[28]—and should proceed on separate tracks.

★   ★   ★

Impeachment is not the end of the process—it is just the
beginning.

The Constitution distinguishes "impeachment" from
"conviction." Impeachment is essentially a formal accusa-
tion—a decision to bring charges. The Constitution provides
that the House decides whether and on what grounds to impeach, and then the Senate holds a trial.[29]

Since the founding of the republic, the House has started
dozens of impeachment proceedings—three against presidents, more than sixty against federal judges, and two against
other officials. Of these, nineteen individuals were impeached
by the House; sixteen proceeded through a full Senate trial;
and eight (all judges) were convicted by the Senate.[30] But this
number understates the total number of officials who have
left office owing to impeachment. Several judges, and one
president (Richard Nixon), decided not to wait out the full
impeachment process—they resigned partway through.[31]

The Constitution does not impose any particular procedure on how the House may go about its decision. The actual vote to impeach must be made by a majority vote, like
any other bill. But the process *before* that vote comes from the
House's own internal rules and precedent.

Generally, the House prefers to assign a committee to investigate charges first—typically, the Judiciary Committee.[32]
The Judiciary Committee has the power to subpoena wit-

nesses and documents in the course of its investigation. The Committee must consider not only evidentiary matters, but also "whether the acts shown probably to have been committed are 'impeachable' within the meaning of the constitutional text."[33] The ultimate question for the Committee is whether "one or more impeachable offenses are shown with sufficient clarity to justify trial."[34]

The Committee has wide flexibility in crafting proposed articles of impeachment. Unlike a criminal indictment, for articles of impeachment there is no requirement that "an official's course of conduct must be divided into offenses, and then each offense must be judged separately as to whether it is impeachable."[35] Rather, "[a]lthough the House has returned multi-count impeachments in the past, it has been well understood that the official's course of conduct as a whole should be the subject of judgment."[36] In fact, "[i]n the early impeachments, the articles were not prepared until after impeachment had been voted by the House, and it seems probable that the decision to impeach was made on the basis of all the allegations viewed as a whole, rather than each separate charge."[37] As John Labovitz, who had served as staff counsel on the House Judiciary Committee's Nixon impeachment inquiry, wrote in 1978:

> The most pertinent precedent in this nation's history for framing a case for the removal of a chief executive may well be the earliest—the Declaration of Independence. In expressing reasons for throwing off the government of George III, the Continental Congress did not claim that there had been a single offense justifying revolution. Instead, it pointed to a course of conduct . . . It was this pattern of wrongdoing taken together, not each specification considered alone, that showed the unfitness of George III to be the ruler of the American people. Impeachment, to be sure, is hardly revolution, and a president is not a king. But the unfitness of a president

to continue in office is to be judged in much the same way: with reference to totality of his conduct and the common patterns that emerge, not in terms of whether this or that act of wrongdoing, viewed in isolation, is an impeachable offense.[38]

The important point is that, *together*, the offenses form "patterns that turn individually troubling acts into a dangerous abuse of office."[39] For example, in the first article of impeachment against President Richard Nixon, the Judiciary Committee combined nine distinct offenses (each of which was arguably individually impeachable) into *one* article with nine paragraphs or "specifications."[40] The Committee decided that those offenses presented a stronger case for an impeachable offense when combined into a single article. In fact, the House has often found it useful to include "'catch-all' or 'omnibus'" articles, which may enable it to "combine charges, restating facts and rewording allegations from separate articles, in hopes of gaining two-thirds support of the senators to convict."[41]

Ultimately, the Judiciary Committee takes a vote on whether to report articles to the full House. If the Judiciary Committee reports articles of impeachment, then the next step is a full House vote. (President Nixon resigned at this point.) The House can approve some or all of the articles by simple majority. And if the House votes to approve one or more articles of impeachment, the official has been impeached.

But the process is far from over. After the House votes to impeach, then the Senate conducts a trial. The House appoints "managers," who act like prosecutors, to present the charges in the Senate. The impeached official can present his own legal defense. The procedures in the Senate come from rules, practices, and the senators' own determinations; the Constitution provides only one procedural rule, namely that when the *president* is tried, the chief justice presides.[42] But this role is largely ceremonial, and the Senate can overrule any decision by the chief justice. For example, Chief Justice William H. Rehnquist, who presided over the impeachment trial of President Bill Clinton, issued only one nontrivial ruling—that House managers not call the senators "jurors." As Rehnquist later remarked, "I did nothing in particular, and I did it very well."[43]

The chief justice's limited role helps emphasize that although we call the Senate proceeding a "trial," it is not a criminal proceeding. For example, courtroom rules of evidence, such as the rule against hearsay, do not apply.[44] Similarly, the "beyond a reasonable doubt" standard of proof in criminal trials does not apply.[45] The fundamental questions that the senators must answer are: "Did the president do what he is charged in this Article with having done?" and "If he did, did that action constitute an impeachable offense within the meaning of the constitutional phrase?"[46]

In the end, the Senate votes. The Constitution requires at least a two-thirds majority of the Senate to convict in an impeachment trial.[47] Yet despite the term "conviction," a "conviction" by the Senate does not put anyone in prison. Any criminal charges proceed (or do not proceed) on a separate track. The one potential interaction between impeachment proceedings and criminal proceedings is that, according to long-standing policy of the Department of Justice's Office of Legal Counsel, and the position of certain legal scholars, the Constitution prohibits the criminal prosecution of a sitting president until after the president is removed from office—although that question is far from settled.[48]

The most relevant precedent here is President Richard Nixon, who in some ways set the model for the Trump presidency. Nixon was not actually impeached; after the House Judiciary Committee approved articles of impeachment against him, he resigned rather than face a full House vote on impeachment and a Senate trial. As Barbara A. Radnofsky notes in her study of past impeachment proceedings, in the modern era, Congress has increasingly streamlined its

procedures to ensure that it can conduct impeachment proceedings efficiently and transparently while simultaneously
allowing Congress to continue the business of the country.
This streamlined process has, as a side effect, also facilitated
conclusion of the impeachment process through resignation.[49]
Here, too, the constitutional purposes of the impeachment
process would be equally well served by Trump's resignation
as by a full Senate trial and conviction.

THE CONSTITUTION
DEMANDS IT

ONE

ACCEPTING UNCONSTITUTIONAL

FOREIGN AND DOMESTIC

EMOLUMENTS

The first ground for impeachment hearings arose from the moment that Donald Trump swore the oath of office. Trump had been warned, before his inauguration, that he would need to separate himself from his businesses. But he chose to ignore that advice. And because he profits from business with foreign governments, the federal government, and even state and local governments, he has been violating two different prohibitions of the U.S. Constitution—the Foreign Emoluments Clause and the Domestic Emoluments Clause—since day one.

★   ★   ★

The framers of the Constitution "were obsessed with corruption," and for good reason—they had seen it in recent British history, in their study of ancient Greece and Rome, and in their own nascent republic.[1] To defend against this ever-present danger, they built bulwarks into the Constitution itself, including the emoluments clauses.

The *Foreign* Emoluments Clause prohibits emoluments from foreign governments: "[N]o Person holding any Office of Profit or Trust under [the United States], shall, without the Consent of the Congress, accept of any present, Emolument, Office, or Title, *of any kind whatever*, from any King, Prince, or

foreign State."² And the *Domestic* Emoluments Clause prohibits emoluments from the federal, state, and local governments:
"The President shall, at stated Times, receive for his Services,
a Compensation, which shall neither be encreased nor diminished during the Period for which he shall have been elected,
and *he shall not receive within that Period any other Emolument
from the United States, or any of them.*"³

The somewhat old-fashioned word "emoluments" may suggest that this is an arcane or technical topic. But it is not. The
Constitution was designed to be understood by ordinary people, and at the time of the founding, the word "emolument"
meant nearly any form of profit, income, or financial advan-
tage.⁴ For practical purposes, when you read the word "emolument," you can mentally substitute "financial benefit."⁵

It is certainly true that most people had never heard of the
emoluments prohibitions before the Trump presidency. But
that does not mean that these constitutional requirements are
obscure or unimportant. To the contrary, they are essential
anticorruption provisions designed to safeguard the republic
by preventing improper influence or corruption, and the conflicts of interest and improper dependence that arise when a
president's policy considerations and actions are intermingled
with his interest in personal financial benefits. The only reason
most people had never encountered this issue before is that no
previous presidents—even those of great wealth—have trampled over the emoluments prohibitions like Trump does.

*   *   *

Shortly after the election, a *Washington Post* analysis of Trump's
financial filings found that at least III Trump companies do
or have done business in eighteen countries and territories
around the world.⁶ Many of the Trump Organization's extensive business dealings include receipt of payments or other
benefits from foreign governments, businesses owned by
foreign governments, and other foreign leaders. That creates

the appearance that foreign governments can gain favorable treatment from the United States by doing business with the Trump Organization. Similarly, many of Trump's businesses benefit financially from the federal government that he now heads (as well as from state and local governments), and several result in his receiving income or other benefits from the federal government (beyond his salary), or from state and local governments.

The president's refusal to disclose his tax returns means that we do not have a complete picture of the sources of his income, and it would be entirely appropriate for congressional impeachment hearings to conduct further fact-finding. But the central point is undisputed: the president's businesses receive substantial profits and other financial benefits from foreign and domestic governments.

On January 11, 2017, the Trump Organization's tax law firm announced a plan to transfer *management* control of the Trump Organization to Trump's grown sons and a senior executive, without removing Trump's *ownership* stake.[7] Instead, Trump transferred his ownership stakes in various Trump business entities to "The Donald J. Trump Revocable Trust." This trust, of which Trump's son Don Jr. and the Trump Organization's chief financial officer are trustees, has as its purpose "to hold assets for the 'exclusive benefit' of the president," and uses Trump's Social Security number as its taxpayer identification number.[8] The trust is run not by an independent trustee, but by his own son and longtime chief financial officer. And he can revoke the trust at any time.[9] Similarly, on February 3, 2017, the Trump Organization filed paperwork to transfer *management* of the LLCs and corporations that operate the Trump International Hotel in Washington, D.C., to Trump's sons, without removing Trump's *ownership* stake.[10]

These arrangements do not diminish Trump's ability to enrich himself during his presidency with funds from constitutionally prohibited sources, and even to shape U.S. policy to preserve and promote his business assets—an outcome the framers expressly intended to prevent. Trump knows which businesses his trust owns (indeed, most of them say "TRUMP" above the front door) and how his actions as president may affect their income and value.

The list of prohibited emoluments continues to expand. Some of the most egregious examples include the following.[11]

EMOLUMENTS FROM FOREIGN GOVERNMENTS
Foreign payments at the Trump International Hotel in Washington, D.C.

In September 2016, Trump used the opportunity of a campaign press conference (at which he renounced his previous claim that President Obama was not a natural-born U.S. citizen) to announce the opening of his new hotel in Washington, D.C.[12] The hotel is physically located in Washington, D.C.'s historic Old Post Office pavilion, which is owned by the federal government and administered by the General Services Administration; in 2013, Trump won the contract to redevelop the historic building into a hotel with a sixty-year lease.[13]

Because new hotels typically do not turn a profit at first, the Trump Organization had estimated that Trump's D.C. hotel would lose $2.1 million in the first four months of 2017. The hotel instead netted $1.97 million in that period.[14] What changed?

Shortly after the election, "[a]bout 100 foreign diplomats, from Brazil to Turkey, gathered at the Trump International Hotel [in Washington, D.C.] to sip Trump-branded champagne, dine on sliders and hear a sales pitch about the U.S. president-elect's newest hotel."[15] The motivation was not hard to discern:

> In interviews with a dozen diplomats, many of whom declined to be named because they were not authorized to speak about anything related to the next U.S. presi-

dent, some said spending money at Trump's hotel is an easy, friendly gesture to the new president.

"Why wouldn't I stay at his hotel blocks from the White House, so I can tell the new president, 'I love your new hotel!' Isn't it rude to come to his city and say, 'I am staying at your competitor?'" said one Asian diplomat.[16]

Indeed, according to one report, at least one foreign embassy was actively pressured to change an existing reservation by the Trump Organization:

> The Embassy of Kuwait allegedly cancelled a contract with a Washington, D.C. hotel days after the presidential election, citing political pressure to hold its National Day celebration at the Trump International Hotel instead . . . [The embassy] abruptly canceled its reservation after members of the Trump Organization pressured the ambassador to hold the event at the hotel owned by the president-elect.[17]

But Kuwait—whose emissaries would later return to the Trump International Hotel for its National Day celebration in 2018—was not alone.[18] Nor is the Trump Organization alone in pumping the hotel for ambassadorial functions. In late October 2017, Mexico's former ambassador to the United States reported that he had learned from a former U.S. diplomat that the U.S. State Department's *official protocol* now emphasizes to world leaders that they should use Trump's D.C. hotel for official visits.[19]

This use of both the Trump Organization and (apparently) the State Department to encourage foreign governments to use Trump's hotel is working. Just a few days after the inauguration, on January 23–26, 2017, a lobbying firm working for, and reimbursed by, the government of Saudi Arabia spent about $270,000 at Trump's D.C. hotel—including $190,273 on lodging and $78,204 on catering.[20] These Saudi government payments came as the kingdom lobbied to modify U.S. law to limit the ability of American families to file lawsuits against Saudi Arabia related to the terrorist attacks of 9/11.[21]

Other examples include:

- In May 2017, the Turkey-U.S. Business Council, reportedly an arm of the Turkish government's Foreign Economic Relations Board, cosponsored a conference at the hotel that prominently advertised the attendance of Turkish government ministers and members of parliament. Similar events in the past had cost approximately $400,000.[22]
- In September 2017, Malaysia's prime minister and an entourage of dozens stayed at the hotel and were seen using meeting rooms (including "a white-tablecloth breakfast in the hotel's Lincoln Library meeting room") and a lounge area for hotel guests. According to *The Washington Post*, bookings of this nature "would probably mean hundreds of thousands of dollars in revenue for the Trump Organization."[23]
- Ambassadors from Russia, the United Arab Emirates, and Turkey have also been seen at Trump's D.C. hotel, and the Romanian president dined at the hotel.[24]
- In June 2018, the Philippine Embassy hosted its invitation-only Independence Day reception at the hotel.[25]

What about Trump's supposed plan to donate the profits from foreign governments to the Treasury? A few days before the inauguration, Trump's tax law firm announced a plan to "voluntarily donate all profits from foreign government payments made to his hotel to the United States Treasury."[26] But the Foreign Emoluments Clause does not provide an exception for receiving foreign government payments, calculating and deducting operating costs, and then donating the "profits" to the Treasury. That is not how anticorruption law works in *any* context, even in local laws against pay-to-play for municipal government contractors, and certainly not in the U.S. Constitution.

In any event, the Trump Organization soon watered down its pledge. When the House Committee on Oversight and Government Reform asked for details about this plan, the Trump Organization claimed that it would be "impractical" to "fully and completely identify" all foreign-government customers and that doing so would "impede upon personal privacy and diminish the guest experience of our brand."[27] Furthermore, the Trump Organization decided that, even for self-identified foreign-government patrons, the company would not calculate actual profits. Apparently, complying with Trump's pledge "is not practical" and would require "time, resources, and specialists." Instead, the Trump Organization would just *estimate* costs.[28] Ultimately, in February 2018, the Trump Organization sent the Treasury a check for $151,470, purportedly representing its estimate of profits from 2017 foreign government business at its hotels and similar businesses, but without any explanation or accounting.[29]

Foreign payments at other Trump properties in the United States

Foreign governments also spend money at Trump's other U.S. properties. For example, at Trump Tower, Trump's flagship skyscraper at 725 Fifth Avenue in Manhattan, one of the largest tenants is the Industrial and Commercial Bank of China. This bank—controlled by the Chinese government—leases the entire 20th floor, and its lease will not expire until October 2019, after which it could be renewed.[30] (The Industrial and Commercial Bank of China should not be confused with the separate, but also state-controlled, Bank of China, discussed below, which is *also* a source of foreign emoluments through the Trump Organization.) Given the price of renting that space, "[t]he Trump Organization makes more money from the Chinese bank alone than it could ever expect from hotel visits by members of a foreign government. And the president has made no pledge to hand over that money."[31]

Other examples include:

- The Kingdom of Saudi Arabia owns the 45th floor of another Trump building in Manhattan: Trump World Tower at 845 United Nations Plaza. The Saudi mission to the United Nations is housed there. The kingdom pays annual building amenity charges that exceeded $85,000 per year in 2001 (the last publicly available figure), and may be considerably higher now. [32]
- The Bank of India, an Indian state-owned entity, leases space in a partly Trump-owned property in San Francisco. This lease will expire in 2019.[33]
- On September 18, 2017, the Trump National Golf Club in northern Virginia hosted the "Turkish Airlines World Golf Cup," sponsored by the state-owned Turkish Airlines.[34]

The Trump Organization and the White House have both refused to disclose Trump's tenants and their payments, so it is impossible to discern the extent of foreign government patronage of Trump's properties.[35] Walter Shaub, who served as the Director of the U.S. Office of Government Ethics until July 2017, has pointed out that "the public reading the [president's financial disclosure] form doesn't know who is paying the president."[36]

Foreign credit

Other forms of foreign emoluments include extensions of credit from banks owned or controlled by foreign governments. For example, the state-owned Bank of China—not to be confused with the Industrial and Commercial Bank of China, the major tenant in Trump Tower—holds part of a $950 million loan on 1290 Sixth Avenue in Manhattan, in which the Trump Organization holds a 30 percent ownership stake.[37] This ongoing foreign government loan benefiting the Trump Organization (i.e., benefiting Trump himself) is also a foreign emolument.

Foreign trademarks

Not all emoluments are cash. In February and March 2017, the Chinese and Mexican governments granted the Trump Organization several long-sought (and long-denied) trademarks.[38] These trademarks have a substantial economic value, and count as foreign emoluments. Moreover, the publicly reported timeline of Trump's statements and actions concerning U.S. foreign policy with respect to China, and the Chinese government's granting of trademarks to the Trump Organization, raise serious questions about the possibility of bribery and extortion involving the president of the United States and the government of China.

Starting in 2006, the Trump Organization sought to persuade Chinese authorities to award the right to register dozens of trademarks, starting with a trademark for construction services.[39] During the decade that followed, the Trump Organization made little headway. The Chinese trademark office rejected Trump's application in 2009, and rejected an appeal in 2014.[40] Later in 2014, a court in Beijing rejected an appeal, and then in May 2015, two months before Trump announced his candidacy, a higher Chinese court issued a final judgment rejecting Trump's appeal, even as he continued to apply for additional trademarks.[41]

Then in September 2016, the Chinese trademark office reversed course after more than a decade and invalidated a rival claim for some of the trademarks that Trump wanted.[42] Finally, on November 13, 2016, just five days after the election, the Chinese government granted preliminary approval to the Trump Organization to register a construction services trademark.[43]

On December 2, 2016, Trump accepted a call from the president of Taiwan, making him the first U.S. president or president-elect to do so since the United States broke off diplomatic relations with Taiwan in 1979.[44] The call prompted a domestic and international outcry that he had broken with the United States' long-standing "One China" policy.[45] China lodged a formal complaint with the United States.[46] Following his telephone call with the president of Taiwan, Trump publicly stated that he might change the One China policy if the United States did not receive trade concessions from China.[47]

In a sudden reversal, on February 9, 2017, Trump spoke with China's president, after which Trump publicly announced that he would honor the One China policy.[48] The BBC perplexedly noted that it was not clear "what, if anything, the Trump Administration . . . won in return."[49] But on February 15, after the expiration of a three-month objection period and just six days after Trump made his official One China declaration, the Chinese government granted the Trump Organization final approval for its construction services trademark.[50]

On February 27, Trump held his first face-to-face meeting with a member of the Chinese leadership as he met China's top diplomat at the White House.[51] That same day, and also on March 6, in an apparent break with usual protocol and ten years of prior rulings, the Chinese trademark office gave preliminary approval for the Trump Organization to register thirty-eight more trademarks.[52] Just one week later, the Trump administration announced plans for Trump to host China's president at a two-day summit in April.[53]

Besides the unconstitutional foreign emoluments, these events, as reported, may violate the federal law against extortion or bribery, and/or gratuities.[54]

Foreign government permits and approvals

Trump's properties abroad supply another source of foreign emoluments. Forbes estimates that the Trump Organization is paid more than $5 million annually by foreign magnates—including many who have ties to local and federal governments—for the right to use the Trump name for branding.[55] And, perhaps more subtly, many Trump projects abroad require foreign government permits and approvals. These approvals are noncash (but substantial) financial benefits that also constitute foreign presents or emoluments.

Although the Trump Organization's tax lawyer announced before the inauguration that "[n]o new foreign deals will be made whatsoever during the duration of President Trump's presidency,"[56] the Trump Organization later retracted the essence of that assurance. It asserted that "[i]mplementing future phasing of existing properties does not constitute a new transaction."[57] The Trump Organization has continued, is continuing, and by all accounts intends to continue to expand its existing foreign properties.[58] Trump's sons continue to forge ahead with Trump Organization business and benefit from official escorts of U.S. embassy and presidential protective staff as they do so.[59]

These projects and approvals give foreign governments points of leverage—whether explicitly or implicitly—over the president. Consider Turkey. The Trump Organization has licensing deals with two Trump Towers in Istanbul. In December 2015, in response to a question as to Turkey's NATO membership and reliability as a partner, Trump admitted that "I have a little conflict of interest, because I have a major, major building in Istanbul."[60] After the U.S. election in 2016, shares in Trump's Turkish partner on the project surged almost 11 percent.[61]

Trump's "little conflict of interest" has turned out to be not so little.[62] In May 2017, Washington, D.C.'s Sheridan Circle was the site of an unprecedented attack by agents of a foreign government. Turkish president Recep Erdoğan was in town, and about twenty peaceful protesters assembled in a grassy area on public property across the street from the Turkish ambassador's residence. Some of them held the flag of a Kurdish political party. Without provocation (or, more precisely, without provocation other than the act of protesting the Turkish president's visit), black-suited men from Erdoğan's security detail assaulted the protesters.[63] As videos from the scene show, the Turkish presidential bodyguards kicked and punched the demonstrators while Erdoğan watched.[64] Eventually, the D.C. police intervened and (after some time) were able to stop the attack.

The point here is not what the Turkish bodyguards did, but what Trump *did not* do: neither he nor his White House said a word about this foreign government attack on U.S. soil. In fact, on the day of the assault, the only government agencies to report the event were the D.C. fire department and the Turkish-language edition of Voice of America. After some delay, a State Department spokesperson eventually issued a short statement, and the department summoned the Turkish ambassador to its offices.[65] (Turkey's Foreign Ministry, for its part, summoned the U.S. ambassador in Istanbul to complain that the D.C. police failed to stop a "provocative" demonstration.[66])

As for Trump and his prolific Twitter feed—silence. Was this a considered diplomatic de-escalation strategy or "a little conflict of interest"? It's hard to peer into a president's soul, so the Foreign Emoluments Clause is designed to prevent the "little conflict of interest" in the first place.

And that is not the only Trump property abroad that creates "a little conflict of interest." Since the election in 2016, more Trump properties have continued to open abroad, such as a new golf course in Dubai.[67] And there are many more. Additional foreign government permits and approvals will inevitably be required for ongoing and planned Trump projects, including:

1. **Dominican Republic:** The Trump Organization appears to

be finalizing a partnership agreement to build in the Dominican Republic. In January 2018, the Cap Cana Group, which partners with the Trump Organization, was granted permits to construct seventeen buildings, including condominiums with links to the Trump Organization. Cap Cana recently released a statement announcing, "We are enthusiastic to work with the Trump Organization in future phases of the project." Meanwhile, lawyers from the Trump Organization have argued that the project is part of a preexisting licensing deal that was signed in 2007.[68]

2. **India:** The Trump Organization reportedly has five projects in India, including a Trump Tower, an apartment project in Mumbai, and an apartment block; Trump has leased his name to each of the projects.[69]

3. **Indonesia:** The Trump Organization plans to open two new luxury hotels in Indonesia. And he has reportedly "forged relationships with powerful political figures in Indonesia, where such connections are crucial to pushing through big projects."[70]

4. **Philippines:** The Trump Organization has a business interest in a Trump Tower in the Philippines that is on the verge of completion.[71] Right after the November 2016 election, the Philippine government announced that it had appointed Jose E. B. Antonio, a real estate developer who partnered with Trump on the $150 million tower, as the country's special envoy to the United States.[72]

5. **United Arab Emirates:** There are two Trump-branded and -operated golf clubs in the Emirates. All services, including electricity, water, and roads, "come at the discretion of the government," including "government approvals to serve alcohol, not to mention other regulatory issues."[73]

6. **United Kingdom:** Trump appears to have tried to exploit his position and access to leaders of the United Kingdom in the service of his two golf resorts in Scotland: Trump Turnberry, and Trump International Golf Links Scotland in

Aberdeenshire.[74] The Trump Organization plans to extend the Aberdeenshire course by "extending its boutique hotel and building a second 18-hole golf course."[75] Trump told *The New York Times* that he "might have" mentioned an off-shore wind farm near the Aberdeenshire course with Nigel Farage, the former leader of the U.K. Independence Party, whom Trump has recommended as an ambassador to the United States.[76] For years, Trump had complained about the wind farm supposedly spoiling the view from the golf course, and he tried to prevent it from being developed.[77]

In addition to providing permits and approvals for Trump properties abroad, foreign governments have also aided in the development of these projects more directly.

For example, the Panamanian government supported a project that connected sewer and water pipes to the new Trump Ocean Club International Hotel and Tower Panama City, when the company that was originally contracted went out of business.[78] And when that property—a hotbed of money-laundering, later dubbed "Narco-a-Lago"[79]—ran into problems with the owners of its condominium units, the Trump Organization appealed directly to the president of Panama for assistance.[80]

Trump's two Indonesia projects highlight even further the danger of the president's businesses abroad. For Trump's Bali resort, the Indonesian government has prioritized shortening the driving time between Bali's primary airport and the Trump International Hotel and Tower Bali.[81] And the business plan for his Lido (West Java) resort is financially dependent on a flagship theme park that will be built by a Chinese state-owned construction firm and is backed by $500 million in loans from the Chinese government.[82]

Two days after that loan was announced, Trump surprised

his own government by tweeting that he would direct the Department of Commerce to lift penalties on ZTE, a Chinese phone maker that has violated sanctions on North Korea and Iran, and repeatedly lied to the U.S. government. In fact, the Department of Defense had just two weeks earlier banned ZTE phones from being sold on U.S. bases because of their security risks.[83] This unprecedented and unexplained presidential reversal of a Commerce Department enforcement action, and its curious timing, leaves little doubt that the president's official actions are being influenced (if not dictated) by his personal financial interests. That is the precise danger the framers sought to avoid through the Foreign Emoluments Clause. It further suggests that the Chinese payments to support Trump's Indonesia development may be more than just a foreign emolument—they may also be a bribe.[84]

The Foreign Emoluments Clause does contemplate that Congress can consent to a particular foreign emolument. But Trump has not asked for, and Congress certainly has not given, consent for *any* of the foreign emoluments that Trump has received or will receive during his time in office.

EMOLUMENTS FROM FEDERAL, STATE, AND LOCAL GOVERNMENTS
Profiting personally from official government travel

When Trump visits a Trump golf club, as he has on about a quarter of the days since his inauguration,[85] he is accompanied by a protective detail of the U.S. Secret Service. The Secret Service, in turn, uses taxpayer funds to pay the Trump golf club at market rates. Neither the Trump administration nor the Trump Organization have been forthcoming with details, but we know, for example, that the Secret Service paid $63,700 in hotel costs at Mar-a-Lago in the three-month period of February–April 2017.[86] And as of November 29, 2017, the Secret Service had spent $144,975 on *golf cart rentals alone* at Trump golf courses.[87]

Other government officials accompany the president on these visits, and incur similar expenses. Defense Department employees spent $58,876 on lodging and food at Mar-a-Lago during the twenty-five days that Trump spent there between February and April 2017, and $9,619 at his Bedminster, New Jersey, golf club during his four-day visit there in May 2017.[88] And in March 2017, the Coast Guard paid $1,092 ($546 per night at rack rate) for an official to stay at Mar-a-Lago, apparently for an off-site meeting of the National Security Council.[89]

While all presidents' travel results in other officials incurring expenses (including for protective details on presidents' vacation travel), it is unprecedented for taxpayer money for travel expenses to be paid to a facility owned by the president from which he personally profits.

Even when Trump himself is not traveling, he profits from official taxpayer-funded travel when other government officials travel to his properties. (Of course, it is theoretically possible that these officials would choose to stay at Trump hotels when they traveled even if Trump were not president, but that does not square with reality.) One study found that "70 executive branch officials [made] nearly 200 visits to Trump Organization properties in the first year of the Trump administration."[90] These include:

- The Department of Defense spent almost $53,000 at Trump hotels when the president wasn't even there—$35,652 at the Trump International Las Vegas Hotel, and $17,103 at the Trump International Hotel Panama City (no longer a Trump property as of the spring of 2018).[91]
- An employee of the General Services Administration, which owns the Old Post Office building that houses

Trump's Washington, D.C., hotel and is thus Trump's landlord, spent $900 for a stay there.[92]

- The Governor of Maine reportedly spent thousands of state dollars at Trump's D.C. hotel for members of his security team.[93]
- A group of some 250 students, staff, and administrators from the University of Wisconsin-Madison (a public university with almost $900 million in annual federal funding) paid about $100,000 to stay at the Trump National Doral in Miami for a week in December 2017.[94]
- In the United Kingdom, unnamed Trump administration officials paid $7,585 in taxpayer funds (approved by the Department of State and paid through the U.S. Embassy in London) for a "VIP visit" to the Trump Turnberry golf resort in Scotland.[95]

Executive branch action to benefit Trump businesses

Trump's control over the vast modern powers of the executive branch means that favorable federal regulatory action benefiting his businesses also counts as a government benefit.

For example, Trump's ongoing lease of Washington, D.C.'s Old Post Office Pavilion violates an explicit clause in the General Services Administration lease contract providing: "No . . . elected official of the Government of the United States . . . shall be admitted to any share or part of this Lease, or to any benefit that may arise therefrom . . ."[96] In late November 2016, members of Congress wrote to the GSA, requesting information about the "imminent breach-of-lease and conflict of interest issues created by President-elect Donald Trump's lease with the U.S. Government for the Trump International Hotel building in Washington, D.C."[97] The GSA responded in mid-December that it could not make a determination "until the full circumstances surrounding the president-elect's business arrangements have been finalized and he has assumed office."[98] After he assumed office, the GSA announced that it had concluded that this clause somehow did not apply.[99] The reasoning is fatuous, but the basic idea is that since the Trump Organization nominally transferred management of the LLCs and corporations that operate the hotel to Trump's sons, Trump will not "benefit" from the lease during his term in office—a conclusion at odds with the fact that Trump remains the *beneficial* owner of the Trump Organization and, by definition, is currently benefiting from the lease.[100] The GSA's decision not to enforce the unambiguous term in the lease contract is a government benefit.

Perhaps the most disturbing use of executive branch action to benefit Trump's businesses involves the military. The president famously ordered an airstrike on a Syrian airbase during dessert at Mar-a-Lago. Secretary of Commerce Wilbur Ross, who was present for Trump's order along with Chinese president Xi Jinping, commented that the engagement was "after-dinner entertainment."[101] True, it did not involve cash going from the Treasury directly to Trump's pocket. But it is not hard to see how Trump's use of presidential power helps generate additional income—it is the only golf club where paying members get to experience the equivalent of being in the White House Situation Room.

Subsidies, tax breaks, and other direct and indirect payments

Many of Trump's businesses receive federal and state government subsidies and tax breaks. For example, since 1980, Trump and his businesses have "reaped at least $885 million in tax breaks, grants and other subsidies for luxury apartments, hotels and office buildings in New York."[102] More recently, in February 2018, the State of Mississippi gave a $6 million tax break to a hotel project that the Trump Organization will manage

and brand. This public subsidy was approved by the Mississippi Development Authority, and is expected to offset a third
of the building costs. One of the local owners of the development project notified personal and government contacts about
the detail with the subject line, "Trump Hotels Coming to the
Mississippi Delta."[103]

But that is barely the start. Consider Trump's troubled
"Trump SoHo" project. The Trump SoHo was announced in
June 2006 in the season finale of *The Apprentice*. Because zoning
laws did not allow a residential development, the Trump SoHo
was billed as a luxury condo-hotel development where condominium owners bought a hotel room and could not occupy it
for more than 120 nights per year. The Trump Organization's
partners in the project were the Bayrock Group and the Sapir
Organization, two real estate development companies helmed
by Soviet-born businessmen with strong connections to potential Russian investors. (One key member of the Bayrock
team was Felix Sater, who had been involved with a Russian
organized-crime scheme and also served as an FBI informant;
he later joined the Trump Organization.)[104]

The Trump SoHo units came on the market in September
2007 as the global economy was collapsing.[105] The timing, along
with the restrictions on occupancy, made the units difficult to
sell, but according to Don Jr. and Ivanka Trump, they had already sold 31 percent of the units in April 2008 and 60 percent
by June 2008.[106] Those claims were apparently false—by March
2010, only 15.8 percent of the units had sold.

In August 2010, unit buyers filed a lawsuit against Donald
Trump, the Trump Organization, Don Jr., Ivanka, and others
for fraud, claiming "consistent pattern of false representa-
tions."[107] Shortly afterward, the Manhattan District Attorney's
office opened a criminal investigation.[108] The civil case settled
in November 2011.[109] In the settlement, the defendants agreed
to refund 90 percent of the $3.16 million in deposits to the unit
buyers; the buyers, for their part, sent a letter to the district

attorney stating that they would no longer provide any assistance in the criminal investigation.[110] (The settlement agreement was not enough to persuade the district attorney to stop the criminal investigation—that took some $40,000 in campaign contributions from Trump's lawyer Marc Kasowitz to the district attorney's reelection campaign. But that is a story for another day.[111])

Because of Trump SoHo's financial troubles, in 2015 it came into the ownership of "CIM Fund III," a private-equity real estate fund run by the CIM Group. About half of the total $2.37 billion investment in CIM Fund III comes from state and local public pension funds.[112] These public investors are required to pay quarterly management and performance fees to CIM Fund III. Meanwhile, under the agreement, CIM Fund III paid Trump's company 5.75 percent of gross hotel operating revenue, and operating and overhead charges on the unsold hotel suite units (about two-thirds of the total units). The total payments from CIM Fund III to Trump's company amounted to millions of dollars per quarter; about half of the payments flowed from public state and local pension funds.[113]

That is a domestic emolument. After this came to light, a concerted public campaign, bolstered by a letter from Representative Ted Lieu and eleven other members of Congress from California, was directed at the California and New York state public pension funds. The campaign urged the public-pension funds to either work with other pension fund investors in CIM Fund III to demand that CIM Fund III sell the Trump SoHo property and end its relationship with the Trump Organization because of these illegal domestic emoluments, or, alternatively, divest their interest in CIM Fund III. In December 2017, the CIM Group bought out its contract with Trump International Hotels Management.[114] The property, now known as the Dominick Hotel, no longer has any association with the Trump Organization.

★　★　★

The facts above show not just a few isolated instances, but a pervasive pattern of the president accepting emoluments from foreign and domestic governments.

The framers of the Constitution considered these clauses to be critical safeguards against foreign and domestic corruption. In Alexander Hamilton's words, a critical purpose of the emoluments clauses was to ensure that the president had "no pecuniary inducement to renounce or desert the independence intended for him by the Constitution."[115] And while some of Trump's emoluments are currently the subject of civil litigation,[116] the framers made clear that violating these anticorruption provisions constitutes grounds for impeachment. (The framers were not breaking new ground in doing so; "incompatible employments" was a basis for impeachment in England.[117])

In July 1787, at the Constitutional Convention in Philadelphia, the delegates debated whether to include a provision for impeaching the president. Gouverneur Morris of Pennsylvania (known as the "Penman of the Constitution") observed that "no one would say that we ought to expose ourselves to the danger of seeing the first Magistrate [the president] in foreign pay, without being able to guard against it by displacing him."[118] James Madison (sometimes called the "Father of the Constitution") thought an impeachment provision would be "indispensable" as a safeguard against a president who "might pervert his administration into a scheme of peculation" or "betray his trust to foreign powers."[119] ("Peculation" means illegal enrichment, such as embezzlement, particularly from public funds.[120]) As Madison explained in arguing for the impeachment power, "corruption" in the presidency "might be fatal to the Republic."[121]

Similarly, at the Virginia ratifying convention in June 1788, Edmund Jennings Randolph (governor of Virginia, a delegate to the Constitutional Convention, and later the first attorney general of the United States and the second secretary of state) argued for ratifying the new Constitution. Randolph acknowledged skeptics' concerns about corruption, but reassured them that the Constitution was designed to prevent this sort of corruption:

> It has too often happened that powers delegated for the purpose of promoting the happiness of a community have been perverted to the advancement of the personal emoluments of the agents of the people; but the powers of the President are too well guarded and checked to warrant this illiberal aspersion.[122]

And when George Mason, now opposing the Constitution, raised concerns about influence over the president, Randolph responded: "There is another provision against the danger, mentioned by the honorable member, of the President receiving emoluments from foreign powers. *If discovered, he may be impeached* . . . It is impossible to guard better against corruption."[123]

This is consistent with the views of other framers, such as Alexander Hamilton, who described impeachable offenses as arising from "the misconduct of public men, or in other words from the abuse or violation of some public trust."[124] Similarly, in the North Carolina ratifying convention, future U.S. Supreme Court justice James Iredell described impeachable conduct as including instances where the president "acted from some corrupt motive," giving the example of a president receiving "a bribe . . . from a foreign power, and under the influence of that bribe . . . [getting Senate] consent to a pernicious treaty."[125]

Finally, this is also consistent with congressional precedent. At least six of the nineteen impeachments in our history have alleged "the use of office for personal gain or the appearance of financial impropriety while in office."[126] Examples of such grounds for impeachment, which congressional historians have grouped under the heading of "Using the Office for an Improper Purpose or Personal Gain,"[127] include the 1912 impeachment of Judge Robert W. Archbald. He was charged with "using his office to secure business favors from litigants and potential litigants before his court." Three other federal judges were charged with "misusing their power . . . for personal profit."[128]

Since there is really no question that taking illegal emoluments is a serious impeachable offense, Trump's defenders must argue that these payments do not actually violate the emoluments clauses. A law professor in Ireland claims, based on his own historical analysis, that the president is not covered by the Foreign Emoluments Clause because he does not hold "any Office of Profit or Trust under [the United States]"—but not even the president's lawyers argue this.[129] And in any event, this would not help with the Domestic Emoluments Clause, which explicitly applies to the president—in fact, it *only* applies to the president.

The other argument that the president and his defenders make is that payments to the president's businesses are not "emoluments" if they are in exchange for goods and services. But this argument does not square with the historical meaning or structural (anticorruption) role of the emoluments clauses. Rather, the better understanding is that "emoluments" is a broad term. It includes "any conferral of a benefit or advantage, whether through money, objects, titles, offices, or economically valuable waivers or relaxations of otherwise applicable requirements," even including "ordinary, fair market value transactions that result in any economic profit or benefit to the federal officeholder."[130]

Trump was warned before the inauguration that, unless he took credible action to address these conflicts, he would be violating the emoluments bans from the *moment he took office*.[131] His refusal to separate his presidential duty from his business interests undermines the integrity of the presidency.

★   ★   ★

BOTTOM LINE: Through his businesses in the United States and abroad, the president receives payments, regulatory approval, and other forms of direct and indirect financial benefits from foreign governments. These include increased foreign bookings at the Trump International Hotel in Washington, D.C.; foreign government payments at other Trump properties in the United States; extensions of credit from foreign-owned banks; foreign trademarks; and foreign government permits and approvals for projects abroad. These violate the Constitution's Foreign Emoluments Clause, which prohibits federal officials, including the president, from receiving a "present" or "emolument" from any foreign government or official.

The president's businesses also act as a conduit for enrichment from federal and state government coffers. This includes the president profiting personally from official government travel, executive-branch action to benefit Trump businesses, and various other subsidies and tax breaks. These violate the Domestic Emoluments Clause, which prohibits the president from receiving, beyond his official salary, any emolument from the United States or any state.

The president was advised between the election and the inauguration that, unless he took credible action to separate himself from his business interests, he would be in violation of these provisions from the moment he entered office. Instead, he chose a weak set of superficial measures that removed him from day-to-day management of his businesses, but retained his ownership interests, so that he continues to profit personally from foreign and domestic emoluments.

It is time for Congress to investigate whether to impeach President Trump for accepting emoluments from foreign governments without the consent of the Congress, and emoluments from the United States and the several states beyond his compensation.

CONSPIRING TO SOLICIT
AND THEN CONCEAL ILLEGAL
FOREIGN ASSISTANCE FOR HIS
PRESIDENTIAL CAMPAIGN

The Russian government engaged in a sophisticated campaign of "active measures" to influence the 2016 election. Trump's senior campaign officials—his campaign manager, son, and son-in-law—and probably Trump himself actively participated in soliciting campaign help from Russian nationals *whom they understood to be Russian government agents.* And Trump helped cover it up.

★ ★ ★

It is now beyond doubt that the Russian government ran a sophisticated influence operation in the 2016 election. But even worse, senior Trump campaign officials were knee-deep in efforts to solicit campaign help from Russian agents. Several campaign officials have already pleaded guilty to federal crimes. What is not yet publicly known—and what impeachment hearings can help bring out—is exactly what the president knew, and when he knew it. But we have a good sense. We have strong evidence that Trump knew about the Russian government's outreach in real time in the summer of 2016, before a critical in-person meeting at Trump Tower. And we also know that Trump later tried to cover up the story with a misleading public explanation.

The facts of the Trump campaign's interactions with Russian operatives—what some call Russiagate, or with more flair *L'Affaire Russe*—continue to emerge at a dizzying pace. The summary below provides only a sketch of what we already know.[1] And by the time you are reading this book, it is virtually certain that additional facts will have been revealed.[2]

The key point is that *we already have enough information to justify a fact-finding impeachment investigation.* The facts on the public record, summarized below, support further inquiry into what the president knew during his campaign and before assuming office, what he knows now, and whether he has participated in, facilitated, or should be held accountable for concealment of engagement with one or more foreign governments as part of his election campaign.

As discussed in detail below, the president may face some serious criminal exposure. But Congress can begin impeachment hearings now, without waiting for the resolution of an ongoing criminal investigation. Congress need not tie itself in knots over the distinctions (discussed below) between "conspiracy" and "aiding and abetting," or between "substantial assistance" and "coordination." These fine statutory distinctions should not obscure the issue for impeachment: the president helped cover up (and probably approved) his campaign's unprecedented efforts to seek Russian electoral help. Furthermore, while congressional impeachment hearings can bring out some additional facts, the publicly available evidence is enough to justify starting those hearings.

If the Trump campaign is, upon investigation, shown to have engaged in unprecedented and previously unimaginable collaboration with foreign governments, this engagement and the later efforts to conceal it amount to a high crime and misdemeanor for which impeachment is appropriate—regardless of the outcome of pending criminal proceedings. Conspiring with representatives of a foreign government to influence an election is *precisely* the type of threat directed at undermining our republic that the founders feared. They worried about the "corruption" of our government through "foreign intrigue."[3] As the Constitutional Convention debated whether to include an impeachment provision, James Madison argued that the Constitution must include an impeachment provision as a safeguard against a president who might "betray his trust to foreign powers."[4]

The framers understood that elections themselves were part of this process. George Mason asked rhetorically: "Shall the man who has practised corruption and by that means procured his appointment in the first instance, be suffered to escape punishment, by repeating his guilt?"[5] Mason's question raises an important point. While impeachment *usually* focuses on conduct that occurs in office, it can also address corruptly obtaining the office in the first place. (Indeed, in 2010, Judge Thomas Porteous was impeached and convicted largely based on conduct that occurred before he assumed federal office—including making false statements to the Senate and FBI in connection with his nomination and confirmation.[6]) Mason was talking about a president who corrupted the electors of the Electoral College, but the same concern applies to other forms of corrupt campaign tactics.

The combination of betrayal of trust to foreign powers and corrupt electioneering—each a ground for impeachment on its own—was sharply described by Alexander Hamilton. He wrote in the Federalist Papers that "the desire in foreign powers to gain an improper ascendant in our councils" could not be "better gratif[ied] . . . than by raising a creature of their own to the chief magistracy of the Union."[7]

That is the issue we must confront.

★   ★   ★

The U.S. intelligence community has concluded, and the bi-partisan Senate Intelligence Committee has confirmed, that Russia engaged in an "influence campaign in 2016 aimed at the US presidential election," which included a social media campaign and the public dissemination of hacked information through the WikiLeaks website.[8] In February 2018, a federal grand jury returned indictments against thirteen Russians and three Russian corporate entities involved in this effort.[9] Later investigations have revealed some of the details of the social media campaign, including paid campaign ads placed by Russian government operatives on Facebook.[10]

But these Russian operatives did not act alone. Throughout the presidential campaign in 2016, Trump campaign officials and advisors engaged in numerous communications and meetings with individuals who they understood to have Russian ties. When later confronted about these communications, Trump campaign officials and advisors denied they took place, and later, denied that they were related to the campaign. And throughout the campaign, *Trump himself* publicly encouraged the ongoing dissemination of hacked information.

Some of the connections go back years and involve Trump's business ties. On October 13, 2015, Felix Sater (a Russian-American businessman who occasionally worked for the Trump Organization and who was also involved in the Trump SoHo project) emailed Trump's lawyer, Michael Cohen, seeking Trump's signature on a letter of intent already signed by a proposed Russian partner for a Trump Tower in Moscow.[11] On October 28, 2015—the day of the third Republican Party presidential debate—Trump signed the letter of intent.[12] On November 3, 2015, Sater emailed Cohen, promising: "I will get Putin on this program and we will get Donald elected . . . Buddy our boy can become President of the USA and we can engineer it. I will get all of Putin's team to buy in on this."[13]

By the spring of 2016, Russian nationals and government operatives had begun their outreach to the Trump campaign to discuss potential assistance. One approach came via George Papadopoulos, a foreign-policy advisor to the Trump campaign, who later pleaded guilty to making false statements to FBI agents regarding his communications with Russian operatives.[14] In March 2016, Papadopoulos was approached by Joseph Mifsud, a Maltese academic linked to Russian intelligence, and a female Russian intelligence agent described to Papadopoulos as the niece of Russian president Vladimir Putin.[15] On March 31, 2016, Papadopoulos informed Trump and other campaign advisors that he could help arrange a meeting between Trump and Putin. And as the spring of 2016 progressed, Papadopoulos repeatedly attempted to arrange a meeting between the campaign and Russian government officials.[16]

Of course, the Russian intelligence services did not put all their eggs in Papadopoulos's basket. Another line of approach came from Rob Goldstone, a music publicist connected to Emin Agalarov, an Azerbaijani-Russian pop singer. Agalarov's father is Aras Agalarov, a Moscow oligarch who was Trump's business partner for the 2013 Miss Universe contest in Moscow. On April 25, 2016, Trump's personal assistant Rhona Graff emailed Rob Goldstone, passing along a handwritten response from Trump to an unspecified email from Aras Agalarov.[17] The next day, April 26, Papadopoulos met with a Russian operative who advised him that the Russians, via "thousands of e-mails," had "dirt" on Hillary Clinton.[18] On April 27, Trump and his campaign surrogate Senator Jeff Sessions met with Sergey Kislyak, the Russian ambassador, at the Mayflower Hotel, and apparently discussed campaign-related matters.[19] (Sessions later failed to disclose this meeting during his confirmation hearings, and ultimately recused himself from the Justice Department's investigation into matters related to the 2016 election due to his own involvement.[20])

A few weeks later, on May 19, 2016, Trump appointed Paul Manafort, who had done extensive business in Russia, as his "unpaid" campaign chairman. (Manafort was later indicted by a federal grand jury on thirty-two counts of tax, financial, and bank fraud charges.[21])

By the early summer of 2016, the FBI had identified four different Trump campaign aides—Papadopoulos; Manafort; Lieutenant General (ret.) Michael Flynn, who was advising Trump on national security; and Carter Page, whom Russian intelligence apparently tried to recruit as early as 2013—with known or suspected links to Russian intelligence.[22] The FBI began a counterintelligence investigation to determine if Russian intelligence was secretly attempting to penetrate the Trump campaign.[23] But, as it turned out, the Trump campaign did not need to be penetrated in secret: it was perfectly happy to accept help from the Russian government in the open.

★   ★   ★

On June 3, 2016, Goldstone sent Donald Trump, Jr., the following email:

> Emin just called and asked me to contact you with something very interesting.
>
> The Crown prosecutor of Russia met with his father Aras this morning and in their meeting offered to provide the Trump campaign with some official documents and information that would incriminate Hillary and her dealings with Russia and would be very useful to your father.
>
> This is obviously very high level and sensitive information but is part of Russia and its government's support for Mr. Trump—helped along by Aras and Emin.
>
> What do you think is the best way to handle this information and would you be able to speak to Emin about it directly?
>
> I can also send this info to your father via Rhona, but it is ultra sensitive so wanted to send to you first. [24]

This was an extraordinary contact. Goldstone identified the source of information as the Russian government and mentioned, almost as an aside, that this was "part of Russia and its government's support for Mr. Trump." But Don Jr. did not consult with a campaign lawyer, let alone alert law enforcement. Rather, just minutes later, Don Jr. responded:

> Thanks Rob I appreciate that. I am on the road at the moment but perhaps I just speak to Emin first. Seems we have some time and if it's what you say I love it especially later in the summer. Could we do a call first thing next week when I am back?[25]

On Monday, June 6, 2016, Goldstone and Don Jr. exchanged a series of emails to schedule the meeting. The time-frame is important. After some preliminary logistical back-and-forth between Goldstone and Don Jr. trying to establish a phone call between Emin Agalarov and Don Jr., at 3:43 p.m. Goldstone wrote: "Ok he's on stage in Moscow but should be off within 20 Minutes so I am sure can call."

The thirty-four-minute period between 4:04 p.m. and 4:38 p.m. is intriguing. At 4:04 p.m., according to cell phone records and confirmed by Don Jr.'s testimony, there was a short phone call between Don Jr. and Emin Agalarov's number. At 4:27 p.m., there was a call between Don Jr. and a blocked number. While the identity of the person at this number is not yet known, Corey Lewandowski testified that Trump's "primary residence has a blocked [phone] line." Shortly afterward, Don Jr. had another call with Emin Agalarov. Finally, at 4:38 p.m., Don Jr. emailed Goldstone to say: "Rob thanks for the help."[26]

The next day, June 7, two important things happened.

First, Goldstone emailed Don Jr. to say: "Emin asked that I schedule a meeting with you and The Russian government attorney who is flying over from Moscow for this Thursday."

He also added, "I believe you are aware of the meeting." After some scheduling back-and-forth, by 6:14 p.m. Don Jr. had confirmed with Goldstone the time (4 p.m. on Thursday, June 9), address (Trump Tower), and Trump campaign representatives in attendance (himself, Manafort, and Jared Kushner, Trump's son-in-law and senior advisor).[27]

And that night, after having won enough state primaries to clinch the Republican nomination, Trump told a crowd: "I am going to give a major speech on probably Monday of next week and we're going to be discussing all of the things that have taken place with the Clintons. I think you're going to find it very informative and very, very interesting."[28]

On Thursday, June 9, 2016, at 4 p.m., Don Jr., Manafort, and Kushner met at Trump Tower with several Russian citizens with the intention of acquiring the information offered in the June 3 emails.[29] The Russian delegation included Natalia Veselnitskaya, a Russian lawyer linked to the Kremlin, who later described herself as a Russian government "informant."[30] According to later testimony by one of the meeting's attendees, Don Jr. specifically asked whether Veselnitskaya had damaging information about Hillary Clinton.[31]

The meeting apparently lasted about twenty minutes.[32] At 4:40 p.m.—in other words, about twenty minutes after the meeting wrapped—Trump tweeted about Hillary Clinton's emails: "How long did it take your staff of 823 people to think that up—and where are your 33,000 emails that you deleted?"[33]

Throughout the campaign, but particularly after that meeting, Russian operatives and/or WikiLeaks released hacked information at opportune times, including one day after Trump fired campaign manager Corey Lewandowski;[34] one day after James Comey announced that the FBI would not bring criminal charges against Hillary Clinton;[35] and just one hour after the release of the *Access Hollywood* recording of Trump admitting to sexually assaulting women.[36] Both Don Jr. and Roger Stone, a Trump associate and advisor, maintained communication with WikiLeaks during the campaign.[37] At least once, Trump tweeted about WikiLeaks immediately following one of Don Jr.'s communications.[38]

Often, WikiLeaks releases were described by Trump associates before they happened. For example, on July 15, 2016, Michael Flynn emailed a colleague with the note that "[t]here are a number of things happening (and will happen) this election via cyber operations (by both hacktivists, nation-states and the DNC)."[39] One week later, on July 22, WikiLeaks publicly released 20,000 email messages hacked from the Democratic National Committee.[40] Meanwhile, Roger Stone hinted about forthcoming WikiLeaks information releases on multiple occasions.[41]

Finally, Trump himself made multiple public statements during the campaign supporting WikiLeaks' ongoing dissemination of hacked information.[42] Notably, on July 27, 2016, Trump appeared to encourage Russia to continue interfering with the election, stating: "Russia, if you're listening, I hope you're able to find the 30,000 emails that are missing, I think you will probably be rewarded mightily by our press."[43]

Later in the summer of 2016, the FBI specifically warned Trump that foreign adversaries, Russia in particular, would probably try to infiltrate his presidential campaign.[44] But the horse was already out of the barn.

If that were not enough, later that summer Don Jr. took *another* meeting with foreign nationals offering campaign assistance. On August 3, 2016, Don Jr. met at Trump Tower with Erik Prince, the former head of the Blackwater private military company; George Nader, a Lebanese-American businessman with a shadowy past, appearing on behalf of the crown princes of Saudi Arabia and the United Arab Emirates; and Joel Zamel, an Israeli social media expert with connections to both the Emirates and Russia.[45] While details of this meeting, any agreement, and the aftermath are not fully known yet, initial reports indicate that Nader told Don Jr. that the two crown princes were eager to help Trump win the election; that Don Jr. responded approvingly; that "after those initial offers of help, Mr. Nader was quickly embraced as a close ally by Trump campaign advisers," including Kushner and Flynn; and that after the election, Nader paid Zamel some $2 million.[46]

THE COVER-UP

Throughout 2016 and well into 2017, the Trump campaign repeatedly denied any contacts with Russia. For example, on July 24, 2016, Paul Manafort (who had been at the Trump Tower meeting the previous month) was asked by the host of ABC's *This Week* whether there were any connections between the Trump campaign and Russia. Manafort answered, "No, there are not. And you know, there's no basis to it."[47] Manafort, Trump himself, Sessions, and other Trump campaign and White House officials publicly denied any Russia contacts at least twenty times.[48]

In March 2017, Don Jr. denied to *The New York Times* that he ever represented the Trump campaign in a meeting with Russian nationals, insisting that he had never "set up" any meetings with Russians and "certainly none that I was representing the campaign in any way, shape or form."[49] However, when the June 9, 2016, Trump Tower meeting was publicly revealed on July 8, 2017, Don Jr. released the following public statement about the circumstances and purpose of the meeting.[50]

It was a short introductory meeting. I asked Jared and Paul to stop by. We primarily discussed a program about the adoption of Russian children that was active and popular with American families years ago and was since ended by the Russian government, but it was not a campaign issue at the time and there was no follow up. I was asked to attend the meeting by an acquaintance, but was not told the name of the person I would be meeting with beforehand.[51]

This statement was, of course, misleading.[52] The next day, July 9, *The New York Times* reported that, in advance of the meeting, Don Jr. was promised damaging information on Hillary Clinton.[53] Don Jr. then issued a second statement, providing slightly more information. By July 11, 2017, it was clear that Don Jr. had been specifically promised damaging information by an attorney working for the *Russian government*.[54]

President Trump was closely involved with issuing the misleading public statement on July 8, 2017. In fact, as reported at the time and later confirmed by Trump's lawyers, Trump *personally dictated* his son's statement about the meeting.[55] As for Don Jr., he admits that he spoke with his father about his public statement, but before Congress he claimed "attorney-client privilege" to avoid testifying about the conversation, even though neither Don Jr. nor the president is an attorney.[56]

WHAT DID THE PRESIDENT KNOW
AND WHEN DID HE KNOW IT?

We know that Don Jr., Manafort, Kushner, Papadopoulos, and a few other Trump associates were involved with the Russian outreach. What about Trump himself?

Current publicly available evidence does not conclusively establish that the president himself was personally aware of his campaign's frequent contacts with Russian-affiliated individuals, including the June 9, 2016, meeting involving his top advisors. However, an impeachment investigation is warranted by the circumstances.

First, well before the June 9, 2016, meeting, Trump was aware of at least some of his team's Russian outreach—at minimum, from the March 31, 2016, campaign meeting in which

Papadopoulos spoke of his efforts to arrange a meeting with Putin.

Second, campaign officials at the very highest levels attended the June 9 meeting. While some of Trump's defenders have dismissed Papadopoulos as a peripheral figure, that cannot be said for Manafort, Don Jr., or Kushner. And as the House Judiciary Committee made clear in its second article of impeachment against President Richard Nixon, a pattern of activity by subordinates may be attributed to the president for purposes of impeachment.[57]

Third, there is suggestive (though not conclusive) evidence that the president himself knew about the true purpose of the June 2016 meeting, either beforehand or shortly afterward. As noted above, call logs on June 6, 2016, suggest that Don Jr. may have called his father in between calls with Emin Agalarov. And right after the meeting with Russian operatives, Trump started tweeting about Hillary Clinton's emails.

Finally, at the very least, the fact that the president appears to have dictated his son's misleading July 8, 2017, public statement about the meeting suggests that he knew the true purpose of the meeting before it was reported in the newspapers.

★   ★   ★

Let's start with the president and his team's *criminal* exposure. While impeachable offenses do not need to be crimes, the criminal law can be a helpful starting point. Writing in 1974, just before the passage of the modern Federal Election Campaign Act, Professor Charles Black described "improper campaign tactics" as a potential category of impeachable offense, but warned that the impeachability was highly case-specific. He added: "Congress could do much more than it has done to make clear what the rules are to be."[58]

Just a few months after Black wrote those words—and after the House Judiciary Committee approved articles of impeachment against President Nixon, leading to his resignation—

Congress did, in fact, do much more to "make clear what the rules are to be." In October 1974, Congress passed major amendments to the Federal Election Campaign Act. And two years later, Congress again amended that act to add strict limits on foreign nationals giving or spending money in U.S. elections. During the Watergate investigation, Congress had discovered that the 1972 Nixon presidential election campaign had taken advantage of a loophole that allowed it to raise funds directly from foreign governments, such as the military government of Greece.[59] The Federal Election Campaign Act amendments aimed to close this loophole. Senator Lloyd Bentsen, the lead sponsor of a key amendment on this point, put it simply: "I do not think foreign nationals have any business in our political campaigns."[60]

The critical provision of the Federal Election Campaign Act strictly limits foreign nationals from giving or spending money in U.S. elections. It forbids a foreign national from making, or promising to make, "a contribution or donation of money or other thing of value . . . in connection with a Federal, State, or local election," or from making a campaign "expenditure [or] independent expenditure."[61] It also makes it illegal for anyone (such as a campaign official) to "solicit, accept, or receive a contribution or donation" from a foreign national for election campaign purposes.[62]

Since then, federal courts have understood that the ban on foreign money in U.S. elections is critical to preserving democratic self-government. In the 2010 case of *Bluman v. Federal Election Commission*, two foreign nationals in the United States on temporary work visas—one a Canadian citizen, the other a dual citizen of Canada and Israel—challenged these prohibitions as supposedly violating their First Amendment rights.[63] But a specially convened three-judge court rejected their argument. The court's opinion, written by Judge Brett Kavanaugh (a President George W. Bush appointee, whom Trump has floated as a potential Supreme Court nominee[64]) explained the importance of "preserv[ing] the basic conception of a political community" and "preventing foreign influence over the U.S. political process" to protect democratic self-government.[65] The Supreme Court then affirmed the lower court's opinion without further comment. (Perhaps nothing more needed to be said about the obvious reasons why the public should be able to protect democratic self-government against foreign influence.)

The facts of the *Bluman* case were considerably less disturbing than what happened in 2016. *Bluman* involved Canadians who lived full-time in the United States, one of whom hoped to "print flyers . . . and to distribute them in Central Park."[66] By contrast, the Trump campaign engaged in secretive communications with a hostile intelligence service about high-stakes efforts to influence the national election. While most violations of the Federal Election Campaign Act are resolved with fines rather than criminal charges, knowing and willful violations are punishable by up to five years in prison, depending on the offense, and recent years have seen several high-profile criminal prosecutions for violating this law.[67]

There are at least three distinct criminal threads at issue here: efforts by the Trump campaign to help shape Russian influence operations, such as paid social media, by providing useful guidance *to* Russian operatives; the Trump campaign's efforts to solicit valuable information *from* Russian operatives; and the cover-up.

SHAPING RUSSIAN INFLUENCE OPERATIONS: "SUBSTANTIAL ASSISTANCE" AND "COORDINATION"

Two different legal prohibitions under the Federal Election Campaign Act apply to the Trump campaign's efforts to supply useful information *to* Russian operatives: "substantial assistance" and "coordination."

The law prohibits anyone from providing "substantial assistance in the solicitation, making, acceptance, or receipt of a contribution or donation . . . [or] the making of an expenditure, independent expenditure, or disbursement" by a foreign national.[68] So for example, if a foreign national wants to target and schedule an operation for maximum impact, and the campaign gives substantial assistance, the campaign has violated the law.

A separate provision, which is not limited to foreign nationals, bans "coordination" between political campaigns and supposedly "outside" spenders. If a supposedly independent political operative spends money (such as by hiring people to make social media posts) to influence an election, and that spending is "made in cooperation, consultation or concert with, or at the request or suggestion of, a candidate [or] a candidate's [campaign] committee," or qualifies as a "coordinated communication," that expenditure is considered a "contribution" to the candidate even if no money changes hands.[69]

In essence, coordination converts what may look like a freelance third-party expenditure into an illegal campaign contribution. This is not a minor offense. For example, in 2012, a congressional campaign manager coordinated with a political action committee on $325,000 worth of political advertising opposing a rival candidate. He eventually pleaded guilty and was sentenced to twenty-four months in prison for illegal campaign coordination.[70] And because it is illegal for a campaign to accept *any* campaign contribution from foreign nationals, coordination with a foreign national is *always* illegal.

SOLICITATION OF A "THING OF VALUE" FROM FOREIGN NATIONALS

Trump campaign officials attended the June 9, 2016, meeting with the clear expectation and intention of receiving politically damaging information about Hillary Clinton from self-described Russian government agents. In political campaigns, opposition research is a valuable commodity—campaigns normally pay for it. Receiving it for free makes it a contribution of a "thing of value."[71] And in political campaigns, soliciting a thing of value from foreign nationals is flatly illegal.[72]

The publicly available evidence suggests that senior officials in the Trump campaign violated this provision multiple times and in several different ways. Nonpublic information about a candidate's opponent—hacked emails, or the "dirt" (in Joseph Mifsud's words) or opposition research that campaigns might normally pay for—is a "thing of value." As former White House counsel Bob Bauer notes, "[t]he President and others associated with the campaign made no bones about the value to them of [Democratic Party officials'] purloined email communications," citing them repeatedly at campaign events and in presidential debates.[73] And while the regulations provide a means for campaigns and campaign officials to defend themselves on the basis that they could not have reasonably known that the source of assistance was a foreign national, Trump and team have no such excuse.[74] The Trump campaign knew quite well that it was dealing with Russian nationals and government agents.

If Trump approved the meeting beforehand, he may have committed several different crimes. The first is *conspiracy*. The main federal conspiracy statute applies when, "two or more persons conspire either to commit any offense against the United States, or to defraud the United States, or any agency thereof in any manner or for any purpose, and one or more of such persons do any act to effect the object of the conspiracy."[75] In this case, that would be a conspiracy to solicit a thing of value (opposition research) from foreign nationals. It is subject to up to five years' imprisonment.[76] And contrary to the common usage of the term "conspiracy," which can suggest a complex scheme years in the making, federal conspiracy law does not require a detailed master plan. It simply requires that each conspirator share in the common purpose of committing the act that is unlawful, and that at least one of them take an "overt act" in furtherance of committing the unlawful act.[77]

Alternatively, Trump may have *aided and abetted* his son and associates in attempting to procure opposition research from foreign agents. Under the main federal "aiding and abetting" statute, someone who "aids, abets, counsels, commands, induces or procures [the] commission" of an offense is punishable as if he had done it himself.[78]

THE COVER-UP

The efforts to conceal and mislead the public about the June 2016 Trump Tower meeting with Russian operatives probably involved several crimes. The conspiracy statute's "fraud" prong prohibits conspiring "to defraud the United States, or any agency thereof."[79] As the Supreme Court has explained, this includes not only "to cheat the government out of property or money," but also "to interfere with or obstruct one of its lawful governmental functions by deceit, craft or trickery, or at least by means that are dishonest."[80] That would include a conspiracy to conceal an action from a regulatory agency, such as the Federal Election Commission.[81] Indeed, a federal grand jury indicted the Russian government operatives on this very charge.[82]

Trump could also be criminally liable for being an accessory after the fact and/or for misprision of felony. A defendant is guilty of being an accessory after the fact if he knows that a federal crime has been committed and then "relieves, comforts or assists the offender in order to hinder or prevent his apprehension, trial or punishment."[83] And a defendant is guilty of misprision of felony if he knows that a federal felony was committed but "conceals and does not as soon as possible make known the same to some judge or other person in civil or military authority under the United States."[84] Finally, Trump's efforts to throw law enforcement off the trail with a misleading public statement could constitute obstruction of justice, discussed in more detail later in this book.

★   ★   ★

Whether or not the president's personal actions in this area, by themselves, would amount to impeachable conduct, the president is also responsible for the acts of his subordinates. While "no president can or should be held responsible for the wrongs of all persons working under him," actions by subordinates may be attributed to the president in impeachment proceedings based on "the extent of the president's knowledge and moral culpability."[85] James Madison explained in the debates of the First Congress that the president's supervisory role over subordinates makes him subject to impeachment "if he suffers them to perpetrate with impunity high crimes or misdemeanours against the United States, or neglects to superintend their conduct, so as to check their excesses."[86]

The question is at what point the president becomes responsible for subordinates' wrongdoing. Professor Black argued that while "simple carelessness in supervision" would not make the president liable for the acts of those working on his behalf, "the president (like anybody else) is totally responsible for what he commands, suggests, or ratifies" and that "[w]hen carelessness is so gross and habitual as to be evidence of *indifference* to wrongdoing, it may be in effect equivalent to ratification of wrongdoing."[87] Notably, in the second article of impeachment against President Nixon, Congress set a precedent by including a pattern of activity by subordinates.[88]

★   ★   ★

What about treason? Given the documented Russian influence operations in the 2016 election and the strong evidence that the Trump campaign (probably including Trump himself) illegally conspired or coordinated with Russian government operatives, Trump's notable unwillingness to criticize or act against Russian interests, [89] and his apparent complete lack of interest in taking action to secure the United States against *future* election interference, people have begun to ask about treason.

As a criminal matter, treason has a precise definition, specified in the Constitution itself: "Treason against the United States, shall consist only in levying War against them, or in adhering to their Enemies, giving them Aid and Comfort." [90] There is an open legal question as to whether Russia could be considered an "enemy," and some authorities suggest a narrow definition of that term. [91]

But that may not matter for impeachment purposes. In the past, the Constitution's precise definition of treason (and special proof requirements) have led Congress to avoid specifically impeaching officials for treason even where it is clearly an appropriate description of the offense. In 1862, in the middle of the Civil War, Congress conducted impeachment proceedings against Judge West H. Humphreys, a federal judge in Tennessee who advocated secession, accepted a judicial appointment in the Confederacy, helped organize the armed rebellion, and levied war against the United States—all without resigning his judgeship. [92] Congress impeached and convicted Humphreys, but not for treason, which might have suggested a higher burden of proof. Rather, it impeached and convicted him for high crimes and misdemeanors that essentially encompassed that charge, including conspiring "to oppose by force the authority of the Government of the United States" and "organiz[ing] armed rebellion against the United States." [93]

A similar approach may be appropriate here. As noted earlier, the framers worried about the "corruption" of our government through "foreign intrigue."[94] Trump appears to be in foreign pay, through foreign emoluments and (in-kind) campaign contributions. As discussed above, each of those constitutes a separate impeachable offense. And Trump has suspiciously failed to secure our elections from future foreign election interference. (As it happens, in 1974 Professor Charles Black listed as an example of impeachability a president who "dangerously denuded the United States of its defenses, on some occasion of international tension."[95]) Whether or not we call Trump's conduct "treason," it is remarkably close to a scenario discussed in 1787 by Gouverneur Morris at the Constitutional Convention debates on the impeachment power:

> [The president] may be bribed by a greater interest to betray his trust; and no one would say that we ought to expose ourselves to the danger of seeing the first Magistrate in forign [sic] pay, without being able to guard agst. it by displacing him. One would think the King of England well secured agst. bribery. He has as it were a fee simple in the whole Kingdom. Yet Charles II was bribed by Louis XIV. The Executive ought therefore to be impeachable for treachery . . .[96]

The evidence suggests that Trump has "betray[ed] his trust to foreign powers" in myriad ways that merit an immediate impeachment investigation. Whether or not it meets the technical definition of "treason," it certainly carries the stench of "treachery," and that is plenty.

BOTTOM LINE: In the 2016 election, the senior-most officials of Trump's presidential campaign (including his campaign chairman, his son, and his son-in-law) met with Russian nationals after an invitation to receive compromising information about his campaign opponent, Hillary Clinton, that they were told would be of great value to the campaign. Federal campaign finance law prohibits a candidate or campaign from soliciting a foreign national (including a foreign government) for a thing of value. In 2017, after this meeting was revealed, Trump personally dictated a misleading public statement on behalf of his son as to the intended purpose of the meeting.

It is time for Congress to investigate whether to impeach President Trump for conspiring with others to solicit things of value from a foreign government and other foreign nationals, and to conceal those violations.

THREE

OBSTRUCTING JUSTICE

Since his first week in office, Trump has repeatedly tried to interfere with FBI and congressional investigations into his conduct and that of his subordinates by (variously) cajoling, threatening, misleading, and in some cases firing investigators with the intent of disrupting ongoing federal investigations. That is obstruction of justice—conduct intended to frustrate or impede an investigation.

★   ★   ★

Congress can establish obstruction of justice from facts that are already well known from the public record. Even if any one item standing alone is not conclusive, together they form a clear pattern. Much of the evidence comes from Trump's own mouth on camera, or his Twitter feed. (His tweets matter. According to the White House, Trump's tweets "are considered official statements by the president of the United States."[1] And as a recent federal court decision pointed out, his tweets are official presidential records and are considered "state action."[2]) The House Judiciary Committee can investigate the rest through documents and examination of witnesses—including, potentially, Trump himself. Furthermore, the House's impeachment investigation will not require advanced investigative techniques, such as forensic science or signals intelligence, or evidence from Special Counsel Robert Mueller's criminal investigation.

Nor does congressional investigation need to be held up until Mueller's report is completed.

The principal facts are publicly available from Trump's own statements, from testimony given in Congress, and from news reports in reliable mainstream outlets.[3] The account of FBI Director James Comey comes from his oral testimony to Congress, his written statement for the record, and contemporaneous memos that he wrote after several disturbing conversations with Trump. (Trump, for his part, has described these memos as "phony memos," adding that Comey "didn't write those accurately, and they have a lot of phony stuff."[4])

Here are the key points. We have not included every single detail, but enough to lay out the case.[5] If accurate, they indicate the following course of conduct.

IMPROPER DEMAND FOR LOYALTY

On January 26, 2017, Trump learned that the FBI was investigating then National Security Advisor Michael Flynn for suspicious communications with the Russian ambassador. That day, then Acting Attorney General Sally Yates warned White House Counsel Don McGahn about dishonest statements made by Flynn that she believed made Flynn a risk to national security.[6] As the White House later stated, "[i]mmediately after the Department of Justice notified the White House Counsel of the situation, the White House Counsel briefed the president and a small group of senior advisors."[7]

The very next day, January 27, Trump invited Comey to a private one-on-one dinner at the White House. At that dinner, as Comey later testified:

> The President began by asking me whether I wanted to stay on as FBI Director, which I found strange because he had already told me twice in earlier conversations that he hoped I would stay, and I had assured him that I in-

tended to. He said that lots of people wanted my job and, given the abuse I had taken during the previous year, he would understand if I wanted to walk away. *My instincts told me that the one-on-one setting, and the pretense that this was our first discussion about my position, meant the dinner was, at least in part, an effort to have me ask for my job and create some sort of patronage relationship.* That concerned me greatly, given the FBI's traditionally independent status in the executive branch . . .

A few moments later, the President said, "I need loyalty, I expect loyalty." . . .

Near the end of our dinner, the President returned to the subject of my job, saying he was very glad I wanted to stay, adding that he had heard great things about me from Jim Mattis, Jeff Sessions, and many others. *He then said, "I need loyalty."*[8]

The president's statements appear to be an attempt to gain influence over and/or intimidate the official in charge of a pending investigation. They can also be viewed as a form of bribery: offering to allow Director Comey to keep his job, on the condition that he would be "loyal" to the president.

FALSE STATEMENTS TO FBI DIRECTOR
REGARDING RUSSIA VISIT

At the January 27, 2017, dinner with James Comey, Trump made a false statement to Comey. Earlier, on January 6, 2017, Comey had alerted then President-elect Trump that some sources were claiming that the Russian government had video of Trump with prostitutes at the Ritz Carlton Hotel from when Trump visited Moscow for the Miss Universe pageant in 2013.[9] During the January 27 dinner, Trump brought up the topic unsolicited and claimed that during his 2013 trip to Moscow he did not stay overnight but rather departed by plane to

New York the same night.[10] Later, on February 8, the president repeated this claim to Comey in the presence of then Chief of Staff Reince Priebus.[11]

This was demonstrably false, as confirmed by flight records.[12] Indeed, a year later, on April 26, 2018, during a phone interview with the *Fox and Friends* show, Trump denied having told Comey that he had not stayed overnight in Moscow.[13]

Trump's lie to Comey was almost certainly intended to cast doubt on the validity of a broader set of allegations concerning Trump and his campaign's interactions with Russian nationals and the Russian government, and to induce Comey or the FBI not to further investigate these allegations.

IMPROPER REQUEST TO ABANDON
INVESTIGATION OF FLYNN

On February 13, 2017, Michael Flynn was forced to resign after some of the facts regarding his false statements became public. (As Trump explained months later, "I had to fire General Flynn because he lied to the Vice President and the FBI. He has pled guilty to those lies."[14])

The next day, Trump met in the Oval Office with Comey and other top officials: Vice President Mike Pence, Attorney General Jeff Sessions, the deputy director of the CIA, the director of the National Counter-Terrorism Center, the secretary of Homeland Security, and Trump's son-in-law and senior advisor, Jared Kushner. At the end of the meeting, the president asked everyone but Comey to leave the room.

Comey observed that Sessions hesitated before leaving. Comey later testified: "My sense was the attorney general knew he shouldn't be leaving, which is why he was lingering."[15]

Soon the president was alone with Comey. Trump asked Comey to abandon the investigation into Flynn. According to Comey's testimony:

When the door by the grandfather clock closed, and we were alone, the President began by saying, "I want to talk about Mike Flynn." . . . [After discussing other topics, the] President then returned to the topic of Mike Flynn, saying, "He is a good guy and has been through a lot." He repeated that Flynn hadn't done anything wrong on his calls with the Russians, but had misled the Vice President. He then said, *"I hope you can see your way clear to letting this go, to letting Flynn go. He is a good guy. I hope you can let this go."*

I immediately prepared an unclassified memo of the conversation about Flynn and discussed the matter with FBI senior leadership. *I had understood the President to be requesting that we drop any investigation of Flynn in connection with false statements about his conversations with the Russian ambassador in December.* I did not understand the President to be talking about the broader investigation into Russia or possible links to his campaign. I could be wrong, but I took him to be focusing on what had just happened with Flynn's departure and the controversy around his account of his phone calls. Regardless, *it was very concerning, given the FBI's role as an independent investigative agency. The FBI leadership team agreed with me that it was important not to infect the investigative team with the President's request,* which we did not intend to abide.[16]

Comey later explained that, when the president expressed a "hope" that Comey would "let this go," he took it as more than a suggestion: "I took it as a direction. He's the president of the United States, with me alone, saying, 'I hope this.' I took it as this is what he wants me to do."

As Trump later admitted, he had fired Flynn for lying to the FBI—a criminal offense. In fact, on December 1, 2017, Flynn pleaded guilty to making false statements to the FBI regarding interactions with the Russian government.[17] Trump's direction to Comey to "let this go" was an impermissible attempt to interfere with the ongoing FBI investigation into Flynn.[18]

IMPROPER REQUEST FOR ATTORNEY GENERAL TO PROTECT HIM FROM INVESTIGATION

On March 1, 2017, *The Washington Post* reported that Attorney General Jeff Sessions had not been candid with the Senate about his meetings with the Russian ambassador.[19] As public pressure mounted for Sessions to recuse himself from the investigation into Russian election interference and Trump campaign involvement, Trump directed Don McGahn to try to stop Sessions from recusing himself.[20]

However, on March 2, in accordance with advice from Department of Justice lawyers, Sessions recused himself "from any existing or future investigations of any matters related in any way to the campaigns for President of the United States."[21] This put Rod Rosenstein in charge of the Russia investigation.

Trump was displeased. At a meeting in Mar-a-Lago later in March, he reportedly berated Sessions and asked him to retake control of the investigation.[22] Sessions refused.

Trump's purpose in asking Sessions to un-recuse himself was simple but improper: he hoped that Sessions, a political ally, would be able to protect him from the investigation. To aides, Trump reportedly lamented, "Where's my Roy Cohn?,"[23] and to *The New York Times*, Trump explained that his preferred model for an attorney general was Eric Holder, whom he believed had "totally protected" President Obama.[24]

As Trump later told the *Times*, "Sessions should have never recused himself, and if he was going to recuse himself, he should have told me before he took the job and I would have picked somebody else."[25] Indeed, for much of July 2017, Trump publicly attempted to pressure Sessions to resign.[26] Even a year later, he was still tweeting, "The Russian Witch Hunt Hoax continues, all because Jeff Sessions didn't tell me he was going to recuse himself . . . I would have quickly picked someone else."[27]

In short, Trump first attempted to pressure Sessions to reassert control over an investigation from which Sessions had properly recused himself due to a conflict of interest. When Sessions refused to do that, Trump attempted to pressure him to resign. The fact that Sessions resisted that as well does not diminish the fact that Trump's efforts were transparently motivated by a desire to influence the course and outcome of the Department of Justice's investigation into his campaign.

IMPROPER PRESSURE TO MAKE PUBLIC STATEMENTS REGARDING INVESTIGATION

On March 30, 2017, Trump called Comey and asked him when federal authorities were going to state publicly that Trump was not personally under investigation.[28] This was not a new request; on February 15 Trump's then White House chief of staff, Reince Priebus, had reportedly called Comey to ask for help in countering news reports that Trump's associates had been in contact with Russian intelligence officials during the campaign.[29]

Comey did not agree to the president's request, in part because such a statement could potentially be misleading, depending on what the ongoing investigation might reveal. As he testified:

> I did not tell the President that the FBI and the Department of Justice had been reluctant to make public statements that we did not have an open case on President Trump for a number of reasons, *most importantly because it would create a duty to correct, should that change.*[30]

Trump's request was an attempt to prevent, or interfere with, an FBI investigation into Trump and his associates. So too was the call made by the president's chief of staff, which, according to precedent from the Nixon impeachment investigation, is attributable to the president himself because the chief of staff was acting as the president's agent.[31]

ATTEMPT TO MISUSE INTELLIGENCE OFFICIALS TO INTERFERE WITH INVESTIGATION

In March 2017, Trump reportedly asked two top intelligence officials to publicly deny the existence of any evidence against him in the matter under FBI investigation.[32] According to news reports, the following sequence unfolded.

On March 22, shortly after Comey's March 20 testimony to the House Intelligence Committee that the FBI was investigating "the nature of any links between individuals associated with the Trump campaign and the Russian government and whether there was any coordination between the campaign and Russia's efforts," Director of National Intelligence Dan Coats and then CIA director (now secretary of state) Mike Pompeo attended a briefing at the White House along with other government officials. At the end of the briefing, Trump reportedly asked everyone to clear the room except for Coats and Pompeo. Then he complained to them about the FBI's Russia investigation.[33]

On March 22 or 23, Trump personally called Coats and asked him to publicly deny any evidence of collusion between the Trump campaign and Russian officials.[34] Coats deemed the request inappropriate, and refused to comply. Shortly afterward, Trump made a similar request to Admiral Michael Rogers, the director of the National Security Agency, who similarly refused. (Trump's conversation with Rogers was documented in a contemporaneous internal memo written by a senior NSA official.)

At about the same time, "senior White House officials sounded out top intelligence officials about the possibility of intervening directly with Comey to encourage the FBI to drop its probe of Michael Flynn." The line of questioning was reportedly paraphrased by one official as "Can we ask him to shut down the investigation? Are you able to assist in this matter?"[35]

If these news reports are accurate, this was an attempt to misuse federal officials to interfere with another agency's investigation.[36] It is even more direct than President Nixon's infamous "smoking gun" tape, in which (among other things) he asked his chief of staff to ask the Central Intelligence Agency to help derail an FBI investigation.[37] Here, Trump called the intelligence officials himself.

IMPROPER ATTEMPT TO
ENFORCE "LOYALTY" COMMITMENT

On April 11, the president called James Comey and asked him what he had done to convey publicly that Trump was not personally under investigation. Comey recommended that Trump convey his request to Department of Justice leadership. According to Comey:

> [Trump] said he would do that and added, *"Because I have been very loyal to you, very loyal; we had that thing you know."* I did not reply or ask him what he meant by "that thing."[38]

In trying to box Comey into making a public statement with references to being "loyal to you" because of "that thing," Trump was trying to enforce the improper loyalty commitment that he demanded (and may have thought he received) from Comey on January 27, apparently in exchange for his continued employment.

At the same time, Trump sought loyalty from Michael Flynn. On April 25, the president reportedly told Flynn to "stay strong."[39]

MISUSE OF FEDERAL OFFICIALS
TO PROVIDE FALSE PRETEXT

By his own later admission, Trump decided to fire Comey on or before May 8, 2017, because of the investigation in question.

Reportedly, President Trump and political aide Stephen Miller drafted a letter that reflected the president's actual thinking. White House Counsel Don McGahn apparently prevailed on the president not to issue that letter.[40]

Instead, Trump first enlisted Sessions and Deputy Attorney General Rod Rosenstein to create pretextual memos offering an unrelated basis to fire Comey. Rosenstein, who apparently received a copy of the original letter drafted by Trump and Miller, wrote a completely different memo, based on the fact that Comey had improperly disclosed information about a separate investigation involving Hillary Clinton before the 2016 election and before the president's decision to retain Comey as the FBI director. Rosenstein later told Congress in a prepared statement:

> On May 8, I learned that President Trump intended to remove Director Comey and sought my advice and input . . . I wrote a brief memorandum to the Attorney General summarizing my longstanding concerns about Director Comey's public statements concerning the Secretary Clinton email investigation. I chose the issues to include in my memorandum.[41]

The timing and order of those events are extremely significant. Trump *first* decided to fire Comey, *then*, at the president's direction, Rosenstein wrote a memo describing a rationale for the firing based on grounds *that Rosenstein himself identified*. The grounds set forth in Rosenstein's memo therefore could not have formed the basis for Trump's earlier decision to fire Comey. To the extent that the president pointed to the Rosenstein memo, the grounds contained in that memo were pretextual.

Trump's use of federal employees to create a false pretext is independent evidence of obstruction of justice. The president intended to mislead any future investigation and thereby impede or obstruct the administration of justice.

FIRING FBI DIRECTOR TO INTERFERE WITH AN ONGOING INVESTIGATION

On May 9, 2017, Trump fired James Comey. While the president initially claimed this was for reasons cited in the pretextual memos, that explanation quickly unraveled.

On May 10 (the day after the Comey firing), the president revealed his motive for the firing to the Russian ambassador and foreign minister in the Oval Office, in the presence of several American officials. According to meeting notes that the White House does not dispute, the president stated: "I just fired the head of the F.B.I. He was crazy, a real nut job. I faced great pressure because of Russia. That's taken off. I'm not under investigation."[42] This unsolicited statement confirms that his reason for firing Director Comey was because the president personally "faced great pressure" from the FBI's investigation. With Comey gone, he believed, "[t]hat's taken off."

And on May 11, Trump explained the real reason to NBC interviewer Lester Holt:

> I—I was going to fire Comey. Uh I—there's no good time to do it by the way . . . [Deputy Attorney General Rosenstein] made a recommendation but regardless of recommendation I was going to fire Comey knowing, there was no good time to do it. *And in fact when I decided to just do it, I said to myself, I said you know, this Russia thing with Trump and Russia is a made-up story*, it's an excuse by the Democrats for having lost an election that they should have won.[43]

On its face, Trump's on-camera statement constitutes an admission that he fired Comey to impede the course of a specific investigation ("this Russia thing with Trump and Russia"). The inference is compelling that the president fired Comey to inhibit or end that investigation.

As Comey later testified: "I was fired in some way to change, or the endeavor was to change, the way the Russia investigation was being conducted. And that is a very big deal."[44]

Trump's decision to fire Comey because of his claim that "this Russia thing with Trump and Russia is a made-up story," and that by firing Comey the "great pressure" he faced "because of Russia" would be "taken off," was an attempt to interfere with the conduct of an FBI investigation by firing its director.

Much later, Trump and his team would attempt to backtrack his admission. In June 2018, Trump contradicted his earlier words to Lester Holt by now claiming, "Not that it matters but I never fired James Comey because of Russia! The Corrupt Mainstream Media loves to keep pushing that narrative, but they know it is not true!"[45] Trump's criminal defense lawyer, Rudy Giuliani, provided a different explanation of why Trump fired Comey: "He fired Comey because Comey would not—among other things—say that [Trump] wasn't a target of the investigation . . . He fired him and he said, 'I'm free of this guy.'"[46] Under this account, Trump fired Comey for refusing to comply with Trump's demand to prematurely end a law-enforcement investigation out of Trump's own self-interest. This is hardly an improvement from what Trump said in May 2017.[47]

Trump's firing of Comey also set the stage for a consequential development: Rosenstein's decision, just eight days later, to appoint Robert Mueller, a distinguished former federal prosecutor and FBI director, as special counsel to continue Comey's investigation.[48]

ATTEMPT TO INTIMIDATE
AND DISCREDIT A WITNESS

On May 12, 2017, after widespread negative reaction to the Comey firing among the public, media, and members of Congress, Trump tweeted: "James Comey better hope that there are no 'tapes' of our conversations before he starts leaking to the press!"[49]

This tweet was almost certainly intended to deter Comey (now no longer a law enforcement officer, but a witness in a potential obstruction case) from speaking out. It was designed (even if it did not succeed) to threaten and intimidate Comey to discourage him from sharing unfavorable information about the president.

In short, Trump engaged in a sustained course of attempts to interfere with ongoing FBI investigations. He first asked Comey to abandon his investigations; when Comey would not, he tried to enlist other government officials to get Comey to abandon the investigations; when that did not work either, Trump enlisted federal officials to develop a pretextual rationale and fired him. And even after the firing, Trump attempted to intimidate Comey over Twitter. The evidence is compelling, does not require sophisticated investigative techniques, and in several instances, comes from the president's own mouth on video, on Twitter, or in the presence of reputable witnesses.

ATTEMPT TO INTERFERE
WITH CONGRESSIONAL INVESTIGATIONS

Over the summer of 2017, Trump repeatedly urged leaders in Congress to end their investigations. According to Senator Richard Burr of North Carolina, the chairman of the Senate Intelligence Committee, Trump in essence told him: "I hope you can conclude this as quickly as possible."[50] Trump also reportedly told Senate Majority Leader Mitch McConnell of

Kentucky, and Senator Roy Blunt of Missouri, a member of the Intelligence Committee, to end the investigation swiftly.[51] Apparently, he "complained frequently to Mr. McConnell about not doing enough to bring the investigation to an end."[52] And, while on a flight with Blunt on Air Force One in August 2017, the president urged Blunt "to wrap up this investigation."[53] Trump also asked other Republican senators to lobby Burr to close the Russia investigation.[54]

ATTEMPT TO USE PARDONS TO DISCOURAGE WITNESSES FROM TESTIFYING

In the late summer or fall of 2017, Trump's then criminal-defense lawyer, John Dowd, reportedly contacted the lawyers representing Flynn and Paul Manafort, the Trump campaign's one-time campaign manager, regarding potential pardons for their clients.[55] Reports suggest that Dowd may have been "offering pardons to influence their decisions about whether to plead guilty and cooperate in the investigation."[56]

"Dangling" pardon offers is a classic case of presidential obstruction of justice. For example, the first article of impeachment against President Richard Nixon included a specification for "endeavouring to cause prospective defendants, and individuals duly tried and convicted, to expect favoured treatment and consideration in return for their silence or false testimony, or rewarding individuals for their silence or false testimony," which specifically included discussions of presidential pardons.[57]

Yet at the same time, a president who wants to convey his willingness to offer pardons to former aides who may already be cooperating with prosecutors, or under surveillance, faces a conundrum. Contacting them *directly* to offer a pardon in exchange for silence is legally risky. But he can *indirectly* send that message by pardoning someone else—someone convicted of similar crimes, or someone equally (or more) controversial.[58]

On Friday evening, August 25, 2017, Trump issued his first

presidential pardon to Joe Arpaio, the former sheriff of Maricopa County, Arizona. Arpaio had been convicted of criminal contempt of court for willfully disobeying a court order to stop violating individuals' constitutional rights. (This pardon, which is deeply problematic independent of the obstruction of justice issues, is discussed in greater detail in Chapter 5.)

The timing of the pardon was significant. Most presidents save controversial pardons for late in their terms. The fact that Trump was willing to issue a "hot" pardon so early in his term indicates that he is not going to fret about political blowback from pardoning his associates.

Next, consider the offense itself—contempt of court. In a complex criminal investigation, like Mueller's, prosecutors sometimes want a low-level witness to testify against higher-ups. If the witness refuses to testify, claiming the Fifth Amendment right against self-incrimination, prosecutors can grant that witness immunity from prosecution. If the witness *still* refuses to testify, then he or she can be prosecuted for criminal contempt.[59] But Trump has signaled that he will pardon criminal contempt. So Trump's pardon of Arpaio sent a clear message to Trump's current and former associates: "Stay strong."

Then on April 13, 2018, Trump pardoned Lewis "Scooter" Libby. During the second Bush administration, Libby had been the chief of staff to Vice President Dick Cheney. In 2007, Libby was convicted of obstruction of justice, perjury, and making false statements to the FBI, stemming from an investigation into leaking classified information about an undercover CIA agent. Yet Trump's pardon had little practical effect on Libby himself. In 2007, President Bush commuted Libby's sentence, so he served no prison time. And while Libby initially suffered some collateral effects of the conviction, including suspension of his license to practice law, these collateral effects had ended before Trump was even elected.[60]

By 2018, therefore, a pardon for Libby was entirely symbolic—to send a message. Notably, Bush had pointedly refused to pardon

Libby, despite Cheney's entreaties. The most obvious message to Trump's associates is this contrast: unlike Bush, who refused to pardon a top aide when it could have made a difference in his life, Trump will dispense pardons to aides as needed. In other words, loyalty comes with a get-out-of-jail-free card.

If the message was not sufficiently clear, in May 2018, Trump pardoned political commentator Dinesh D'Souza (who had pleaded guilty to violating the Federal Election Campaign Act), and publicly floated the idea of extending clemency to both former Illinois governor Rod Blagojevich (who had been impeached and then convicted on federal corruption charges, including lying to the FBI) and celebrity lifestyle mogul Martha Stewart (who had completed a prison sentence after conviction for lying to federal investigators).[61] Given the uncanny similarity between the crimes of these individuals and the actual or potential criminal charges against Trump's associates, these moves were widely understood as signals to Trump aides.

Taken together, the pardon offers to Flynn and Manafort, the pardons granted to Libby and D'Souza, and the continued discussions of potential clemency for others convicted of similar offenses to those of Trump's own aides are part of a concerted effort to use the presidential pardon power to induce witnesses not to cooperate with law enforcement.

If that were not enough, Trump has warned that he may even attempt to pardon *himself*. On June 4, 2018, he tweeted, "As has been stated by numerous legal scholars, I have the absolute right to PARDON myself, but why would I do that when I have done nothing wrong?"[62] The idea of a presidential self-pardon fundamentally contradicts the basic premise that no one, not even the president, is above the law. A president who can pardon himself could commit federal crimes without the slightest fear of punishment. Indeed, in 1974, just four days before Nixon resigned, the Department of Justice's Office of Legal Counsel issued an opinion concluding that "[u]nder the fundamental rule that no one may be a judge in his own case, the President cannot pardon himself."[63] But regardless of whether Trump ever attempts to pardon himself, his announcement sent a clear message that he has no compunctions against using the pardon power to protect himself from a criminal investigation.

ATTEMPTS TO IMPEDE OR TERMINATE SPECIAL COUNSEL'S INVESTIGATION

Ever since Robert Mueller began his work on May 17, 2017, Trump has made several efforts to impede Mueller's investigation. In June 2017, just a few weeks after Mueller's appointment, Trump attempted to fire him.[64] In discussions with White House counsel Don McGahn, Trump asserted that Mueller had a conflict of interest due to his resignation from Trump National Golf Club in Sterling, Virginia, some years earlier. Trump also claimed that Mueller could not be impartial due to work his former law firm had provided for Jared Kushner. Trump demanded that McGahn order the Department of Justice to fire Mueller. But Trump's arguments were so specious and inappropriate that McGahn refused and threatened to resign.[65]

In December 2017, Trump again attempted to fire Mueller.[66] Reportedly, Trump had frequently discussed with his staff his desire to remove Mueller, and his hesitation to make the decision came only after his lawyers convinced him that doing so would further imperil his public and legal standing.[67] Nonetheless, on December 28, 2017, Trump told *The New York Times*, "I have absolute right to do what I want to do with the Justice Department," while offering the hedged assurance that "for purposes of hopefully thinking I'm going to be treated fairly, I've stayed uninvolved with this particular matter."[68]

The June 2017 firing attempt first came to public light in a January 25, 2018, *New York Times* article. In the last days of January 2018, Trump told an aide to convey that McGahn should issue a statement denying the *Times* report—specifically, to deny that Trump had ordered McGahn to have Mueller fired.[69] But as McGahn reminded the president, Trump *had* asked McGahn to arrange Mueller's dismissal. McGahn refused to lie publicly as requested by Trump.[70]

On April 26, 2018, Trump once again made a veiled threat to interfere with Mueller's investigation. In an interview with the television program *Fox and Friends*, Trump stated, "I've taken the position—*and I don't have to take this position and maybe I'll change*—that I will not be involved with the Justice Department."[71] This comment came after he criticized the Department of Justice for spending "8 Million Dollars investigating [him]."[72]

These comments make his intentions clear. While it is unclear at this time what, if anything, Trump will do to Department of Justice officials, a decision to fire Mueller, Rosenstein, or even Sessions would add even more fuel to the obstruction of justice case against him.[73]

FIRING DEPUTY FBI DIRECTOR ANDREW MCCABE

Late on Friday night, March 16, 2018, Attorney General Jeff Sessions fired Andrew McCabe, the deputy director of the FBI.

McCabe had been involved in several recent high-profile investigations, including the investigation of Hillary Clinton's email mismanagement, and the counterintelligence investigation of Russian interference in the 2016 election. He had also authorized a criminal investigation, begun in 2017 but not publicly revealed until March 2018, into whether Sessions had lied to the U.S. Senate Judiciary Committee during his confirmation hearings about his contacts with Russian officials.[74]

Furthermore, James Comey had told McCabe contemporaneously about his own interactions with Trump, and McCabe may thus be a key witness to obstruction of justice.[75] For example, as McCabe later testified to the House Intelligence Committee, Comey had recounted his April 11, 2017, conversation with the president to McCabe shortly after it occurred. As Mc-

Cabe later explained, he interpreted the president's statement (to Comey) that "I have been very loyal to you, very loyal; we had that thing you know" as a "veiled threat" against Comey.[76]

For months before the firing, Trump had publicly insisted that Andrew McCabe be fired. Trump based this demand on what has been described as "an unwholesome conspiracy theory about McCabe's wife."[77] In 2015, Dr. Jill McCabe ran (unsuccessfully) for the Virginia State Senate. At this point, her husband, Andrew, was not deputy director of the FBI, nor did he have any role in the investigation of Hillary Clinton's email mismanagement.[78] During 2015, Jill McCabe's campaign received $467,500 from a political action committee associated with then Governor Terry McAuliffe (a Clinton ally) and another $207,788 from the Virginia Democratic Party.[79] Later, after the November 2015 election (which Jill McCabe lost), Andrew McCabe was named deputy director and joined the executive leadership team under Comey, with some oversight role for the Clinton investigation.[80]

After Trump fired Comey, Andrew McCabe became acting director of the FBI. But just two months later, Trump began calling for McCabe to be fired. Over the course of 2017–18, Trump repeatedly tweeted on this subject. Most of his tweets tied together (albeit with little regard for factual accuracy) Jill McCabe's 2015 acceptance of campaign contributions from Clinton allies, Andrew McCabe's 2016 role in the Clinton email investigation, and Andrew McCabe's 2017 role in witnessing Trump's own obstruction of justice. For example, in the latter half of 2017, Trump tweeted:

- "Problem is that the acting head of the FBI and the person in charge of the Hillary investigation, Andrew McCabe, got $700,000 from H for wife!" (July 25, 2017)[81]
- "Why didn't A.G. Sessions replace Acting FBI Director Andrew McCabe, a Comey friend who was in charge of Clinton investigation but got . . . big dollars ($700,000)

for his wife's political run from Hillary Clinton and her representatives. Drain the Swamp!" (July 26, 2017)[82]

- "How can FBI Deputy Director Andrew McCabe, the man in charge, along with leakin' James Comey, of the Phony Hillary Clinton investigation (including her 33,000 illegally deleted emails) be given $700,000 for wife's campaign by Clinton Puppets during investigation?" (Dec. 23, 2017)[83]

- "FBI Deputy Director Andrew McCabe is racing the clock to retire with full benefits. 90 days to go?!!!" (Dec. 23, 2017)[84]

In February 2018, the Department of Justice's inspector general wrote a report (not made public until April 2018) regarding McCabe's role in public disclosures regarding Clinton investigations.[85] The report centered on how certain law enforcement–sensitive information (in particular, an August 2016 conversation in which a Department of Justice official expressed concerns about the FBI's investigation of the Clinton Foundation, and McCabe "pushed back, asking 'are you telling me that I need to shut down a validly predicated investigation?'"[86]) came to be disclosed to a *Wall Street Journal* reporter. Ultimately, the report concluded that McCabe had authorized a disclosure to the reporter that violated FBI policies on commenting on ongoing investigations—and then misled both Comey and investigators about his having authorized the disclosure.[87]

Late on Friday night, March 16, 2018, two days before McCabe was scheduled to retire, Sessions fired him, ostensibly based on the findings of the inspector general's report. But the president left little doubt of his *own* motivations. Trump tweeted:

- "Andrew McCabe FIRED, a great day for the hard working men and women of the FBI—A great day for

Democracy. Sanctimonious James Comey was his boss and made McCabe look like a choirboy. He knew all about the lies and corruption going on at the highest levels of the FBI!" (Mar. 16, 2018)[88]

- "The Fake News is beside themselves that McCabe was caught, called out and fired. How many hundreds of thousands of dollars was given to wife's campaign by Crooked H friend, Terry M, who was also under investigation? How many lies? How many leaks? Comey knew it all, and much more!" (Mar. 17, 2018)[89]

On March 17, it emerged that McCabe, like Comey, had kept detailed memos of his interactions with Trump.[90] Trump then tweeted: "Spent very little time with Andrew McCabe, but he never took notes when he was with me. I don't believe he made memos except to help his own agenda, probably at a later date. Same with lying James Comey. Can we call them Fake Memos?"[91]

On April 13, the Department of Justice publicly released the inspector general report. The president then tweeted: "DOJ just issued the McCabe report—which is a total disaster. He LIED! LIED! LIED! McCabe was totally controlled by Comey—McCabe is Comey!! No collusion, all made up by this den of thieves and lowlifes!"[92]

It strains credibility to suggest that Trump and Sessions were genuinely exercised by McCabe's lack of candor with Comey or internal investigators as to who had approved telling the media that McCabe insisted on investigating the Clinton Foundation. Sessions had *himself* misled the Senate about his contacts with Russian government officials, and in fact was under a criminal investigation *authorized by McCabe* for that lack of candor. As for Trump, he can hardly be believed to be concerned about FBI sources insisting on investigating the Clinton Foundation. And in any event, his tweets make clear that this was not his real concern. Rather,

the *most credible* interpretation of Trump's action here was
to discredit McCabe as a potential witness against him regarding obstruction of the investigation into Russian interference in the presidential election.

PUBLIC ATTACKS ON SPECIAL COUNSEL
INVESTIGATION AND DEPARTMENT OF JUSTICE

Trump has also made public statements designed to undermine the special counsel's credibility and independence. For
example, on March 17, 2017, he tweeted:

> The Mueller probe should never have been started in
> that there was no collusion and there was no crime. It
> was based on fraudulent activities and a Fake Dossier
> paid for by Crooked Hillary and the DNC, and improp-
> erly used in FISA COURT for surveillance of my cam-
> paign. WITCH HUNT![93]

But Trump's attacks on the Justice Department are not limited to the special counsel—he also makes public statements
attacking the Department of Justice as a whole, designed to
undermine its credibility and independence.

- "The top Leadership and Investigators of the FBI and the
  Justice Department have politicized the sacred investigative
  process in favor of Democrats and against Republicans—
  something which would have been unthinkable just a short
  time ago. Rank and File are great people!" (Feb. 2, 2018)[94]
- "As the House Intelligence Committee has concluded,
  there was no collusion between Russia and the Trump
  Campaign. As many are now finding out, however,
  there was tremendous leaking, lying and corruption
  at the highest levels of the FBI, Justice and State.
  #DrainTheSwamp" (Mar. 17, 2018)[95]

- "Why is A.G. Jeff Sessions asking the Inspector General to investigate potentially massive FISA abuse. Will take forever, has no prosecutorial power and already late with reports on Comey etc. Isn't the I.G. an Obama guy? Why not use Justice Department lawyers? DISGRACEFUL!" (Feb. 28, 2018)[96]

- "Look how things have turned around on the Criminal Deep State. They go after Phony Collusion with Russia, a made up Scam, and end up getting caught in a major SPY scandal the likes of which this country may never have seen before! What goes around, comes around!" (May 23, 2018)[97]

Trump has even publicly inserted himself into congressional oversight disputes between members of Congress and the Department of Justice:

- "Lawmakers of the House Judiciary Committee are angrily accusing the Department of Justice of missing the Thursday Deadline for turning over UNREDACTED Documents relating to FISA abuse, FBI, Comey, Lynch, McCabe, Clinton Emails and much more. Slow walking— what is going on? BAD!" (Apr. 7, 2018)[98]

- "What does the Department of Justice and FBI have to hide? Why aren't they giving the strongly requested documents (unredacted) to the HOUSE JUDICIARY COMMITTEE? Stalling, but for what reason? Not looking good!" (Apr. 7, 2018)[99]

- "A Rigged System—They don't want to turn over Documents to Congress. What are they afraid of? Why so much redacting? Why such unequal 'justice?' At some point I will have no choice but to use the powers granted to the Presidency and get involved!" (May 2, 2018)[100]

USE OF PRESIDENTIAL AUTHORITY TO OBTAIN
CONFIDENTIAL LAW ENFORCEMENT INFORMATION
IN INVESTIGATION AGAINST HIMSELF

On May 16, 2018, *The New York Times* reported on the early stages of the FBI's counterintelligence investigation into attempted Russian intelligence penetration of the Trump campaign in 2016.[101] In particular, the report revealed that the FBI had used a confidential source (later identified as Stefan Halper, a professor who had served in the Reagan administration) to approach Trump aides who were suspected of being compromised by, if not agents of, Russian intelligence.[102]

Trump reacted negatively. Notwithstanding explanations that the FBI used a confidential source to *protect* the Trump campaign,[103] Trump increasingly criticized the FBI as the week progressed. On Friday, May 18, 2018, he tweeted: "Reports are there was indeed at least one FBI representative implanted, for political purposes, into my campaign for president. It took place very early on, and long before the phony Russia Hoax became a 'hot' Fake News story. If true—all time biggest political scandal!"[104] After members of Congress began to demand FBI law enforcement records, on Saturday, May 19, he further stated: "If the FBI or DOJ was infiltrating a campaign for the benefit of another campaign, that is a really big deal. Only the release or review of documents that the House Intelligence Committee (also, Senate Judiciary) is asking for can give the conclusive answers. Drain the Swamp!"[105]

Finally, on Sunday, May 20, Trump tweeted: "I hereby demand, and will do so officially tomorrow, that the Department of Justice look into whether or not the FBI/DOJ infiltrated or surveilled the Trump Campaign for Political Purposes—and if any such demands or requests were made by people within the Obama Administration!"[106]

Later that day, Rod Rosenstein announced that he had asked the Department of Justice's inspector general to investigate whether "there was any impropriety or political motivation in how the FBI conducted its counterintelligence investigation of persons suspected of involvement with the Russian agents who interfered in the 2016 presidential election."[107] However, Trump was not satisfied. On Monday, May 21, 2018, Trump summoned Rosenstein and FBI director Christopher Wray to the White House. As Trump's lawyer Rudy Giuliani explained, Trump conducted that meeting in his official capacity as president.[108]

While the exact details of Trump's meeting with Rosenstein and Wray are not known at the time of this writing, later that day the White House issued a statement announcing that "White House Chief of Staff Kelly will immediately set up a meeting with the FBI, DOJ, and [Director of National Intelligence] together with Congressional Leaders to review highly classified and other information they have requested."[109] This suggests that Trump may have used his executive authority over Rosenstein and Wray to order them to turn over law-enforcement materials to which the subject of an investigation would not ordinarily have access at this stage. (Kelly and Emmett Flood, a White House lawyer who is helping defend the president in the special counsel's investigation, attended part of the meeting.[110]) That information could help Trump and other potential defendants who have not yet been interviewed by investigators to understand what the FBI already knows and prepare accordingly. Furthermore, Trump's ordering an investigation of the investigators was intended to attack the credibility of federal law enforcement and thereby undermine the investigation of himself and his associates.

★   ★   ★

The framers of our Constitution knew obstruction of justice to be a serious offense against society. For example, William Blackstone's influential *Commentaries on the Laws of England*— published just a few years before the Revolution, and widely read among the founders—listed some of those "crimes and misdemeanors, that more especially affect the common-wealth." Blackstone's third example was "*obstructing* the exe-cution of lawful *process*," which he described as "at all times an offence of a very high and presumptuous nature."[111] Soon afterward, the Declaration of Independence listed, among its charges against King George, that "[h]e has obstructed the Ad-ministration of Justice."[112]

Obstruction of justice has played a central role in ear-lier impeachment proceedings against U.S. presidents. It grounded the first article of impeachment against President Nixon approved by the House Judiciary Committee in 1974.[113] That article cited President Nixon for, among other things, "interfering or endeavouring to interfere with the conduct of investigations by the Department of Justice of the United States, the Federal Bureau of Investigation, the office of Watergate Special Prosecution Force and Congressional Committees."[114] Nixon himself, while vigorously proclaim-ing his innocence, had earlier acknowledged that "obstruc-tion of justice is a serious crime and would be an impeachable offense."[115] Similarly, in 1998 the House of Representatives ap-proved an article of impeachment against President Clinton for obstruction of justice.[116] And in 2009, the House of Repre-sentatives impeached Judge Samuel B. Kent (who resigned a few days later) for obstruction of justice.[117]

Obstruction of justice is one of the areas where there is a strong overlap between federal criminal law and the concept of an impeachable high crime or misdemeanor. Congress has defined twenty-one distinct criminal offenses under the head-ing of obstruction of justice.[118] And it is indeed likely that some of Trump's conduct may violate one or more federal criminal obstruction of justice statutes.[119]

But while broadly applicable existing obstruction-of-justice statutes certainly can help clarify the impeachable offense, the president's criminal liability is not the end of the question. When Congress drafts criminal statutes, it generally does not write specific provisions to cover the president of the United States. The primary question here is not whether Trump has violated standard federal criminal statutes that could put him at risk of imprisonment. The question is whether he has violated the public trust in a manner warranting removal from office. The *high crime or misdemeanor* of obstruction of justice is separate from, and broader than, the *federal criminal offense* of obstructing justice. Indeed, as noted earlier, scholars and Congress broadly agree that impeachable offenses need not even be crimes.[120] And as Professor Steve Vladeck has noted, "a debate on the finer points of federal obstruction of justice law" can miss the forest for the trees because "the Constitution leaves it to Congress, not the courts, to decide whether a president should be 'removed from Office' for 'Treason, Bribery, or other high Crimes and Misdemeanors.'"[121]

For this reason, Congress may properly find that the president's abuse of his power to impede investigations was an impeachable offense whether or not his conduct meets each of the technical requirements necessary for a criminal conviction. For example, some of the criminal-obstruction statutes involve some fairly technical niceties, such as whether a particular statute should be interpreted to require an implied prerequisite of an ongoing "proceeding" and whether a particular investigation qualifies as such a "proceeding."[122] Congress need not tie itself in such knots when considering the broader question of whether the president has attempted to undermine the justice system that he is sworn to uphold by abusing his power to frustrate an investigation into himself, his campaign, and his administration.

Similarly, securing a conviction under the various federal obstruction-of-justice statutes typically requires that the defendant "corruptly" intended to interfere with a specific or foreseeable proceeding.[123] Courts have differed on the meaning of "corruptly," with some interpreting it to mean that the prosecution "only has to establish that the defendant should have reasonably seen that the natural and probable consequences of his acts was the obstruction of justice,"[124] and others interpreting it to mean that the defendant was "motivated by an improper purpose."[125] For prosecutors contemplating a criminal case against Trump, these questions are critical. But, as Professor Laurence Tribe has noted, Congress can cut through this thicket. Obviously, Congress should only impeach the president if he exercised his powers wrongfully. But in making that determination, Congress could take a broader view of the intent necessary for obstruction for impeachment purposes than would be appropriate in a criminal proceeding.[126]

It is also important not to lose sight of the big picture. The conduct described above is not a set of completely isolated and unrelated incidents; it is a course of conduct. Take, for example, Trump's repeated false statement to FBI director Comey about his overnight in Moscow. In some contexts, making false statements to the FBI is itself a criminal offense, if calculated to influence or induce government action.[127] But regardless of whether Trump's lie to Comey was an independently prosecutable criminal offense, it was almost certainly intended to cast doubt on the validity of a broader set of allegations concerning Trump and his campaign's interactions with Russian nationals and the Russian government, and induce Comey or the FBI not to further investigate these allegations. Thus, Trump's lying to Comey is evidence of an improper intent in his entire obstructionist course of conduct, and consciousness of guilt.[128] Impeachment proceedings do not require proof of intent, but understanding how Trump's lies fit in with the larger course of conduct helps put individual incidents into perspective.

The same goes for Trump's *public* lies. Indeed, in the Nixon impeachment articles, the House Judiciary Committee specifically cited, as an element of obstruction of justice:

> making or causing to be made false or misleading public statements for the purpose of deceiving the people of the United States into believing that a thorough and complete investigation had been conducted with respect to allegations of misconduct on the part of personnel of the executive branch of the United States and personnel of the [president's campaign committee] and that there was no involvement of such personnel in such misconduct.[129]

An objection occasionally stated is that much of the president's conduct at issue, if viewed from a distance in abstract terms, fits within the scope of presidential power. For example, no one disputes, in general, that presidents have the authority to fire FBI directors. But that does not mean that there are no limits on how the president can exercise that power.

Focusing for the moment on the criminal law of obstruction of justice, an action that might be legal in one context—such as shredding office documents, or knocking on someone's door to say, "You have a lovely house, and I hope nothing bad happens to it"—can form the basis of an obstruction of justice charge if done corruptly to influence or impede a proceeding. The same goes for presidential authority: a particular exercise of presidential authority may become illegitimate if done for the purpose of obstructing an investigation.[130]

Looking more broadly at the standard for impeachment, the framers intended impeachment to be available for *misuse* of powers that were granted to the president. In fact, in the very first Congress, James Madison himself, in arguing *why presidents should have the authority to fire subordinates in the first place*, noted as a safeguard that the president would be subject to impeachment for "wanton removal of meritorious officers."[131] Madison's views were not unopposed, but they carried the day. Against this background, the argument that firing an FBI director can never constitute an impeachable obstruction of justice is thoroughly unpersuasive.

BOTTOM LINE: Beginning soon after the inauguration, the president engaged in a course of conduct that sought to obstruct justice in the FBI's investigations of Michael Flynn and of his own campaign's potential involvement with Russian activity in the 2016 election. In short course, the president first improperly demanded loyalty from then FBI Director James Comey; asked him to abandon his investigation; tried to persuade the attorney general to seize control of the investigation; pressured Comey to make public statements regarding the investigation; attempted to misuse intelligence officials to interfere with the investigation; and attempted to enforce a supposed personal "loyalty" commitment. When these failed, Trump fired Comey in the hope of interfering with the investigation, and then attempted to intimidate him to dissuade him from speaking publicly. That led to the appointment of Special Counsel Robert Mueller. Trump then attempted to impede or stop the special counsel's investigation, attacked the special counsel and the Department of Justice more broadly, pressured his underlings to fire the deputy director of the FBI, attempted to interfere with investigations in Congress, dangled pardons to discourage witnesses from testifying, and used his presidential authority to obtain law enforcement–sensitive information about an investigation into himself, his campaign, and his administration.

It is time for Congress to investigate whether to impeach President Trump for preventing, obstructing, and impeding the administration of justice.

FOUR

DIRECTING LAW ENFORCEMENT

TO INVESTIGATE AND PROSECUTE

POLITICAL ADVERSARIES AND CRITICS

FOR IMPROPER PURPOSES

The Department of Justice is not the president's personal law firm. Its mission is to ensure public safety and fairly and impartially enforce the law. But Trump views federal law enforcement as a weapon to be turned against his political adversaries. That is a dangerous threat to the rule of law and an established ground for impeachment.

★ ★ ★

Since taking office, Trump has repeatedly pressured the Department of Justice to investigate and prosecute political adversaries, especially but not limited to former campaign opponent Hillary Clinton. Here is a sampling of those efforts.

On February 14, 2017, Trump told James Comey that "we need to go after the reporters" by "put[ting] them in jail to find out what they know."[1] Comey responded that he "was a fan of pursuing leaks aggressively but that going after reporters was tricky, for legal reasons and because DOJ tends to approach it conservatively."[2] (Comey was correct on the law, in two ways that Trump appears not to understand. First, most of what Trump calls "leaks" are not illegal in the first place.[3] Second, the Supreme Court has held that if a reporter comes into possession of information of public interest that *someone else* obtained or disclosed illegally, and the reporter did not herself violate any laws in obtaining it, the reporter has a First Amendment right to publish it.[4]) Trump instructed Comey to speak to Attorney General Sessions to "see what we can do about being more aggressive."[5]

On July 24, 2017, Trump tweeted: "So why aren't the Committees and investigators, and of course our beleaguered A.G., looking into Crooked Hillarys crimes & Russia relations?"[6]

On November 3, 2017, the president stated in a radio interview:

> You know, the saddest thing is, because I am the president of the United States I am not supposed to be involved with the Justice Department. I'm not supposed to be involved with the FBI. I'm not supposed to be doing the kind of things I would love to be doing and I am very frustrated by it . . .
>
> I look at what's happening with the Justice Department, why aren't they going after Hillary Clinton with her emails and with her dossier, and the kind of money . . . I don't know, is it possible that they paid $12.4 million for the dossier . . . which is total phony, fake, fraud and how is it used? It's very discouraging to me. I'll be honest.[7]

The next day, the president issued a remarkable series of public statements pressuring the U.S. Department of Justice to investigate Hillary Clinton, the Democratic Party, and other political adversaries. He tweeted:

> Everybody is asking why the Justice Department (and FBI) is not looking into all of the dishonesty going on with Crooked Hillary & the Dems.
>
> . . . New Donna B book says she paid for and stole the Dem Primary. What about the deleted E-mails, Uranium, Podesta, the Server, plus, plus . . .

. . . People are angry. At some point the Justice Department, and the FBI, must do what is right and proper. The American public deserves it!

The real story on Collusion is in Donna B's new book. Crooked Hillary bought the DNC & then stole the Democratic Primary from Crazy Bernie!

Pocahontas just stated that the Democrats, lead by the legendary Crooked Hillary Clinton, rigged the Primaries! Lets go FBI & Justice Dept.[8]

Later that morning, Trump told reporters that he was "disappointed" with the Department of Justice and was open to firing Sessions, if prosecutors failed to investigate Democrats. "Honestly," he added, the Department of Justice "should be looking at the Democrats."[9] Ten days later, on November 13, 2017, the Department of Justice announced that it was considering whether to appoint a special counsel to investigate the Clinton Foundation.[10]

That was hardly the end. Trump carried on like this all winter and into the spring:

- "Many people in our Country are asking what the 'Justice' Department is going to do about the fact that totally Crooked Hillary, AFTER receiving a subpoena from the United States Congress, deleted and 'acid washed' 33,000 Emails? No justice!" (Dec. 2, 2017)[11]
- "Crooked Hillary Clinton's top aid, Huma Abedin, has been accused of disregarding basic security protocols. She put Classified Passwords into the hands of foreign agents. Remember sailors pictures on submarine? Jail! Deep State Justice Dept must finally act? Also on Comey & others" (Jan. 2, 2018)[12]
- "Question: If all of the Russian meddling took place during the Obama Administration, right up to January 20th, why aren't they the subject of the investigation? Why

didn't Obama do something about the meddling? Why aren't Dem crimes under investigation? Ask Jeff Sessions!" (Feb. 21, 2018)[13]

- "The big questions in Comey's badly reviewed book aren't answered like, how come he gave up Classified Information (jail), why did he lie to Congress (jail), why did the DNC refuse to give Server to the FBI (why didn't they TAKE it), why the phony memos, McCabe's $700,000 & more?" (Apr. 15, 2018)[14]

- "The so-called leaks coming out of the White House are a massive over exaggeration put out by the Fake News Media in order to make us look as bad as possible. With that being said, leakers are traitors and cowards, and we will find out who they are!" (May 4, 2018)[15]

- "Why isn't disgraced FBI official Andrew McCabe being investigated for the $700,000 Crooked Hillary Democrats in Virginia, led by Clinton best friend Terry M (under FBI investigation that they killed) gave to McCabe's wife in her run for office? Then dropped case on Clinton!" (May 18, 2018)[16]

- "Our Justice Department must not let Awan and Debbie Wasserman Schultz off the hook. The Democrat I.T. scandal is a key to much of the corruption we see today. They want to make a 'plea deal' to hide what is on their Server. Where is Server? Really bad!" (June 7, 2018)[17]

And it was not just on Twitter. On January 11, 2018, Trump accused an FBI agent of treason. During the 2016 election, the agent had sent text messages critical of Trump to his lover. Trump told *The Wall Street Journal* that these text messages were "a treasonous act."[18] Then on February 5, Trump accused congressional Democrats of "treason" for failing to applaud his State of the Union speech. As he put it, "Can we call that treason? Why not?"[19] (See Chapter 2 for why not.)

On April 26, 2018, Trump called into the *Fox and Friends*

THE CONSTITUTION DEMANDS IT

television program for a wide-ranging interview. Speaking of James Comey, who had recently appeared on television to promote his book and criticized the president, Trump said:

> This is a big mistake, this book. He is guilty of crimes, and if we had a Justice Department that was doing their job instead of spending $8 million trying to find —... I've taken the position—*and I don't have to take this position, and maybe I'll change*—that I will not be involved with the Justice Department . . . And you look at the corruption at the top of the FBI. It's a disgrace. And our Justice Department, which I try and stay away from, *but at some point I won't*. Our Justice Department should be looking at that kind of stuff [i.e., investigating Democrats and FBI officials], not the nonsense of collusion with Russia.[20]

On April 28, 2018, Trump told a campaign-style rally: "And if our Justice Department was doing the right thing, they'd be a lot tougher right now on those people [Democrats and the press] because there's tremendous crime and corruption on the *other* side."[21]

Of course, Trump's efforts to undermine the traditional independence of prosecutors and courts haven't focused *entirely* on Democrats and the press. For example, the president called U.S. Army soldier Bowe Bergdahl a "dirty, rotten traitor" while court-martial charges were pending, and declared that Bergdahl should be executed.[22] After Bergdahl was convicted, he avoided a jail sentence, in part because of what the military judge called "troubling" remarks from the president.[23] In response, the president tweeted: "The decision on Sergeant Bergdahl is a complete and total disgrace to our Country and to our Military."[24] And on May 24, 2018, he seemed to suggest that professional football players who kneel during the national anthem should be deported, telling the *Fox and Friends*

TV show that those players "shouldn't be in the country."[25] But mostly he focuses on his political opponents and the press.

★   ★   ★

In 1940, Attorney General Robert Jackson (who would later serve as a Supreme Court justice and chief prosecutor at the Nuremberg trials after World War II) warned that "the greatest danger of abuse of prosecuting power" was "picking the man"—or, in this case, woman—"and then . . . putting investigators to work, to pin some offense on [her]."[26] A chief executive who uses law enforcement to persecute political enemies is characteristic of an authoritarian regime, not a constitutional republic. As Professor Charles Black wrote in the summer of 1974, "the harassing use of any governmental power meant to be neutrally employed" is an impeachable offense:

> This offense . . . strikes close to the heart of what the Framers most feared in a president—abuse of power. Enforcement of any law . . . must be to some extent discretionary. Perhaps the most dangerous (and certainly the most immoral) line of conduct an official can follow is that of using this discretion, which is given him for public purposes and is meant to be used neutrally, for the grossly improper purposes of menace and revenge . . . [C]learly evidenced and persistent misconduct of this kind is impeachable beyond a doubt.[27]

That is why Republican and Democratic presidents alike have respected the independence of law enforcement. In military courts-martial, such as Bergdahl's, this limit is formalized in the prohibition of "command influence."[28] In civilian law, the First and Fifth Amendments prohibit law enforcement targeting based on political opposition, and guarantee due process of law and equal protection of the laws. Due process of law includes the right to a disinterested prosecutor—not a prosecutor who "has, or is under the influence of others who have, an axe to grind against the defendant, as distinguished from the appropriate interest that members of society have in bringing a defendant to justice with respect to the crime with which he is charged."[29] As a further bulwark, after Watergate, the government established norms to protect the Justice Department's institutional independence *precisely* to protect against presidents using law enforcement to settle vendettas.[30]

Over the course of the nineteenth and twentieth centuries, Congress impeached three federal judges on charges categorized as "vindictive use of power."[31] These included impeaching Judge James H. Peck in 1826 for a single instance of retaliation against a lawyer who had criticized one of his decisions; Judge Charles Swayne in 1903 for maliciously using the criminal contempt power to imprison two lawyers and a litigant; and Judge George W. English in 1926 for "threatening to jail a local newspaper editor for printing a critical editorial."[32] And in 1974, Congress's second article of impeachment against President Richard Nixon cited his use of federal investigative agencies (including the Internal Revenue Service and the FBI) against political opponents "for purposes unrelated to national security, the enforcement of laws, or any other lawful function of his office."[33]

The Nixon impeachment article provides a template for the impeachable offense.[34] Like Nixon, Trump has attempted to direct the criminal investigative powers of the federal government against political opponents. Like Nixon, Trump has done this "for purposes unrelated to national security, the enforcement of laws, or any other lawful function of his office."[35] Based on this precedent, Trump's attempts to direct the criminal investigative powers of the federal government against political opponents "for purposes unrelated to national security, the enforcement of laws, or any other lawful function of his office" are grounds for impeachment. That is true regardless of whether these attempts have yet succeeded—like Trump, Nixon also faced some refusal by law enforcement officials.[36] As Professor Frank Bowman notes, "it is not acceptable for a president either to *employ*, or *threaten to employ*, the agents and ministers of the criminal law of the United States against his enemies for political gain. A president who does so engages in precisely the class of misconduct perilous to the maintenance of republican government for which the founders designed the remedy of impeachment."[37]

Trump's efforts to direct law enforcement, including the Department of Justice and the Federal Bureau of Investigation, to investigate and prosecute political adversaries and others, for improper purposes not justified by any lawful function of his office, simultaneously erode the rule of law, undermine the independence of law enforcement from politics, and compromise the constitutional right to due process of law.

BOTTOM LINE: Trump has repeatedly pressured the Department of Justice and the Federal Bureau of Investigation to investigate and prosecute political adversaries, including former campaign opponent Hillary Clinton and the Democratic Party. The president's attempts to employ the criminal investigative powers of the federal government against political opponents for purposes unrelated to national security, the enforcement of laws, or any other lawful function of his office are grounds for impeachment, regardless of whether they have yet succeeded in influencing law enforcement.

It is time for Congress to investigate whether to impeach President Trump for knowingly misusing the executive power by directing or endeavoring to direct law enforcement, including the Department of Justice and the Federal Bureau of Investigation, to investigate and prosecute political adversaries and others, for improper purposes not justified by any lawful function of his office, thereby eroding the rule of law, undermining the independence of law enforcement from politics, and compromising the constitutional right to due process of law.

FIVE

ABUSING THE PARDON POWER

The president has the power to pardon crimes, and most presidents issue a few pardons that stir up some controversy. But in his very first pardon, Trump crossed a line that had never been breached in the history of the republic.

★   ★   ★

On Friday evening, August 25, 2017, Trump issued his first presidential pardon, to Joe Arpaio, the former sheriff of Maricopa County, Arizona. (This pardon was discussed briefly in Chapter 3.)

For over twenty years, Arpaio had run the Maricopa County Sheriff's Office with shocking cruelty and lawlessness, particularly against Latinos.[1] In 2011, the U.S. Department of Justice found that the Sheriff's Office engaged in systemic unconstitutional policing.[2] Later in 2011, a federal judge in Arizona issued a preliminary injunction barring the Sheriff's Office from enforcing federal immigration law or from detaining persons they believed to be in the country without authorization but against whom they had no state charges.[3] In 2012, the judge issued findings of fact and conclusions of law determining that the Sheriff's Office had violated the constitutional rights of Latinos by targeting them during raids and traffic stops, and issued a permanent injunction.[4] However, Arpaio refused to obey the injunction, and in May 2016, the judge found him in civil contempt of court for deliberately disobeying the order.[5]

The judge also referred the matter to a different federal judge in Arizona for an investigation of *criminal* contempt. On July 31, 2017, after a five-day trial, this second judge determined that Arpaio had "willfully violated the order by failing to do anything to ensure his subordinates' compliance and by directing them to continue to detain persons for whom no criminal charges could be filed," and found him guilty of criminal contempt of court. Sentencing was set for October 2017.[6]

Trump made clear that he was displeased with this course of events. In the spring, Trump reportedly had asked Sessions whether the Department of Justice might abandon the criminal contempt case; when rebuffed, Trump decided to let the case go to trial with the plan of pardoning Arpaio if he was convicted.[7]

Two weeks after the verdict, Trump told Fox News that he was considering a pardon for Arpaio, and that Arpaio "doesn't deserve to be treated this way" because he "has protected people from crimes and saved lives."[8] On August 22, just days after the white supremacist rally in Charlottesville, Virginia, Trump rhetorically asked a Phoenix campaign audience, "Was Sheriff Joe convicted for doing his job?"[9]

On August 25, 2017, Trump pardoned Arpaio. In a two-paragraph statement, the White House stated: "Throughout his time as Sheriff, Arpaio continued his life's work of protecting the public from the scourges of crime and illegal immigration. Sheriff Joe Arpaio is now eighty-five years old, and after more than fifty years of admirable service to our Nation, he is [a] worthy candidate for a Presidential pardon."[10] Trump also added in a tweet, "He kept Arizona safe!"[11]

★   ★   ★

The Constitution grants the president "Power to grant Reprieves and Pardons for Offences against the United States, except in Cases of Impeachment."[12] But that power is not without limits.

The founders understood this. At the Virginia ratifying convention in 1788, George Mason (who was opposed to the Constitution) criticized the pardon power: "Now, I conceive that the President ought not to have the power of pardoning, because he may frequently pardon crimes which were advised by himself. It may happen, at some future day, that he will establish a monarchy, and destroy the republic."[13]

James Madison responded that impeachment would be the appropriate response to such an abuse of power: "There is one security in this case to which gentlemen may not have adverted: if the President be connected, in any suspicious manner, with any person, and there be grounds to believe he will shelter him, the House of Representatives can impeach him; they can remove him if found guilty; they can suspend him when suspected, and the power will devolve on the Vice-President . . . This is a great security."[14]

Much later, in the 1925 Supreme Court case of *Ex parte Grossman*, Chief Justice (and former president) William Howard Taft opined that if a president abused the pardon power, that "would suggest a resort to impeachment."[15]

Why is the Arpaio pardon so egregious? In 1974, Professor Black gave the following hypothetical:

> Suppose a president were to announce and follow a policy of granting full pardons, in advance of indictment or trial, to all federal agents or police who killed anybody in line of duty, in the District of Columbia, whatever the circumstances and however unnecessary the killing . . . [C]ould anybody doubt that such conduct would be impeachable?[16]

Trump's pardon of Arpaio is not far off. The matter might have been cloudier if Arpaio had displayed, as those seeking presidential pardons typically must demonstrate, "[a]cceptance of responsibility, remorse, and atonement," and if he had been "genuinely desirous of forgiveness rather than vindication."[17] But quite to the contrary, Arpaio remains unrepentant, and Trump described him as having been "convicted for doing his job" while he "kept Arizona safe" by "protecting the public from . . . illegal immigration."

In other words, Trump's pardon of Arpaio *endorses* the very activity that was enjoined by a federal court as violating Latinos' constitutional rights. The pardon "sends a message to Latinos that they do not deserve equal rights, and affirms to the judiciary"—and the public at large—"that Trump has no respect for the rule of law."[18] As Professor Noah Feldman noted before Trump issued the pardon:

> An Arpaio pardon would express presidential contempt for the Constitution. Arpaio didn't just violate a law passed by Congress. His actions defied the Constitution itself, the bedrock of the entire system of government. For Trump to say that this violation is excusable would threaten the very structure on which his right to pardon is based.
>
> Fundamentally, pardoning Arpaio would also undermine the rule of law itself.
>
> The only way the legal system can operate is if law enforcement officials do what the courts tell them. Judges don't carry guns or enforce their own orders. That's the job of law enforcement . . . When a sheriff ignores the courts, he becomes a law unto himself. The courts' only available recourse is to sanction the sheriff. If the president blocks the courts from making the sheriff follow the law, then the president is breaking the basic structure of the legal order.[19]

That is what happened here. The exercise of the pardon power in the circumstances of Arpaio's case undermines judicial protection of constitutional rights and tramples constitutional constraints on the president's authority to pardon.[20]

It is important to distinguish the Arpaio pardon from the many thousands of pardons that previous presidents have issued over the past two centuries. In the entire history of the United States, this was the first time that a president issued a pardon: (1) for criminal contempt (2) for violating an injunction (3) issued to a government official (4) to cease a systemic practice of violating (5) individuals' constitutional rights.

To understand why Trump's pardon of Arpaio is such a dangerous affront to our constitutional order, step back to 1962.[21] That summer, a federal court ordered the all-white University of Mississippi to admit James Meredith, a black college student who had been denied admission because of his race.[22] But Governor Ross Barnett ordered state officials to refuse to comply with the court order, and block Meredith from Ole Miss.[23] Eventually, the federal government sent the National Guard to escort Meredith onto campus and protect him from a violent riot. The court found that Governor Barnett had willfully interfered with the court order, and directed the Department of Justice to prosecute him for criminal contempt of court.[24]

As the court understood, public officials must face personal consequences for deliberately violating a court order if that order is to be worth anything. Many anti-integration governors were promising "massive resistance" to court-ordered desegregation.[25] As then Attorney General Nicholas Katzenbach later explained, "the problem was not whether [the Department of Justice] had legal power. It was always how to get compliance with the law. The best bet was litigation and a court order requiring certain specified conduct from state or local officials under pain of imprisonment for contempt."[26] Indeed, the legal struggle against segregation relied on the power of court orders enforceable by imprisonment for contempt.

Now imagine a president like Donald Trump pardoning the governor for criminal contempt, while praising him (as Trump did for Arpaio) for "doing his job." The message to segregationist officials would have been loud and clear: just ignore federal court integration orders; the president will have your back if the court tries to enforce them through its contempt power. The result would have empowered massive resistance to desegregation, and eviscerated judicial protection of individual rights.

The pardon power is broad, but, like every power in the Constitution, it cannot be used to subvert constitutional rights. As the Supreme Court stated in 1968:

> [T]he Constitution is filled with provisions that grant Congress or the States specific power to legislate in certain areas; these granted powers are always subject to the limitation that they may not be exercised in a way that violates other specific provisions of the Constitution. For example, Congress is granted broad power to "lay and collect Taxes," but the taxing power, broad as it is, may not be invoked in such a way as to violate the privilege against self-incrimination. Nor can it be thought that the power to select electors could be exercised in such a way as to violate express constitutional commands that specifically bar States from passing certain kinds of laws.[27]

The constitutional value that Trump's pardon of Arpaio trampled is the right to due process of law. Courts protect individual rights against violation by the other branches of government. The civil-rights era showed that the power of contempt is a crucial part of the system by which the judiciary enforces constitutional rights. As a federal court of appeals explained in 2014:

> [T]he purpose of contempt proceedings is to uphold the power of the court . . . and to ensure that the court's vindication of litigants' rights is not merely symbolic. Our

orders would have little practical force, and would be rendered essentially meaningless, if we were unable to prevent parties bound by them from flagrantly and materially assisting others to do what they themselves are forbidden to do.[28]

Trump's pardon of Arpaio undermines due process of law by casting doubt on courts' ability to enforce constitutional limits on government action.[29] It signaled that government officials can engage in massive violations of individuals' constitutional rights, if their actions please the president.[30] Sheriffs and other government officials who are contemplating or engaged in abusive practices now know that the federal courts pose little threat to them—Trump will pardon them if they get into legal trouble.[31]

But racist sheriffs are not the only ones who heard that message. As discussed in Chapter 3, the pardon also sent a message to Trump's current and former aides: "Stay loyal and I will pardon you."

As of this writing, Trump's pardon of Arpaio is under challenge in federal court.[32] But regardless of the outcome of that court proceeding, Congress has an independent obligation to act when the president abuses the pardon power.

BOTTOM LINE: Trump pardoned former Arizona sheriff Joseph Arpaio, who had been convicted of criminal contempt of court for willfully disobeying a court order to stop violating the constitutional rights of Latino drivers. This unprecedented pardon, and the president's public statements explaining the rationale, expressed contempt for equal protection of the laws and the ability of the courts to protect constitutional rights. The president's very first pardon sent a dangerous message that similarly inclined unscrupulous law-enforcement officials could not only violate individual rights, but could also violate court orders requiring them to stop violating those rights with impunity because the president would support them.

It is time for Congress to investigate whether to impeach President Trump for abusing the pardon power.

ADVOCATING ILLEGAL VIOLENCE

AND UNDERMINING EQUAL PROTECTION

OF THE LAWS

Since entering office, Trump has urged police to be "rough" with suspects, given aid and comfort to neo-Nazis and other white supremacists, and suggested that the military should commit war crimes against Muslims. Coming from the president, words matter.

★   ★   ★

On July 28, 2017, in a speech to police officers, Trump openly encouraged police to be "rough" with people they arrest:

> And when you see these towns and when you see these thugs being thrown into the back of a paddy wagon—you just see them thrown in, rough—I said, please don't be too nice. (Laughter.) Like when you guys put some-body in the car and you're protecting their head, you know, the way you put their hand over? Like, don't hit their head and they've just killed somebody—don't hit their head. I said, you can take the hand away, okay?[1]

This speech was widely understood, including by police chiefs nationwide, as endorsing police brutality—that is, encouraging police to cause bodily harm to arrested persons and violate their constitutional rights.[2] Furthermore, since statements by the president can establish executive branch policy, it also implies that the Department of Justice will, at a minimum, deprioritize enforcement of laws protecting the citizenry from police misconduct. Indeed, the Department of Justice appears to have done just that, by taking steps to end its investigations of, and remedial support for, local police departments with a history of police misconduct.[3]

On August 12, 2017, Trump gave a statement after the white supremacist rallies and terrorist attack in Charlottesville, Virginia, in which one woman was killed and more than fifty people were injured at the hands of a self-proclaimed white nationalist. Trump criticized violence "on many sides, on many sides," thus equating violent white supremacists with counterprotesters.[4] On August 15, he insisted that there were "very fine people" among the marching white supremacists.[5] On August 22, the president publicly bemoaned the firing of a CNN commentator for tweeting the Nazi salute "sieg heil."[6] This pattern of statements has been widely understood, particularly by the white supremacists and neo-Nazis themselves, as an expression of support for white supremacist views.

On August 17, the president tweeted: "Study what General Pershing of the United States did to terrorists when caught. There was no more Radical Islamic Terror for 35 years!"[7] The president was almost certainly repeating an internet urban legend that he had recited during the presidential campaign:

They were having terrorism problems, just like we do. And he caught 50 terrorists who did tremendous damage and killed many people. And he took the 50 terrorists, and he took 50 men and he dipped 50 bullets in pigs' blood—you heard that, right? He took 50 bullets, and he dipped them in pigs' blood. And he had his men load his rifles, and he lined up the 50 people, and they shot 49 of those people. And the 50th person, he said: You go back to your people, and you tell them what happened. And

for twenty-five years, there wasn't a problem. Okay?
Twenty-five years, there wasn't a problem.[8]

While no evidence supports this anecdote about General
Pershing, if military service-members did anything like this
today, their actions would likely constitute war crimes.[9] An
imperative to "study" this incident issued by the president,
whom the Constitution designates as "Commander in Chief
of the Army and Navy of the United States,"[10] cannot be dismissed as merely a suggestion that the history faculty at the
military academies should add it to a course syllabus. To the
contrary, the president's imperative could be interpreted as an
order to commit war crimes.[11]

On November 28 and 29, 2017, Trump shared three inflammatory and misleading anti-Muslim videos on Twitter. He
retweeted three posts by a leader in Great Britain's far-right
"Britain First" party who had previously been convicted and
imprisoned in England for religiously motivated harassment.[12]
After the president's tweets, British prime minister Theresa
May stated: "It is wrong for the president to have done this . . .
Britain First seeks to divide communities by their use of hate-
ful narratives that peddle lies and stoke tensions."[13] The aid
and comfort to white supremacists in the United States constituted by the president's tweets was unmistakable. For example, white supremacist leader David Duke welcomed the
president's tweets with the message "Thank God for Trump!
That's why we love him!"[14]

Furthermore, the anti-Muslim bigotry evident in Trump's
suggestion, when combined with his campaign promise for
a "total and complete shutdown" of Muslims entering the
country and his administration's various immigration orders
that have been held by multiple federal courts to discriminate
against Muslims on the basis of religion,[15] foments religious
hatred and undermines the constitutional guarantee of equal
protection of the laws.

★   ★   ★

Trump's conduct here does not correspond to a specific statutory crime. Unlike, for example, obstruction of justice, these actions probably could not land Donald Trump in prison after he is removed from office.

But, as we saw at the beginning, impeachable offenses are not just crimes. And the president's conduct flies in the face of at least three constitutional obligations.

First, he has a duty to "take care that the laws be faithfully executed."[16] Second, he has a constitutional obligation to protect the citizenry against "domestic Violence."[17] Third, he has an obligation to ensure that the federal government (and, less directly, state and local governments) not "deny to any person within [their] jurisdiction the equal protection of the laws."[18] That includes not giving aid and comfort to white supremacists and neo-Nazis in their efforts toward aims that the Supreme Court has called "directly subversive of the principle of equality at the heart of the Fourteenth Amendment."[19]

No previous president has ever tested these principles as severely as Donald Trump; consequently, there is no directly applicable precedent. But taken as a whole, this pattern and course of conduct constitutes an abuse of public trust that justifies a congressional investigation and hearings on whether impeachment is warranted. As Professor Laurence Tribe and his coauthor Joshua Matz have noted, "[w]holly apart from what a court would say, Congress is free to decide in an impeachment hearing that some of Trump's public comments have violated [constitutional protections including] the Equal Protection Clause."[20]

The president's open advocacy of illegal violence—evidently endorsing police misconduct against arrested persons, and war crimes—violates his obligations to "take care that the laws be faithfully executed" and to ensure "the equal protection of the laws." Furthermore, his expressions of sympathy and support to supposed "very fine people" who were marching alongside neo-Nazis and white supremacists in the streets of Charlottesville gives them aid and encouragement in the future.

Trump's words matter, and have led to what some call "the Trump Effect":

- A survey of more than 10,000 K–12 educators by the Southern Poverty Law Center found that the 2016 presidential election led to increases in "verbal harassment, the use of slurs and derogatory language, and disturbing incidents involving swastikas, Nazi salutes and Confederate flags," with "[o]ver 2,500 educators describe[ing] specific incidents of bigotry and harassment that can be directly traced to election rhetoric."[21]
- A peer-reviewed epidemiological study of the 2016 election found that cities experienced a 12-percent increase in assaults on days when Trump held a rally, as compared to days when there was no campaign rally.[22]
- The Center for the Study of Hate and Extremism at California State University San Bernardino found a sharp increase in the number of hate crimes in most of the nation's largest cities from 2016 to 2017.[23]
- During the first half of 2017, there was a 91-percent increase in anti-Muslim hate crimes as compared to the same time period in 2016.[24]
- The president's name ("Trump! Trump! Trump!") has become a racial jeer at schools, sporting events, and elsewhere.[25]

To be sure, hate crimes preceded Trump, and there are multiple lines of causation involved. But it requires willful blindness to deny that Trump's advocacy of illegal violence and undermining of the equal protection of the laws has had a substantial harmful effect on the people of the United States.

BOTTOM LINE: The president has made a series of public statements that, together, constitute a dangerous pattern. For example, he has openly encouraged police officers to physically mistreat arrested persons; encouraged the military to execute Muslim prisoners of war; equated the violent white supremacists and neo-Nazis in Charlottesville, Virginia, with the protesters against them; and shared inflammatory anti-Muslim videos on Twitter from the account of a far-right white supremacist. Taken as a whole, this pattern of conduct violates his constitutional obligation to "take care that the laws be faithfully executed," protect the citizenry against "domestic Violence," and ensure "the equal protection of the laws."

It is time for Congress to investigate whether to impeach President Trump for advocating illegal violence, giving aid and comfort to white supremacists and neo-Nazis, and undermining constitutional protections of equal protection under the law.

SEVEN

RECKLESS ENDANGERMENT BY

THREATENING NUCLEAR WAR

In the conduct of diplomacy, presidents sometimes take calculated risks. But in the nuclear age, there is a line between calculated risks and reckless endangerment likely to cause mass deaths. And Trump has crossed that line by issuing nuclear threats without considering, or even understanding, the consequences.

★ ★ ★

Beginning in the late summer of 2017, Trump made a series of reckless public threats against North Korea. These included that "[m]ilitary solutions" are "locked and loaded";[1] that "Rocket Man is on a suicide mission" and the United States might "have no choice but to totally destroy" North Korea;[2] that North Korea or its leadership "won't be around much longer";[3] that "[b]eing nice to Rocket Man hasn't worked";[4] that he had instructed the secretary of state he was "wasting his time" negotiating with North Korean leadership because "we'll do what has to be done";[5] that North Korea "will be met with fire and fury like the world has never seen";[6] and that diplomacy had failed and "only one thing will work."[7]

Meanwhile, in a departure from North Korea's customary pause in missile testing during the last three months of the year, on November 29, 2017, North Korea tested an intercontinental ballistic missile with an estimated range of 8,100 miles, reportedly capable of reaching any part of the United States.[8]

At times, Trump's threats have veered into Freudian territory. On January 2, 2018, Trump tweeted: "North Korean Leader Kim Jong Un just stated that the 'Nuclear Button is on his desk at all times.' Will someone from his depleted and food starved regime please inform him that I too have a Nuclear Button, but it is a much bigger & more powerful one than his, and my Button works!"[9]

Worse yet, available public evidence suggests that Trump does not fully understand, and/or is unwilling or unable to understand (or is indifferent to), the risks accompanying the use of nuclear weapons, or of how the North Korean leadership could interpret or misinterpret his verbal threats or movement of military forces as military attacks that could lead them to respond with conventional or nuclear attacks on the United States, our allies in the region, or other nations.

Senior administration officials have voiced serious concerns about whether Trump understands the ramifications of his threats. After a July 20, 2017, meeting in which Trump reportedly told senior advisors that he wanted to increase the country's nuclear-weapons stockpile eightfold, then Secretary of State Rex Tillerson was so alarmed by the president's lack of understanding of the risks of nuclear weapons that he reportedly called Trump a "moron."[10] That same month, during a dinner with a business executive, then national security advisor General H. R. McMaster reportedly referred to Trump variously as an "idiot" and a "dope" with the intelligence of a "kindergartner."[11] On an earlier occasion, General McMaster reportedly stated that Trump lacks the necessary brainpower to understand the matters before the National Security Council.[12] This assessment seems to have been confirmed by John Kelly, the White House chief of staff, who reportedly has also privately described Trump as an "idiot."[13]

Senator Bob Corker, the chairman of the Senate Foreign Relations Committee, stated in an interview that "I don't think he appreciates that when the president of the United States speaks and says the things that he does, the impact that it has around the world, especially in the region that he's addressing," and that "he doesn't realize that . . . we could be heading towards World War Three with the kinds of comments that he's making."[14]

Fortunately, a nuclear confrontation has not erupted so far. And in the spring of 2018, Trump announced a summit with North Korea, before canceling it with a letter telling its leader that "You talk about your nuclear capabilities, but ours are so massive and powerful that I pray to God they will never have to be used."[15] This was followed by a dizzying and sometimes conflicting set of messages suggesting that a summit might, or might not, take place after all, capped by Trump's claim that Matthew Pottinger, a Marine officer and National Security Council official who had provided an official White House media briefing on this matter, "doesn't exist."[16]

Ultimately, the summit went forward, though Trump and the North Korean leader later provided "differing versions of what they had accomplished and where they go from here."[17] But whatever may or may not come of diplomatic efforts long after the fact, neither these efforts nor the fact that nuclear war has not yet occurred does not change the recklessness of Trump's threats. Indeed, he continues to make public statements that run a reckless risk of nuclear powers misinterpreting his intentions and reacting in response. For example, on April 11, 2018, he tweeted: "Russia vows to shoot down any and all missiles fired at Syria. Get ready Russia, because they will be coming, nice and new and 'smart!'"[18]

★★★

Nuclear gamesmanship is no laughing matter. In a tense international situation, where each side lacks an accurate understanding of the leadership of the other party's intentions, threats of invasion or bombing could easily lead to a misunderstanding or miscalculation resulting in the use of nuclear weapons by either or both sides. Such a conflagration could quickly spread to South Korea, Japan, China, and/or Russia. Those last two also have—and might be drawn into an exchange of—nuclear weapons. High-ranking government officials with access to classified materials not available to the public have suggested that the risk of escalation is serious.

There is no directly applicable precedent. Obviously, the founders, who designated the president as the "Commander in Chief of the Army and Navy of the United States,"[19] anticipated neither weapons of mass destruction nor the technological developments that can accelerate the pace of modern events. But by all accounts, the country appears not to be in the hands of a well-informed president who, after carefully considering detailed factual information and the counsel of senior advisors, with full information and full decisional capacity, could take a calculated risk involving strategic gamesmanship. Nor, on the other hand, is this merely a matter of "maladministration."

Reckless or wanton endangerment with the potential for millions of deaths constitutes an abuse of power. Reckless endangerment takes place when the conduct occurs, regardless of whether the death or grievous bodily harm actually results. By analogy, military service-members may be charged with "reckless endangerment" for engaging in conduct that is "reckless or wanton," "likely to produce death or grievous bodily harm to another person," and "of a nature to bring discredit upon the armed forces."[20] In a recent court-martial prosecution, affirmed by the U.S. Court of Appeals for the Armed Forces in 2017, a sergeant was convicted of reckless endangerment (and sentenced to ten months' confinement) for failure to properly inspect parachutes—a matter far less grave than reckless conduct that could trigger nuclear war.[21] As it happened, the sergeant's reckless endangerment did not lead to any injuries, because another soldier "became suspicious about the speed with which some of these parachutes had been packed," and they were opened and inspected (and found to contain unsafe deficiencies) without being used.[22] The fact that the reckless conduct did not lead, in fact, to any injuries was no defense.

While the president is of course not subject to the Uniform Code of Military Justice, the gravity of his reckless or wanton conduct likely to lead to nuclear war is far greater than that of one sergeant who failed to inspect some parachutes. And just as no one died in that case because another soldier caught the problem before the jump, the fact that a nuclear exchange has not yet occurred does not diminish the reckless endangerment caused by the president's careless threats. Indeed, the fact that he has done it once makes it more likely that he will do it again—perhaps with worse results.

Impeachment hearings could probe whether (as it indeed appears) the president's unilateral actions are so ill-informed and in disregard of the risks of deaths on a massive scale as to be not merely negligent, but reckless or wanton. As Professor Charles Black noted in 1974, at some point "insensate abuse of the commander-in-chief power [could] amount to a 'high Crime' or 'Misdemeanor' for impeachment purposes."[23]

★   ★   ★

The elephant in the room is that the president's reckless or wanton conduct may stem from *incapacity* to perform his duties.

Since the 2016 election, many people have become familiar with section four of the Twenty-fifth Amendment, which provides a process for temporarily removing a president who is "unable to discharge the powers and duties of his office."[24] This procedure was intended for very serious losses of ability, and it is far more difficult than impeachment. Relieving the president of his duties through section four of the Twenty-fifth Amendment requires the vice president, a majority of the Cabinet, and two-thirds of *both* houses of Congress.

But incapacity may play a role in impeachment as well. In the debates at the Constitutional Convention, as the founders discussed an impeachment provision, James Madison argued that it was "indispensable that some provision should be made for defending the Community agst. the *incapacity*, negligence or perfidy of the chief Magistrate."[25] Madison later repeated this "incapacity" point, noting that the president "might *lose his capacity*" and "[i]n the case of the Executive Magistracy which was to be administered by a single man, *loss of capacity* or corruption was more within the compass of probable events, and either of them might be fatal to the Republic."[26] Another Founder, Gouverneur Morris, who began the debates skeptical of impeachment, later changed his mind, and cited "incapacity" as grounds for impeachment.[27]

Notably, the first successful impeachment conviction in our history was of a federal judge (John Pickering, in 1804) who had slipped into senile dementia. Ultimately, the vigorous congressional debate as to whether his dementia constituted grounds for impeachment was left unsettled because he was impeached and convicted for drunkenness and mishandling cases.[28] In fact, Pickering's defenders conceded his mental incapacity, and (unsuccessfully) used it as a *defense* against impeachment, suggesting that he could not form the legal intent necessary to commit wrongdoing. (Congress rejected that argument, and in doing so helped establish that there is no intent requirement for high crimes and misdemeanors.)

Whatever the answer might be in the abstract, when a president whose closest advisors doubt his mental capacity issues threats of nuclear war with reckless or wanton disregard for the risk of millions of deaths, the protective purposes of impeachment are well suited to address this concern. As noted above, Trump's own national security and international affairs teams have called him a "moron," "idiot," and "dope." Trump's inability or unwillingness to understand the consequences of his threats of nuclear war is sufficiently serious to justify impeachment hearings into his reckless nuclear threats.

BOTTOM LINE: Through a series of public statements (including on Twitter), and beginning particularly in the late summer of 2017, Trump has made increasingly reckless public threats that create an unacceptable risk of nuclear war. It is not clear whether Trump understands the ramifications of his actions. Reported statements indicate that the White House chief of staff, the ex–secretary of state, the ex–national security advisor, and perhaps other senior leaders, believe that the president does not understand (and is incapable of understanding) the facts necessary to make an informed decision regarding nuclear weapons or matters involving North Korea. Tense international situations, lack of accurate understanding of intentions of national leadership, and a willfully ignorant and wanton president combine to mean that threats of invasion or bombing could easily lead to a misunderstanding or miscalculation resulting in the use of nuclear weapons by either or both sides. While the president is the "Commander in Chief of the Army and Navy of the United States," reckless or wanton conduct with the potential for millions of deaths constitutes an abuse of power.

It is time for Congress to investigate whether to impeach President Trump for recklessly threatening nuclear war against foreign nations and engaging in other conduct that grossly and wantonly endangers the peace and security of the United States, and its people and people of other nations, by heightening the risk of hostilities involving weapons of mass destruction, with reckless disregard for the risk of death and grievous bodily harm.

EIGHT

UNDERMINING THE FREEDOM

OF THE PRESS

As strongman leaders in other countries have discovered, an authoritarian ruler can undermine the freedom of the press, and ultimately the idea of constitutional democracy itself, even without formal censorship. Donald Trump is taking us down that path.

★ ★ ★

Trump has repeatedly made public statements designed to undermine major U.S. news organizations by describing them as "fake news" and "the enemy of the American people." The number of these statements posted on Twitter alone is overwhelming; one study found that from June 16, 2015 (when Trump announced his candidacy) to late December 2017, he had posted 990 tweets criticizing the press—slightly more than one per day.[1]

Some thought this was just a campaign tactic. But Trump did not change once he took office. On his second day as president, January 21, 2017, Trump described journalists as "among the most dishonest human beings on Earth."[2] Later, on August 22, 2017, an unrepentant Trump told a Phoenix, Arizona, crowd:

It's time to expose the crooked media deceptions, and to challenge the media for their role in fomenting divisions . . . And yes, by the way—and yes, by the way, they are trying to take away our history and our heritage . . . These are truly dishonest people. And not all of them. Not all of them. You have some very good reporters. You have some very fair journalists. But for the most part, honestly, these are really, really dishonest people, and they're bad people. And I really think they don't like our country. I really believe that . . . These are sick people.

You know the thing I don't understand? You would think—you would think they'd want to make our country great again, and I honestly believe they don't. I honestly believe it.

If you want to discover the source of the division in our country, look no further than the fake news and the crooked media . . .[3]

And on April 26, 2018, in a call-in interview with *Fox and Friends*, Trump used the phrase "fake news" six times—in reference to not just one news network, but, essentially, *all* of them except Fox News. He referred twice to "fake news CNN," then later added: "CBS, and NBC, and ABC. They're all fake news."[4]

But one of Trump's favorite venues for attacking the press is Twitter. Here is a small sampling of statements by the president of the United States on matters related to the press:[5]

- "The fake news media is going crazy with their conspiracy theories and blind hatred. @MSNBC & @CNN are unwatchable. @foxandfriends is great!" (Feb. 15, 2017)[6]
- "The FAKE NEWS media (failing @nytimes, @NBCNews, @ABC, @CBS, @CNN) is not my enemy, it is the enemy of the American People!" (Feb. 17, 2017)[7]
- ".@FoxNews is MUCH more important in the United States than CNN, but outside of the U.S., CNN International is still a major source of (Fake) news, and

they represent our Nation to the WORLD very poorly.
The outside world does not see the truth from them!"
(Nov. 25, 2017)[8]

- "We should have a contest as to which of the Networks,
  plus CNN and not including Fox, is the most dishonest,
  corrupt and/or distorted in its political coverage of your
  favorite President (me). They are all bad. Winner to
  receive the FAKE NEWS TROPHY!" (Nov. 27, 2017)[9]

- "I use Social Media not because I like to, but because it is
  the only way to fight a VERY dishonest and unfair 'press,'
  now often referred to as Fake News Media. Phony and
  non-existent 'sources' are being used more often than
  ever. Many stories & reports a pure fiction!" (Dec. 30,
  2017)[10]

- "I will be announcing THE MOST DISHONEST &
  CORRUPT MEDIA AWARDS OF THE YEAR on Monday
  at 5:00 o'clock. Subjects will cover Dishonesty & Bad
  Reporting in various categories from the Fake News
  Media. Stay tuned!" (Jan. 2, 2018)[11]

- "So many positive things going on for the U.S.A. and the
  Fake News Media just doesn't want to go there. Same
  negative stories over and over again! No wonder the
  People no longer trust the media, whose approval ratings
  are correctly at their lowest levels in history! #MAGA"
  (Feb. 11, 2018)[12]

- "The Fake News Networks, those that knowingly have
  a sick and biased AGENDA, are worried about the
  competition and quality of Sinclair Broadcast. The 'Fakers'
  at CNN, NBC, ABC & CBS have done so much dishonest
  reporting that they should only be allowed to get awards
  for fiction!" (Apr. 3, 2018)[13]

- "The Washington Post is far more fiction than fact.
  Story after story is made up garbage—more like a poorly
  written novel than good reporting. Always quoting
  sources (not names), many of which don't exist. Story on

John Kelly isn't true, just another hit job!" (Apr. 8, 2018)[14]

- Can you believe that despite 93% bad stories from the Fake News Media (should be getting good stories), today we had just about our highest Poll Numbers, including those on Election Day? The American public is wise to the phony an[d] dishonest press. Make America Great Again!" (Apr. 20, 2018)[15]

- "The New York Times and a third rate reporter named Maggie Haberman, known as a Crooked H flunkie who I don't speak to and have nothing to do with, are going out of their way to destroy Michael Cohen and his relationship with me in the hope that he will 'flip.' They use non-existent 'sources' and a drunk/drugged up loser who hates Michael, a fine person with a wonderful family. Michael is a businessman for his own account/ lawyer who I have always liked & respected. Most people will flip if the Government lets them out of trouble, even if it means lying or making up stories. Sorry, I don't see Michael doing that despite the horrible Witch Hunt and the dishonest media!" (Apr. 21, 2018)[16]

- "The Fake News is going crazy making up false stories and using only unnamed sources (who don't exist). They are totally unhinged, and the great success of this Administration is making them do and say things that even they can't believe they are saying. Truly bad people!" (Apr. 30, 2018)[17]

- "NBC NEWS is wrong again! They cite 'sources' which are constantly wrong. Problem is, like so many others, the sources probably don't exist, they are fabricated, fiction! NBC, my former home with the Apprentice, is now as bad as Fake News CNN. Sad!" (May 4, 2018)[18]

Perhaps summing up his entire approach to the press, on May 9, 2018, he tweeted: "The Fake News is working overtime. Just reported that, despite the tremendous success we are having with the economy & all things else, 91% of the Network News about me is negative (Fake). Why do we work so hard in working with the media when it is corrupt? Take away credentials?"[19]

As indicated by that threat to "take away credentials" (presumably he meant White House press credentials), many of his attacks on the press come with threats. Some of these are nonspecific, such as when, on October 11, 2017, Trump told reporters in the Oval Office, "It is frankly disgusting the way the press is able to write whatever they want to write, and people should look into it."[20] Other threats are quite specific. Here are some examples.

THREATS TO USE LAW ENFORCEMENT POWER TO PUNISH PRESS

As noted earlier, on February 14, 2017, Trump ordered FBI Director Comey to speak with Attorney General Sessions to "see what we can do about being more aggressive" about "go[ing] after the reporters" and "put[ting] them in jail to find out what they know."[21] Trump often threatens to prosecute newspapers after unfavorable stories.

In a special twist, when there is an unfavorable story in *The Washington Post*, Trump often attacks not the *Post* itself, but the online retailer Amazon. The reason is that *The Washington Post* is owned by Jeff Bezos, Amazon's founder and CEO. Trump's conflation of Amazon and *The Washington Post* dates back to before the election; in December 2015, he tweeted "The @washingtonpost, which loses a fortune, is owned by @JeffBezos for purposes of keeping taxes down at his no profit company, @amazon."[22] (As the *Post* later pointed out, "Amazon is a publicly traded company, and *The Post*, wholly owned by Bezos, is private. The companies' finances are not intermingled."[23]) Since he became president, these attacks have turned into threats. Here is a sample:

- "A new INTELLIGENCE LEAK from the Amazon Washington Post,this time against A.G. Jeff Sessions. These illegal leaks, like Comey's, must stop!" (Jul. 22, 2017)[24]
- "The Amazon Washington Post fabricated the facts on my ending massive, dangerous, and wasteful payments to Syrian rebels fighting Assad . . ." (Jul. 24, 2017)[25]
- "So many stories about me in the @washingtonpost are Fake News. They are as bad as ratings challenged @CNN. Lobbyist for Amazon and taxes?" (Jul. 24, 2017)[26]
- "Is Fake News Washington Post being used as a lobbyist weapon against Congress to keep Politicians from looking into Amazon no-tax monopoly?" (Jul. 24, 2017)[27]

THREATS TO RAISE SHIPPING RATES ON AMAZON TO PUNISH *THE WASHINGTON POST*

As part of his campaign to intimidate *The Washington Post* via Amazon, Trump has long threatened to raise shipping rates on Amazon's packages. For example:

- "Why is the United States Post Office, which is losing many billions of dollars a year, while charging Amazon and others so little to deliver their packages, making Amazon richer and the Post Office dumber and poorer? Should be charging MUCH MORE!" (Dec. 29, 2017)[28]
- "While we are on the subject, it is reported that the U.S. Post Office will lose $1.50 on average for each package it delivers for Amazon. That amounts to Billions of Dollars. The Failing N.Y. Times reports that 'the size of the company's lobbying staff has ballooned,' and that . . . does not include the Fake Washington Post, which is used as a 'lobbyist' and should so REGISTER. If the P.O. 'increased

THE CONSTITUTION DEMANDS IT   117

its parcel rates, Amazon's shipping costs would rise by
$2.6 Billion.' This Post Office scam must stop. Amazon
must pay real costs (and taxes) now!" (Mar. 31, 2018)[29]

- "I am right about Amazon costing the United States Post
Office massive amounts of money for being their Delivery
Boy. Amazon should pay these costs (plus) and not have
them bourne by the American Taxpayer. Many billions of
dollars. P.O. leaders don't have a clue (or do they?)!" (Apr. 3,
2018)[30]

In May 2018, news emerged that Trump had personally
met with the postmaster general "in multiple conversations"
in 2017 and 2018, demanding that she double the rate that the
Postal Service charges Amazon for package delivery.[31] Trump
also met "with at least three groups of senior advisers to discuss Amazon's business practices, probing issues such as
whether they pay the appropriate amount of taxes or underpay
the Postal Service."[32]

THREATS TO REVOKE LICENSES OF TV NETWORK

On October 11, 2017, Trump tweeted, "Fake @NBC News made
up story that I wanted a 'ten-fold' increase in our U.S. nuclear
arsenal. Pure fiction, made up to demean. NBC = CNN!"[33]
and "With all of the Fake News coming out of NBC and the
Networks at what point is it appropriate to challenge their
License? Bad for country!"[34] On October 11, 2017, Trump also
tweeted, "Network news has become so partisan, distorted
and fake that licenses must be challenged and, if appropriate,
revoked. Not fair to public!"[35]

PRESSURE TO FIRE EXECUTIVES AND REPORTERS

On November 29, 2017, Trump asked on Twitter, "[W]hen will
the top executives at NBC and Comcast be fired for putting out

so much Fake News. Check out Andy Lack's past!"[36] Trump has publicly urged the firing of specific reporters at ABC,[37] CNN,[38] and *The Washington Post*,[39] and his White House press secretary said it was a "fireable offense" for an ESPN sports journalist to criticize Trump on Twitter.[40]

THREATS TO "CHANGE LIBEL LAWS" AFTER UNFAVORABLE NEWS STORIES

On March 30, 2017, Trump tweeted: "The failing @nytimes has disgraced the media world. Gotten me wrong for two solid years. Change libel laws?"[41] While this would be difficult to carry out, his administration may take it seriously. On April 30, 2017, his then chief of staff Reince Priebus confirmed that changing libel laws is "something we've looked at," adding that "newspapers and news agencies need to be more responsible with how they report the news."[42]

★   ★   ★

The White House makes good on some of Trump's threats. On February 24, 2017, Trump's White House barred certain news media—CNN, *The New York Times*, the *Los Angeles Times*, and Politico—from attending a White House press briefing.[43] On May 10, 2017, the White House barred American reporters from witnessing his meeting with Russian Foreign Minister Sergey Lavrov and Russian Ambassador to the United Sates Sergey Kislyak in the Oval Office, but allowed a Russian photographer to document the meeting.[44] Indeed, the only reason that the U.S. public even knows that Trump met with the Russian officials in the Oval Office is because Russian state media released a photograph. (And this is the meeting at which he revealed his motive for firing former FBI director Comey to the Russian officials.[45]) In June 2017, his administration prohibited video recordings of White House press briefings.[46]

Trump's approach has started to percolate throughout the

government, as his administration has also taken or tried to take concrete retaliatory measures against the independent press, particularly news media that have subjected him to critical coverage. For example, in July 2017, White House staff reportedly discussed using the Department of Justice approval process over a pending merger between Time Warner (CNN's parent company) and AT&T as an opportunity for "leverage" over CNN's news coverage of the president.[47] More recently, the Department of Justice revised the U.S. Attorneys' Manual to remove a section titled "Need for Free Press and Public Trial."[48]

In March 2018, the Reporters Committee for the Freedom of the Press issued a report on press freedoms in the United States.[49] The study catalogued "19 of the most egregious public threats made to reporters and media organizations in 2017 by U.S. politicians and other public figures that could have a chilling effect on journalism," and noted that "[a]ll but two of these were made by either President Trump or a member of his administration."[50] Indeed, Trump's rhetoric has led to a "rising trend of physical violence against journalists."[51] Trump often encourages this. For example, on July 2, 2017, Trump tweeted "#FraudNewsCNN #FNN" and circulated a video of himself violently wrestling a man covered by a CNN logo.[52]

Finally, Trump has undermined the constitutional value of freedom of the press by the way his rhetoric has encouraged authoritarian foreign governments to attack the very U.S. media that Trump criticizes, endangering not only press freedoms but the lives and safety of American journalists. On May 2, 2017, just ahead of World Press Freedom Day, the Committee to Protect Journalists noted that "President Trump's oft-tweeted 'fake news' epithet, for example, has already been adopted by repressive governments such as China, Syria, and Russia. And when Trump attacked a correspondent during a February press conference, he was cheered by Turkey President Recep Tayyip Erdoğan, the world's worst jailer of journalists."[53] On November 26, 2017, the Ministry of Foreign Affairs of Egypt used Twitter to describe CNN's coverage of a terrorist attack in the Sinai Desert as "deplorable."[54] And on November 28, 2017, Libyan media attacked a CNN report on slave auctions in Libya, cited Trump's November 25 tweet ("CNN International is still a major source of (Fake) news") to criticize CNN, and suggested that its government might investigate CNN.[55]

★   ★   ★

The First Amendment to the U.S. Constitution provides that "Congress shall make no law . . . abridging the freedom of speech, or of the press."[56] As Justice Black observed in *New York Times Co. v. United States*:

> In the First Amendment the Founding Fathers gave the free press the protection it must have to fulfill its essential role in our democracy. The press was to serve the governed, not the governors. The Government's power to censor the press was abolished so that the press would remain forever free to censure the Government. The press was protected so that it could bare the secrets of government and inform the people. Only a free and unrestrained press can effectively expose deception in government.[57]

In the past, Republican and Democratic presidents alike—while sometimes chafing at particular news stories—have recognized the centrality of freedom of the press.

In 1961, President John F. Kennedy explained:

> Without debate, without criticism, no Administration and no country can succeed—and no republic can survive . . . And that is why our press was protected by the First Amendment—the only business in America specif-

ically protected by the Constitution—not primarily to amuse and entertain, not to emphasize the trivial and the sentimental, not to simply "give the public what it wants"—but to inform, to arouse, to reflect, to state our dangers and our opportunities, to indicate our crises and our choices, to lead, mold, educate and sometimes even anger public opinion.[58]

Similarly, as President George W. Bush noted on World Press Freedom Day in 2007, "[t]he United States values freedom of the press as one of the most fundamental political rights and as a necessary component of free societies. In undemocratic societies where governments suppress, manipulate, and control access to information, journalists are on the front lines of the people's battle for freedom."[59] In stark contrast to Trump, President Bush also condemned harassment of journalists abroad.[60]

To be sure, many presidents have contentious relations with national media. And Trump is certainly free to criticize particular news stories that he believes are inaccurate. Perhaps the president's defenders might argue that his criticisms of the independent press as "fake news" refer mainly to factually inaccurate stories. But the facts do not bear that out. Rather, the president uses the term "fake news" to describe *unfavorable* stories. Indeed, he effectively *defined* his use of "fake" as "negative" when he complained that "91% of the Network News about me is negative (Fake)."[61]

One tweet will not bring down the republic, and none of the individual tweets or statements cited above, standing in isolation, would constitute an impeachable offense. But Trump's consistent pattern of repeated verbal attacks on news media and journalists crosses a line.

Does this consistent line of attack violate the First Amendment protection of freedom of the press? If Trump were a private citizen rather than the president of the United States, there would be no issue. But for over fifty years, the Supreme

Court has acknowledged that a government entity's "threat of invoking legal sanctions and other means of coercion, persuasion, and intimidation" can violate the freedom of the press under the First Amendment.[62] Courts have found First Amendment violations from even indirect coercion by government officials. For example, in one case, the borough president of New York City's Staten Island sent a letter to a billboard company to complain about certain billboards, stating that their message was "not welcome in our Borough." Even though the borough president made no explicit threats and in fact did not even have regulatory authority over the billboard company, a federal court of appeals held that "[a] public-official defendant who threatens to employ coercive state power to stifle protected speech violates a plaintiff's First Amendment rights, regardless of whether the threatened punishment comes in the form of the use (or, misuse) of the defendant's direct regulatory or decisionmaking authority over the plaintiff, or in some less-direct form."[63]

Of course, not *all* government "disendorsement" of the press violates the First Amendment, and courts have attempted to distinguish "attempts to convince [from] attempts to coerce," finding that mere official discouragement or stigma, without an accompanying implicit threat, does not violate the First Amendment.[64] But this is not the usual case. First, the president "is seeking to discredit or silence core political expression addressing matters of public concern . . . [T]he government is seeking to intimidate news organizations that fail to adhere to the sitting administration's viewpoint."[65] Second, "unlike in typical 'disendorsement' cases, the President's commentary on the way his administration is covered does not advance any [even arguably] legitimate government interest. No public purpose is served by undermining trust in news organizations or denigrating journalists."[66]

By repeatedly criticizing respected and independent journalistic institutions and specific news stories as "fake" and the press itself as "corrupt" based on little or nothing more than dislike of unfavorable coverage, threatening (even if emptily) to somehow change libel laws (i.e., reduce First Amendment protection for the press), "take away credentials," or revoke licenses for television networks with critical coverage, the president is undermining a critical foundation of a free society. Threats against the media undermine a critical foundation of our system. Indeed, in 1926, Congress impeached Judge George W. English for "threatening to jail a local newspaper editor for printing a critical editorial."[67]

It is no defense that Trump's threats may not have deterred journalists visibly so far. As one federal court of appeals noted, "such a threat is actionable [under the First Amendment] and thus can be enjoined even if it turns out to be empty—the victim ignores it, and the threatener folds his tent."[68] Moreover, we can never know how many journalists, editors, and owners of media outlets may have felt a chilling effect and restrained themselves from critical reporting of the president for fear of reprisals.

And even if the president's threats prove ineffective, an impeachable offense may be based on harassment and threats that fail to achieve their goals. By analogy, the fact that President Nixon's efforts to obstruct justice were unsuccessful did not diminish the danger of his efforts. The protective purposes of impeachment are well suited to address a chief executive who endangers this pillar of the First Amendment and the foundational institutions on which democracy relies.

BOTTOM LINE: Trump has repeatedly attacked major U.S. news organizations as "fake news" and "the enemy of the American people." His administration has also taken retaliatory measures against the independent press. Trump's rhetoric has encouraged authoritarian foreign governments to attack the very U.S. media that he criticizes. To be sure, Trump is free to criticize particular news stories that he believes are inaccurate, and no one tweet in isolation constitutes an impeachable offense. But his consistent pattern of denigrating journalistic institutions as "fake news" based on little more than dislike of their coverage, threatening (even if emptily) to somehow change libel laws to reduce First Amendment protection for press, and suggesting revocation of licenses for television networks with critical coverage, undermines a critical foundation of a free society.

It is time for Congress to investigate whether to impeach President Trump for undermining the freedom of the press.

NINE

POTENTIAL ADDITIONAL GROUNDS

We have discussed eight areas where the facts and the law combine for the strongest cases for impeachment hearings at this point. But news of presidential scandal and misconduct continues to emerge at a dizzying pace. Based on Trump's venality, bigotry, and despotic ambitions, we can expect the list of potential grounds for impeachment hearings to continue to expand. Here are some areas to watch in the future.

THE STORMY DANIELS MATTER

In October 2016, as Election Day neared, Donald Trump's personal lawyer, Michael Cohen, negotiated a "hush agreement" with Stormy Daniels, an adult-film actress whose real name is Stephanie Clifford. Under the agreement, Clifford received $130,000 from Essential Consultants LLC, a limited liability company that Cohen set up for the occasion, in exchange for keeping quiet about an extramarital sexual encounter that Trump had with her in 2006.[1]

The issue is not the sexual encounter itself, nor even the fact of the hush money, but rather the fact that the hush money was intended to influence the election. As Trump's lawyer Rudy Giuliani later (perhaps inadvertently) confirmed, the purpose of this expense was obviously campaign-related: "Imagine if that came out on Oct. 15, 2016, in the middle of the, you know, last debate with Hillary Clinton."[2] The agreement, ultimately signed on October 28, 2016, only came to light in 2018. And Trump claims to have reimbursed Cohen for this expense after the election.[3]

While there are a few open factual questions, it is most likely illegal under any scenario. Under campaign finance law, "hush money" to silence unfavorable information that could harm a political candidate's chances in an election is deemed a campaign contribution or expenditure if it was paid "for the purpose of influencing any election for Federal office."[4] Ironically, Trump *could* have done this perfectly legally: he could have paid the money himself and then disclosed it on campaign finance reports. But that is not how it happened.

If Cohen was truly the source of the money, it would count as an in-kind contribution to Trump's campaign, yet one that was forty-eight times higher than the federal campaign contribution limit of $2,700 and which the campaign failed to disclose as required by law.[5] But Trump's story is now that Cohen advanced the money to be later repaid by Trump (plus, presumably, a markup).[6] According to Giuliani, Trump personally owed Cohen several hundred thousand dollars as of the date of the election.[7]

As noted in Chapter 2, conduct before assuming office may properly be grounds for impeachment, particularly if it corrupted the very process by which the official was chosen. But that is not the end of the story. Trump's conduct here continued after he took the oath of office, as he made every effort to conceal this payment. This is illegal. Under the Ethics in Government Act, Trump was legally required to disclose his outstanding personal debts. Trump's May 2018 financial-disclosure form, executed after the payment became public, lists this debt. But his June 2017 financial disclosure form, sworn under penalty of perjury and covering a sixteen-month period that spanned the election, did *not* list any debt to Michael Cohen.[8]

Trump almost certainly violated the Ethics in Government Act by omitting this debt from his 2017 financial-disclosure form.[9] Indeed, on May 16, 2018, the acting director of the U.S. Office of Government Ethics (the federal agency responsible for certifying the president's financial disclosure report) wrote to Deputy Attorney General Rosenstein. As OGE explained, it had concluded that the payment made by Cohen to "a third party" (Stormy Daniels) was required to be reported as a liability.[10] While OGE itself has no enforcement power, the letter noted that "[y]ou may find the disclosure relevant to any inquiry you may be pursuing regarding the President's prior report."[11] As a former OGE director observed, the letter was "tantamount to a criminal referral."[12]

The question here is whether these violations rise to the level of high crimes and misdemeanors. They may. However, based on the currently available facts, we have decided not to include it on the list of grounds for impeachment—yet. But perhaps more importantly, the Stormy Daniels matter helped expose something that could be even more legally serious.

THE MICHAEL COHEN CORPORATE SLUSH FUND

In May 2018, the public learned that Essential Consultants LLC was not *only* used to pay Stormy Daniels to keep silent about her affair with Trump. It also served as a corporate slush fund that received $500,000 from Columbus Nova, a company tied to Russian oligarch Viktor Vekselberg (supposedly for "real estate investment advice"), as well as $600,000 from AT&T (supposedly to advise on "specific long-term planning initiatives as well as the immediate issue of corporate tax reform and the acquisition of Time Warner"), $1.2 million from Swiss pharmaceutical giant Novartis (supposedly for healthcare policy advice), and an undisclosed sum from South Korea's Korea Aerospace Industries (supposedly for accounting advice).[13]

It may be that this was Cohen's side hustle and Trump was not involved. But do not bank on that. We know that Essential Consultants LLC made payments on Trump's behalf in *L'Affaire Stormy Daniels*. The "company" appears to be, to some extent, a corporate slush fund into which outside figures can deposit money for Trump's benefit.

One possibility is that Cohen (after deducting a commission, known in the industry as "juice") simply passes the money directly to Trump. Indeed, in December 2016, Cohen allegedly shook down a Qatari investor at Trump Tower, for "millions" in bribes for "Trump family members."[14] But it is also possible that the corporate slush fund is used *indirectly* to pay off Trump's debts.

It may help to understand this as a scheme with four players. The first player is Donald Trump. Trump owes money, for whatever reason (business debts, hush payments to mistresses, etc.) to the second player—the creditor. The third player is someone who wants something out of Trump—the briber.

A simple bribery scheme would involve the briber paying Trump in exchange for official favors; Trump would then use the money to pay off the creditor. A slightly more sophisticated version of the scheme would have the briber make an arrangement with Trump: the briber pays the creditor directly, and in return gets the official favors from Trump. But this creates a paper trail connecting the briber to the creditor, when they seemingly have no relationship with each other, and they might not want to have to explain it. Or at very least, they'd prefer to cloud the money trail.

So the next level is to add a fourth player—a legitimate-seeming intermediary, such as "Essential Consultants LLC." Now, the briber pays the legitimate-seeming intermediary, with a passable cover story as to why the briber would be writing a check of that type; meanwhile, the legitimate-seeming intermediary pays the creditor, which need not even know the identity of the briber. Through this type of scheme, Trump would receive a financial benefit (debt repayment) from the briber without ever touching the money himself.

Is this what happened with Essential Consultants LLC? We do not know yet. But if it was, then it likely violated the federal bribery statute.[15] Bribery is an impeachable offense—in fact, one of just two offenses specifically listed in the Constitution as grounds for impeachment. And if Trump demanded that the bribers pay up by threatening economic harm or as a price of doing business with the United States, it would also be extortion—"obtaining of property from another, with his consent, induced by wrongful use of . . . fear, or under color of official right."[16] Extortion and conspiracy to commit extortion[17] are almost certainly impeachable offenses as well.

UKRAINIAN MISSILES

Michael Cohen may not be the only potential source of bribes to Trump. As noted in Chapter 1, the curious timing by which the Chinese government announced major financial support for a Trump resort development in Indonesia and then, two days later, Trump stunned his own advisors by announcing that the government would back off sanctioned Chinese phone maker ZTE, suggests the possibility of a quid pro quo.

Yet bribery includes not only *taking* bribes, but also *giving* them. In early April 2018, a U.S. sale of 210 anti-tank missiles to Ukraine was pending but not finalized. That month, the Ukrainian government halted cooperation with Special Counsel Mueller's investigation, as well as four of its own criminal investigations connected to Manafort and his associates for money laundering and other dealings when he worked there. As one Ukrainian lawmaker explained, "In every possible way, we will avoid irritating the top American officials. We shouldn't spoil relations with the administration." On April 30, the missiles were delivered.[18]

It is possible that the Ukrainian government decided, on its own, to freeze its cooperation with the special counsel's investigation. But "[i]t is far more likely that somebody in the administration proposed a quid pro quo, and Ukraine quite rationally decided it would rather have weapons to defend itself against the next Russian aggression than participate in an investigation that the president of the United States regards as a mortal threat."[19]

★   ★   ★

As this book went to press, the Trump administration inflicted a new horror: breaking up migrant families and imprisoning their children in cages. Long after that outrageous practice has ended, the incalculable trauma already inflicted upon thousands of children and their families will remain.

Donald Trump stains not just his office, but America itself. Generations of future historians will study this era and how we allowed Trump to drag the country to these depths. The fundamental question will be: what did we, as a people, do to respond to this abuse of power?

TEN

WHY NOW?

Some argue that Congress should wait until Special Counsel Robert Mueller completes his criminal probe before beginning impeachment hearings. Mueller's investigation could indeed provide evidence relevant to some of the grounds for an impeachment investigation. But Congress must not use that pending investigation as an excuse to shirk its duty to conduct its own independent impeachment hearings.

First, the special counsel's investigation is more limited than the scope of an impeachment investigation. His charge focuses on the Russia investigation, "matters that arose or may arise directly from the investigation," and "crimes committed in the course of, and with intent to interfere with, the Special Counsel's investigation, such as perjury, obstruction of justice, destruction of evidence, and intimidation of witnesses."[1] But that does not cover the majority of Trump's impeachable offenses. Of the eight grounds for impeachment hearings that we have listed, only two—obstruction of justice, and L'Affaire Russe—are within the special counsel's purview. The other six grounds are far more than enough to warrant impeachment hearings. Indeed, some of them, such as violating the emoluments clauses and abusing the pardon power, were specifically identified by the founders as grounds for impeachment. But the special counsel has no jurisdiction with respect to the grounds outside the scope of his appointment; they remain the responsibility of Congress.

Second, Mueller is only authorized to prosecute violations of *federal criminal statutes*. But federal criminal statutes do not include the full range of potential abuses that may constitute "high Crimes and Misdemeanors." The president has unique powers and opportunities for abuse that he shares with literally no one else in the country, and it would not make sense for Congress to pass specific statutes detailing a range of criminal violations that only one person could commit.

Third, even within the area of overlap, the special counsel must focus on criminal violations that he can *prove in federal court*. Trials in federal courts are subject to procedural and evidentiary requirements that do not apply to a congressional impeachment proceeding. When the House Judiciary Committee conducts an impeachment investigation, it can consider whatever evidence the Committee finds appropriate, whether or not a federal judge would allow it to be presented to a jury. The same is true if the matter reaches the Senate for a trial.

Fourth, the federal criminal obstruction-of-justice statutes require proof that the defendant had a particular state of mind. By contrast, Congress is empowered to decide that the president's actions merit impeachment regardless of his intentions or mental state.[2]

Fifth, the special counsel's investigation will, by nature, be conducted in secret, except as particular indictments and pleas are unsealed. Furthermore, since, according to some opinions, a sitting president cannot be indicted, it is possible that the special counsel's analysis of the president's misconduct may come in the form of a confidential recommendation to the Department of Justice, which could bury it so that neither citizens nor journalists nor members of Congress learn its contents until long after Trump's term in office has ended. By contrast, a congressional impeachment investigation will be conducted—at least in part—in the open, laying forth the evidence for the American public as it develops, and in a timely manner.

Finally, in an important sense, an impeachment investigation into the president's corruption and abuses of power does not require a special prosecutor. As we have shown here, the factual evidence supporting many potential bases for impeachment is largely public, and largely undisputed. To be sure, evidence regarding the dealings among Trump, his campaign, and his administration with the Russian government, is still unfolding. Those issues are factually complex and may even involve questions of statutory interpretation. But they do not provide the only basis for impeachment hearings.

Similar reasoning applies to pending litigation involving challenges to the president's violations of the emoluments clauses, and to the pardon of Joe Arpaio. Given the protective purposes of impeachment, the fact that a judicial remedy may be available to halt or undo specific presidential actions does not obviate the need for Congress to act without further delay in order to prevent continuing harm to the rule of law.

As a final note, the fact that President Trump is unrepentant in continuing his corruption and abuse of power militates strongly in favor of opening impeachment proceedings immediately. This is not a case of an isolated instance of wrongdoing, or of a president who retreated from impeachable territory after his malfeasance was exposed.[3] Quite the contrary—if not checked or restrained, Trump will be emboldened to abuse his office even further. As Elbridge Gerry said in the constitutional debates, urging that the new Constitution include provisions for impeaching the president, "[a] good magistrate will not fear them. A bad one ought to be kept in fear of them."[4]

And there is a price to delay. Any impeachment inquiry, and any vote to impeach, as well as the requisite trial that would follow in the Senate, would be a deliberate and deliberative process. Investigation, impeachment, and trial would take months to play out. Waiting to decide, or deciding to wait, enables and emboldens a dangerous authoritarian president who is becoming increasingly unrestrained. Delay in beginning this process is dangerous and irresponsible.

★   ★   ★

Some observers, looking at current levels of public support for impeachment and the current predilections of Congress, have concluded that impeachment is a pipe dream. They are wrong.

To address the obvious, it is certainly correct that if the U.S. House were to hold a floor vote on the date of this writing on articles of impeachment, they would not pass. Indeed, a limited article of impeachment presented by Representative Al Green of Texas *did* go to a floor vote, and it garnered 66 votes—some 152 short.[5]

But the situation is fluid and dynamic, and can change rapidly. And it is far too early to start counting votes before the House has even begun committee investigations. The very process of public House Judiciary Committee impeachment hearings—with careful fact-finding, and serious and credible public discussions of which offenses are impeachable—will change the dynamics in both Congress and public opinion.

In their recent book *To End a Presidency*, Professor Laurence Tribe and his coauthor, Joshua Matz, note that, historically, a critical factor in the success of impeachment proceedings has been public support.[6] For comparison, consider the Nixon impeachment process.[7] Nixon won reelection in 1972 by a landslide, and enjoyed a 68-percent approval rating at his second inauguration in January 1973. The emerging Watergate news caused a notable decline in his approval rating, but at the start of the Senate Watergate hearings in May 1973, he still had a 48-percent approval rating. One month into those widely televised hearings, his approval rating was steady and a mere 19 percent of the public supported impeachment.

As the hearings continued, and the public saw more and more evidence of Nixon's abuses of power, public support for impeachment rose steadily—but slowly. Ten days after the October 20, 1973, "Saturday Night Massacre" (in which Nixon fired several Justice Department officials in an effort to fire the

Watergate special prosecutor), the House voted to authorize the Judiciary Committee to conduct an impeachment inquiry. Yet support for impeachment was still below 40 percent, and remained there during the inquiry's early phases, much of which involved behind-the-scenes staff work.

In May 1974, when the Judiciary Committee opened its formal impeachment hearings, public support for impeachment was still well below 50 percent. In fact, public support for impeachment *never crossed 50 percent* before the House Judiciary Committee finally approved three articles of impeachment in late July 1974. Public support for removing Nixon from office then rose to 57 percent, and Nixon was persuaded that he would be convicted in a Senate trial. On August 8, he resigned.

How does the present situation compare? Impeachment hearings have not yet started—indeed, the House has not even authorized them to start. At this point in the Nixon timeline, public support for impeachment was in the 30s.

By comparison, as of this writing, public support for impeaching President Trump is, depending on which polls you consider and when, just under 50 percent.[8] Of course, this is less than a majority. But the right analysis is to compare it to a comparable stage in Watergate. Public support for impeaching Trump is *already* at levels not seen in the Nixon investigation until the House Judiciary Committee had already concluded its hearings and was debating which articles of impeachment to approve. And we haven't even started hearings yet.

Imagine a pundit in 1973 or early 1974 insisting that Nixon would never be forced from office, based on that day's polls. Now consider that public support for impeaching Trump is much stronger than it was for Nixon at the same point in the process. Anyone who confidently predicts that Trump cannot be impeached or convicted, based on public polls or nose-counting members of Congress before impeachment hearings have even begun, is committing an even bigger error than the pundit who swore Nixon would finish his term.

★   ★   ★

We say that the Constitution demands impeachment proceedings. But Congress is not literally forced to impeach Trump—that decision lies solely in Congress's hands, and no court can force Congress to act. In fact, the Constitution does not really "demand" *anything*. It is a piece of paper; it does not make demands.

Yet there is a deeper sense in which the Constitution *does* demand action. If we care about its principles, then we cannot tolerate a profiteering president who abuses his power to shield his corrupt dealings, reward his cronies, and harass his political opponents and the press while toying erratically with nuclear war.

In the Declaration of Independence, Thomas Jefferson charged that King George had become "unfit to be the ruler of a free people."[9] Today, President Trump's high crimes and misdemeanors put our entire constitutional system at risk. Congress needs to launch hearings now—the Constitution demands it.

AFTERWORD

If you are convinced that protecting our Constitution demands that we press for impeachment proceedings, here's what you can do to help.

1. **Talk to your friends, family, and neighbors about impeachment.** Right now, the message from Washington, D.C., is to shush "impeachment talk." But we can counter that with our own message. Whether on social media or (better yet) in person, talk to friends, family, and neighbors about the dangers of the Trump presidency and why the legal criteria for impeachment hearings have already been met.

2. **Call your Representative in Congress.** Only Congress can start impeachment hearings. Call your Representative (the Capitol Switchboard is 202-224-3121) and urge him or her to support authorizing the Judiciary Committee to begin impeachment hearings. Or better yet, talk to him or her in person during an appointment for a meeting at the district or D.C. office, or at a town hall. The Appendix includes sample scripts. (You may only be able to talk to a staffer. That is fine— convey your concern. They take notes of these calls.)

3. **Write a letter to the editor in your local newspaper supporting impeachment hearings.** We have included a sample letter to the editor (which ran in *The New York Times*) that you can use as a starting point.

4. **Join the Impeachment Project.** Please visit the website

www.impeachmentproject.org to stay updated and learn what you can do as events develop. And if you can contribute a few dollars to the effort, even better!

SAMPLE PHONE SCRIPT
FOR MEMBER OF CONGRESS

Hi, my name is [YOUR NAME], I'm a constituent living in [CITY/TOWN] and my zip code is [ZIP]. I'm calling to ask Representative X to support a resolution calling for the Judiciary Committee to open an investigation into the impeachment of President Trump. It's time to start the investigation. From the moment he was sworn in, President Donald Trump has been in direct violation of the U.S. Constitution's emoluments clauses, and since then the grounds for impeachment hearings have only grown.

And the House shouldn't wait for the special counsel's investigation to finish—it should start now. Most of the grounds for impeachment hearings, such as directing law enforcement to harass political opponents, aren't even within the scope of the special counsel's investigation.

Would Representative X be willing to introduce or cosponsor a resolution calling for the House Committee on the Judiciary to open an impeachment investigation?

SAMPLE LETTER TO
THE EDITOR IN SUPPORT OF
IMPEACHMENT PROCEEDINGS

The following letter was published in the April 11, 2018 New York Times.[1] *Feel free to modify it and use it for your own purposes.*

The argument that we need more proof before pressing for impeachment proceedings against Trump belies the facts.
We already have overwhelming evidence that the

president has committed impeachable offenses, including obstruction of justice; violations of the anticorruption provisions of the Constitution (the emoluments clauses); abuse of the pardon power; undermining the freedom of the press; recklessly threatening nuclear war against foreign nations; directing or seeking to direct law enforcement, including the Department of Justice and the F.B.I., to prosecute political adversaries for improper purposes; and giving aid and comfort to white supremacists and neo-Nazis.

Whether the president was directly involved in a conspiracy with the Russian government to interfere with the 2016 election remains the subject of Robert Mueller's investigation. But we do not need to wait for the outcome of that criminal investigation before moving forward with an impeachment inquiry in the House of Representatives on whether the president has committed crimes against the state: abuse of power and abuse of the public trust.

Our Constitution is facing one of its greatest tests. We must rise to defend it, using the power of the impeachment clause to confront the unprecedented corruption of the presidency. That starts with the launch of an impeachment investigation of Mr. Trump.

JOHN C. BONIFAZ

BEN T. CLEMENTS

The writers are, respectively, the president and chairman of Free Speech For People.

SELECTED BIBLIOGRAPHY

For further reading on the law and history of impeachment, you may find the following helpful.

Charles L. Black, Jr., *Impeachment: A Handbook* (New Haven: Yale University Press, 1974).

Barbara A. Radnofsky, *A Citizen's Guide to Impeachment* (Brooklyn: Melville House, 2017).

House Judiciary Committee, *Constitutional Grounds for Presidential Impeachment* (93d Cong., Feb. 1974), http://bit.ly/CGPI1974.

Laurence Tribe and Joshua Matz, *To End a Presidency* (New York: Basic Books, 2018).

The following white papers help explain important topics related to particular grounds for impeachment hearings.

Barry H. Berke, Noah Bookbinder, and Norman L. Eisen, *Presidential Obstruction of Justice: The Case of Donald J. Trump*, Brookings Governance Studies, Oct. 10, 2017, http://brook.gs/2jadWLb.

Norman L. Eisen, Richard Painter, and Laurence H. Tribe, *The Emoluments Clause: Its Text, Meaning, and Application to Donald J. Trump*, Brookings Governance Studies, Dec. 16, 2016, http://brook.gs/2i1i3Ht.

Brianne J. Gorod, Brian R. Frazelle, and Samuel Houshower, *The Domestic Emoluments Clause: Its Text, Meaning, and Application to Donald J. Trump*, Const. Accountability Ctr., July 2017, http://bit.ly/CACDomesticEmoluments.

NOTES

INTRODUCTION

1. Gerald R. Ford, Speech on Floor of the U.S. House of Representatives, in 116 Cong. Rec. 11, pp. 912–13, 116 Cong. Rec. H3113 (April 15, 1970).
2. U.S. Const. art. II, § 4.
3. See James Madison, *September 8, 1787*, in *The Avalon Project: Madison Debates* (Yale Law Sch. Lillian Goldman Library ed., 2008), http://avalon.law.yale .edu/18th_century/debates_908.asp; Laurence H. Tribe, "Defining 'High Crimes and Misdemeanors': Basic Principles," 67 Geo. Wash. L. Rev., pp. 712, 718–19 (1999).
4. Charles Doyle, Cong. Research Serv., *Impeachment Grounds: A Collection of Selected Materials*, pp. 1, 26 (Oct. 29, 1998); Gary L. McDowell, "'High Crimes and Misdemeanors': Recovering the Intentions of the Founders," 67 Geo. Wash. L. Rev., pp. 626, 638 (1999).
5. The Federalist No. 65, p. 394 (Alexander Hamilton) (New York: Signet Classics, 2003).
6. *Id.*, pp. 394–95.
7. Black, *Impeachment*, p. 37.
8. Cass R. Sunstein, "Impeaching the President," 147 U. Pa. L. Rev., pp. 279, 284–85 (1998).
9. Tribe and Matz, *To End a Presidency*, p. 42.
10. House Judiciary Committee, *Constitutional Grounds for Presidential Impeachment*, pp. 21–25 (93d Cong., Feb. 1974), http://bit.ly/CGPI1974.
11. See Jared P. Cole and Todd Garvey, Cong. Research Serv., *Impeachment and Removal* 1, pp. 7–9 (Oct. 29, 2015), https://fas.org/sgp/crs/misc /R44260.pdf; *Constitutional Grounds for Presidential Impeachment*, pp. 21–25 (93d Cong., Feb. 1974), http://bit.ly/CGPI1974.
12. See, for example, Tribe and Matz, *To End a Presidency*, pp. 44–53; Black, *Impeachment*, pp. 33–35.
13. Joseph Story, *Commentaries on the Constitution* § 764, vol. I, p. 541 (Boston: Little Brown & Co., 1873), http://bit.ly/Story764.
14. Black, *Impeachment*, p. 35.
15. Tribe, 67 Geo. Wash. L. Rev., p. 717.
16. *Id.*; see also Akhil Reed Amar, "On Impeaching Presidents," 28 Hofstra

L. Rev., pp. 291, 295 (1999) ("a President who simply runs off on vacation in the middle of a crisis").

17. Black, *Impeachment*, p. 34.

18. *Id.*, p. 39 (emphasis in original).

19. *Id.* (emphases in original).

20. Story, *Commentaries on the Constitution* § 803, p. 568 (emphasis added).

21. *Id.* § 764, p. 541.

22. While the Constitution is not explicit on the point, it is now widely accepted that the grounds for impeaching judges are the same as the grounds for impeaching presidents and other civil officers. See Radnofsky, *A Citizen's Guide to Impeachment*, pp. 22–23; see Jared P. Cole and Todd Garvey, Cong. Research Serv., *Impeachment and Removal* pp. 1, 9 (Oct. 29, 2015), https://fas.org/sgp/crs/misc/R44260.pdf .

23. House Judiciary Committee, *Impeachment of Judge Samuel B. Kent*, H.R. Rep. No. 111-159, p. 5 (2009), https://www.congress.gov/111/crpt/hrpt159/CRPT-111hrpt159.pdf (quoting House Judiciary Committee, *Impeachment of Walter L. Nixon, Jr.*, H.R. Rep. No. 101-36, p. 5 (1989)) (quotation marks omitted); *id.*, p. 6 ("[T]he phrase 'high Crimes and Misdemeanors' 'refers to misconduct that damages the state and the operations of governmental institutions, and is not limited to criminal misconduct.'") (quoting House Judiciary Committee, *Impeachment of Alcee L. Hastings*, H.R. Rep. No. 100-810, p. 6 (1988)).

24. See Jared P. Cole and Todd Garvey, Cong. Research Serv., *Impeachment and Removal*, p. 9 (Oct. 29, 2015), https://fas.org/sgp/crs/misc/R44260.pdf.

25. House Judiciary Committee, *Constitutional Grounds for Presidential Impeachment*, pp. 21–25 (93d Cong., Feb. 1974), http://bit.ly/CGPI1974.

26. *Id.*

27. See U.S. Senate, *The Impeachment Trial of Alcee L. Hastings (1989) U.S. District Judge, Florida*, http://bit.ly/2rPOwnF.

28. James Wilson, *The Works of the Honourable James Wilson, L.L.D.*, vol. I, p. 452 (Philadelphia: At the Lorenzo Press, printed for Bronson and Chauncey, 1804).

29. U.S. Const. art. I, § 2, cl. 5; *id.*, art. I, § 3, cl. 6.

30. See generally Radnofsky, *A Citizen's Guide to Impeachment* (2017).

31. See, for example, *id.*, pp. 48–54, 67 (discussing impeachment proceedings against Judges Delahay, English, Kent, and Aquilar, and Secretary of War Belknap, each of whom resigned partway through the process).

32. Lewis Deschler, *Precedents of the U.S. House of Representatives*, ch. 14 § 5.11; T. J. Halstead, Cong. Research Serv., *An Overview of the Impeachment Process*, pp. 2–3 (April 20, 2005).

33. Black, *Impeachment*, p. 7.

34. *Id.*

35. John O. McGinnis, "Impeachment: The Structural Understanding," 67 Geo. Wash. L. Rev., pp. 650, 659 (1999)

36. *Id.*

37. House Judiciary Committee, *Constitutional Grounds for Presidential Impeachment*, p. 21 (93d Cong., Feb. 1974), http://bit.ly/CGPI1974.

38. John Labovitz, *Presidential Impeachment*, p. 131 (New Haven: Yale University Press, 1978).

39. Tribe and Matz, *To End a Presidency*, p. 56.

40. House Judiciary Committee, *Impeachment of Richard M. Nixon, President of the United States*, H.R. Rep. No. 93-1305, 120 Cong. Rec. 29,220 (1974), http://bit.ly/HR93-1305.

41. Radnofsky, *A Citizen's Guide to Impeachment*, p. 54.

42. U.S. Const. art. I, § 3, cl., pp. 6–7.

43. Tribe and Matz, *To End a Presidency*, pp. 133–34 (quoting Linda Greenhouse, "William H. Rehnquist, Architect of Conservative Court, Dies at 80," *The New York Times*, Sept. 5, 2005, https://nyti.ms/2LVuGzL).

44. Black, *Impeachment*, p. 18.

45. *Id.*, pp. 14–18; Thomas B. Ripy, Cong. Research Serv., *Standard of Proof in Senate Impeachment Proceedings* (Jan. 7, 1999).

46. Black, *Impeachment*, p. 13.

47. *Id.*

48. See Norman Eisen and Elizabeth Holtzman, "Donald Trump should not assume he's above the law. A sitting president can be indicted," *USA Today*, May 24, 2018, https://usat.ly/2IHfoRh; Adam Liptak, "A Constitutional Puzzle: Can the President Be Indicted?," *The New York Times*, May 29, 2017, https://nyti.ms/2scC27a.

49. Radnofsky, *A Citizen's Guide to Impeachment*, pp. 48, 50, 66.

CHAPTER 1

1. Zephyr Teachout, "The Anti-Corruption Principle," 94 Cornell L. Rev., pp. 341, 348 (2009).

2. U.S. Const. art. I, § 9, cl. 8 (emphasis added).

3. U.S. Const. art. II, § 1, cl. 7 (emphasis added).

4. For a thorough historical exposition of the meaning of the word "emolument" at the time of the founding, see John S. Mikhail, "The Definition of 'Emolument' in English Language and Legal Dictionaries, 1523–1806" (working paper, 2017), https://ssrn.com/abstract=2995693.

5. Of course, readers who wish to plumb the depths may consult detailed expert analyses. For example, see Norman L. Eisen et al., *The Emoluments Clause*; Brianne J. Gorod et al., *The Domestic Emoluments Clause*.

6. Drew Harwell and Anu Narayanswamy, "A scramble to assess the dangers of President-elect Donald Trump's global business empire," *The Washington Post*, Nov. 20, 2016, http://wpo.st/KCmP2.

7. See "Donald Trump's News Conference: Full Transcript and Video," *The New York Times*, Jan. 11, 2017, http://nyti.ms/2kHSolf.

8. Susanne Craig and Eric Lipton, "Trust Records Show Trump Is Still

Closely Tied to His Empire," *The New York Times*, Feb. 3, 2017, https://nyti.ms/2kytJlP.

9. *Id.*

10. See Patrick Madden, "It's Official: Trump's Son Takes Over Pennsylvania Avenue Hotel", WAMU, Feb. 6, 2017, http://bit.ly/2lkv9S5.

11. Many of these are collected in Michael Keller et al., *Tracking Trump's Web of Conflicts, Bloomberg,* https://bloom.bg/2Ae4GfQ (last updated Dec. 22, 2017). But the list continues to expand. For regularly updated lists, see Global Anticorruption Blog, *Tracking Corruption and Conflicts in the Trump Administration,* https://globalanticorruptionblog.com/profiting-from-the-presidency-tracking-corruption-and-conflicts-in-the-trump-administration (last visited June 5, 2018); Citizens for Responsibility and Ethics in Washington, *Trump Inc.: A Chronicle of Presidential Conflicts,* https://www.citizensforethics.org/trump-timeline/ (last visited June 5, 2018).

12. Tina Nguyen, "Donald Trump Trolls the Media, Turns Phony 'Birther' Press Conference Into Hotel Infomercial," *Vanity Fair,* Sept. 16, 2016, http://bit.ly/2jZkAB6.

13. Jonathan O'Connell, "Eleven things you should know about Trump's new D.C. hotel, even if you're not going to go there," *The Washington Post,* Sept. 16, 2016, https://wapo.st/2c7fEDQ.

14. Jonathan O'Connell, "Trump D.C. hotel turns $2 million profit in four months," *The Washington Post,* Jan. 30, 2018, http://wapo.st/2GHpHzi.

15. Jonathan O'Connell and Mary Jordan, "For foreign diplomats, Trump hotel is place to be," *The Washington Post,* Nov. 18, 2016, http://wpo.st/VemN2.

16. *Id.*

17. Judd Legum and Kira Lerner, "Under political pressure, Kuwait cancels major event at Four Seasons, switches to Trump's D.C. hotel," *Think Progress,* Dec. 19, 2016, http://thkpr.gs/1f204315d513. The Kuwaiti ambassador later gave a different reason for moving the event. According to the ambassador, "[n]obody pressured" him; rather, "There is a new hotel in town, and we thought we would give it a try." Jonathan O'Connell, "Kuwaiti Embassy is latest to book Trump D.C. hotel, but ambassador says he felt 'no pressure,'" *The Washington Post,* Dec. 20, 2016, http://wapo.st/2kGKh8D.

18. David A. Fahrenthold and Jonathan O'Connell, "Kuwaiti embassy returns to Trump hotel in D.C. for its national celebration," *The Washington Post,* Jan. 26, 2018, http://wapo.st/2ngqkrc.

19. See Ian Millhiser, "Former Mexican ambassador says State Department is telling world leaders to stay at Trump hotels," *Think Progress,* Nov. 1, 2017, http://bit.ly/2hdWD06; Arturo Sarukhan (@Arturo_Sarukhan), Twitter (Oct. 31, 2017, 11:30 AM), https://twitter.com/Arturo_Sarukhan/status/925429733692727296.

20. Chuck Ross, "Saudis Spent $270K At Trump Hotel In Lobbying Cam-

paign Against 9/11 Bill," *Daily Caller*, June 4, 2017, https://bit.ly/2JoNCsj.

21. Jonathan O'Connell and David A. Fahrenthold, "Nine questions about President Trump's businesses and possible conflicts of interest," *The Washington Post*, Jan. 30, 2018, http://wapo.st/2EUsO6m.

22. Hui-yong Yu, "Trump's Washington Hotel Seen Facing New Set of Legal Challenges," *Bloomberg*, April 12, 2017, https://bloom.bg/2kaK9T8; "36th Annual Conference on U.S.-Turkey Relations," American Turkish Council, http://bit.ly/2kcpX3k (last visited June 7, 2018).

23. Jonathan O'Connell, "From Trump hotel lobby to White House, Malaysian prime minister gets VIP treatment," *The Washington Post*, Sept. 12, 2017, http://wapo.st/2wXTBM4.

24. Citizens for Responsibility and Ethics in Washington (CREW), "Profiting from the Presidency: A Year's Worth of President Trump's Conflicts of Interest," http://bit.ly/CREWProfPres (last visited June 5, 2018).

25. Apparently, the $60,000 reception was paid for by the Philippine government's "friends in private business." Jose Katigbak, "US-NoKor summit takes gloss off Independence Day reception," *The Philippine Star*, June 14, 2018, https://www.philstar.com/headlines/2018/06/14/1824449/us-nokor-summit-takes-gloss-independence-day-reception; Jose Katigbak, "PH Independence Day rites to be held at Trump Hotel in DC," *Manila Mail*, April 18, 2018, http://www.manilamail.us/?p=4665.

26. See "Donald Trump's News Conference: Full Transcript and Video," *The New York Times*, Jan. 11, 2017, http://nyti.ms/2kHSolf.

27. Trump Organization, *Donation of Profits from Foreign Government Patronage*, http://bit.ly/2Gg3I1x (undated).

28. *Id.*

29. "Trump Org donated $151,470 to gov't from foreign profits at hotels," NBC News, March 9, 2018, https://nbcnews.to/2KlWqwt.

30. Michael Keller et al., *Tracking Trump's Web of Conflicts*, Bloomberg, https://bloom.bg/2Ae4GfQ (last updated Dec. 22, 2017); Steve Cuozzo, "China Bank for Trump," *New York Post*, Sept. 16, 2008, http://nyp.st/2kGuHKg.

31. Dan Alexander, "Trump's Biggest Potential Conflict of Interest Is Hiding in Plain Sight," *Forbes*, Feb. 13, 2018, http://bit.ly/2ovCop6.

32. Stephen Rex Brown, "Exclusive: Donald Trump made millions from Saudi Arabia, but trashes Hillary Clinton for Saudi donations to Clinton Foundation," *New York Daily News*, Sept. 4, 2016, http://nydn.us/2kHfjxi.

33. Alexander, "Trump's Biggest Potential Conflict of Interest Is Hiding in Plain Sight," *Forbes*.

34. Alex Howard, "Turkish Airlines event at Trump Golf Course tees off emolumental problems," *Sunlight Found*, Sept. 24, 2017, http://bit.ly/2s1P364; Turkish Airlines, *Venues: Washington, D.C.*, http://bit.ly/2s4daki (last visited June 5, 2018).

35. Alexander, "Trump's Biggest Potential Conflict of Interest Is Hiding

in Plain Sight," *Forbes*. Despite the Trump Administration's unwillingness to disclose tenants and payment amounts, *Forbes* identified 164 of
Trump's global tenants and estimated payments, and also notes that
at least 36 of the 164 have "meaningful relationships with the federal
government." *Id.*; see also Dan Alexander and Matt Drange, *Landlord-
in-Chief*, *Forbes*, Feb. 13, 2018, https://www.forbes.com/trump-tenants.

36. *Id.*

37. Michael Keller et al., *Tracking Trump's Web of Conflicts*, Bloomberg,
     https://bloom.bg/2Ae4GfQ (last updated Dec. 22, 2017); Susanne
     Craig, "Trump's Empire: A Maze of Debts and Opaque Ties", *The New
     York Times*, Aug. 20, 2016, http://nyti.ms/2kpFwRc.

38. For details on the Mexican trademarks, see Carolyn Kenney and John
     Norris, "Trump's Conflicts of Interest in Mexico," Ctr. for Am. Prog-
     ress, June 14, 2017, https://ampr.gs/2GcWbR3.

39. Jethro Mullen et al., "China Grants Trump a Trademark He's Been
     Seeking for a Decade," CNN, Feb. 17, 2017, http://cnnmon.ie/2npCXQ1.

40. Zheping Huang, "A Curious Timeline of Trademarks Granted to Don-
     ald Trump by an Increasingly Helpful China," *Quartz*, March 13, 2017,
     https://qz.com/930896.

41. *Id.*

42. *Id.*; Jethro Mullen et al., "China Grants Trump a Trademark He's Been
     Seeking for a Decade," CNN, Feb. 17, 2017, http://cnnmon.ie/2npCXQ1.

43. "Donald Trump Scores Legal Win in China Trademark Dispute," *The
     Wall Street Journal*, Nov. 14, 2016, http://on.wsj.com/2npMUNv.

44. "Trump Agrees to Honour 'One China' Policy Despite Threats," BBC,
     Feb. 10, 2017, http://bbc.in/2npyBsl; Stephen Collinson et al., "China
     Lodges Complaint over Trump–Taiwan Call," CNN, Dec. 3, 2016,
     http://cnn.it/2girg9W.

45. Stephen Collinson et al., "China Lodges Complaint over Trump–
     Taiwan Call," CNN, Dec. 3, 2016, http://cnn.it/2girg9W.

46. *Id.*

47. "Trump Agrees to Honour 'One China' Policy Despite Threats," BBC,
     Feb. 10, 2017, http://bbc.in/2npyBsl.

48. Mark Landler and Michael Forsythe, "Trump Tells Xi Jinping U.S.
     Will Honor 'One China' Policy," *The New York Times*, Feb. 9, 2017, http:
     //nyti.ms/2npxfh7; "Trump Agrees to Honour 'One China' Policy De-
     spite Threats," BBC, Feb. 10, 2017, http://bbc.in/2npyBs.

49. "Trump Agrees to Honour 'One China' Policy Despite Threats," BBC,
     Feb. 10, 2017, http://bbc.in/2npyBs.

50. Jackie Northam, "China Grants Trump a Valuable Trademark Regis-
     tration," NPR, Feb. 16, 2017, http://n.pr/2nBjZ8g.

51. "US–China Relations: Trump Meets Senior Official Yang Jiechi," BBC,
     Feb. 27, 2017, http://bbc.in/2nFOA4N.

52. Sui-Lee Wee, "In China, Trump Wins a Trove of New Trademarks,"
     The New York Times, March 8, 2017, http://nyti.ms/2mGagyv.

53. "Trump Reportedly Plans to Host China's President in April," CNBC, March 13, 2017, http://cnb.cx/2nmKGhJ.

54. See Ben T. Clements et al., "Did Trump's China trademarks violate the Constitution and federal law?," *Albany Times-Union*, June 5, 2017, http://bit.ly/2IHTJnU. The Hobbs Act prohibits actual or attempted extortion affecting commerce. See 18 U.S.C. §§ 1951(a), (b)(2). A public official commits "color of right" extortion in violation of the Hobbs Act "when he or she encourages or accepts payments prompted by the hope that the official will be influenced in the exercise of his or her powers." *United States v. Davis*, 890 F.2d 1373, 1378 (7th Cir. 1989). The federal bribery statute prohibits a public official from directly or indirectly demanding, accepting, or seeking anything of value in exchange for being influenced in an official act. See 18 U.S.C. §§ 201(a), (b)(2). "The agreement need not be explicit, and the public official need not specify the means that he will use to perform his end of the bargain." *McDonnell v. United States*, 136 S. Ct. 2355, 2371 (2016). The statute also prohibits public officials from accepting gratuities that are given to curry favor, even without a direct quid pro quo. See 18 U.S.C. § 201(c)(1)(B); *United States v. Sun-Diamond Growers*, 526 U.S. 398, 405 (1999).

55. Alexander, "Trump's Biggest Potential Conflict of Interest Is Hiding in Plain Sight," *Forbes*.

56. See "Donald Trump's News Conference: Full Transcript and Video," *The New York Times*, Jan. 11, 2017, http://nyti.ms/2kHSolf.

57. Severin Carrell, "Trump's Scotland golf resort proceeds with expansion despite business pledge," *The Guardian*, Jan. 14, 2017, http://bit.ly/2kkIYOL.

58. See, for example, Anita Kumar, "Despite pledge, Trump company works with a foreign entity. Again.," McClatchy DC Bureau, Dec. 4, 2017, http://bit.ly/2koZ64d; Anita Kumar, "Trump promised not to work with foreign entities. His company just did.," McClatchy DC Bureau, Sept. 11, 2017, http://bit.ly/2khmQa6; Severin Carrell, "Trump's Scotland golf resort proceeds with expansion despite business pledge," *The Guardian*, Jan. 14, 2017, http://bit.ly/2kkIYOL.

59. See Eric Lipton and Susanne Craig, "Trump Sons Forge Ahead Without Father, Expanding and Navigating Conflicts," *The New York Times*, Feb. 12, 2017, http://nyti.ms/2l88CYa; Amy Brittain and Drew Harwell, "Eric Trump's business trip to Uruguay cost taxpayers $97,830 in hotel bills," *The Washington Post*, Feb. 3, 2017, https://wpo.st/-5Hb2 (describing pre-inauguration trip).

60. Lisa Marie Segarra, "Donald Trump told Steve Bannon he has a "conflict of interest" in Turkey in a 2015 interview," *TIME*, April 19, 2017, http://ti.me/2pRHHyb.

61. Michael Keller et al., *Tracking Trump's Web of Conflicts*, Bloomberg.

62. For more on the points that follow, see Ron Fein, "Turkish Bodyguards

Attacked US Demonstrators. Why Has Trump Said Nothing?," *Truthout*, June 24, 2017, http://bit.ly/2s34nPQ.

63. Nicholas Fandos and Christopher Mele, "Erdogan Security Forces Launch 'Brutal Attack' on Washington Protesters, Officials Say," *The New York Times*, May 17, 2017, https://nyti.ms/2qs4MLv.

64. See Malachy Browne et al., "Did the Turkish President's Security Detail Attack Protesters in Washington? What the Video Shows," *The New York Times*, May 26, 2017, https://nyti.ms/2s1wv38; Nicholas Fandos, "In Video, Erdogan Watches as His Guards Clash With Protesters," *The New York Times*, May 18, 2017, https://nyti.ms/2rwPRgD.

65. Elise Labott and Zachary Cohen, "US summoned Turkish ambassador after protester violence," CNN, May 18, 2017, http://cnn.it/2qwBfQs.

66. Kareem Fahim, "Turkey condemns U.S. over 'aggressive' acts against Erdogan's guards during D.C. visit," *The Washington Post*, May 22, 2017, http://wapo.st/2qckdnh.

67. Jonathan O'Connell and David A. Fahrenthold, "Nine questions about President Trump's businesses and possible conflicts of interest," *The Washington Post*, Jan. 30, 2018, http://wapo.st/2EUsO6m.

68. Cristina Maza, "Trump Organization's Dominican Republic Projects Could be Grounds for Impeachment: Experts," *Newsweek*, Feb. 10, 2018, http://bit.ly/2nRRYw3.

69. Kailash Babar, "Donald Trump meets Indian partners, hails PM Modi's work," *Economic Times*, Nov. 17, 2016, http://ecoti.in/owmzxa.

70. Richard C. Paddock and Eric Lipton, "Trump's Indonesia Projects, Still Moving Ahead, Create Potential Conflicts," *The New York Times*, Dec. 31, 2016, http://nyti.ms/2kHiVz5; Keller et al., *Tracking Trump's Web of Conflicts*, Bloomberg.

71. *Id.*; Kurt Eichenwald, "How Donald Trump's Business Ties Are Already Jeopardizing U.S. Interests," *Newsweek*, Dec. 13, 2016, http://bit.ly/2hooq7c.

72. Eichenwald, "How Donald Trump's Business Ties Are Already Jeopardizing U.S. Interests," *Newsweek*, Paddock and Lipton, "Trump's Indonesia Projects, Still Moving Ahead, Create Potential Conflicts," *The New York Times*.

73. Jon Gambrell, "AP Exclusive: Golf club shows pitfalls of Trump presidency," AP News, Jan. 4, 2017, http://bit.ly/2AooeOk.

74. Carrell, "Trump's Scotland golf resort proceeds with expansion despite business pledge," *The Guardian*, Keller et al., *Tracking Trump's Web of Conflicts*, Bloomberg.

75. Carrell, "Trump's Scotland golf resort proceeds with expansion despite business pledge," *The Guardian*.

76. Greg Sargent, "Trump may have just flatly and openly admitted to a conflict of interest," *The Washington Post*, Nov. 22, 2016, http://wpo.st/FRdX2; Danny Hakim and Eric Lipton, "With a Meeting, Trump Renewed a British Wind Farm Fight," *The New York Times*, Nov. 21, 2016,

https://nyti.ms/2jMoGgN; Keller et al., *Tracking Trump's Web of Conflicts*, Bloomberg.

77. Edward Malnick, "Donald Trump's letters to David Cameron complaining wind farms were 'blighting' the landscape in Scotland," *The Telegraph*, May 5, 2018, http://bit.ly/2GdIIZf; Danny Hakim and Eric Lipton, "With a Meeting, Trump Renewed a British Wind Farm Fight," *The New York Times*, Nov. 21, 2016, https://nyti.ms/2jMoGgN. Despite Trump's efforts, the first wind turbine was installed in April 2018; Colin Drury, "The world's most powerful wind turbine goes up off Scottish coast—despite Trump's opposition," *The Independent*, Apr. 11, 2018, https://ind.pn/2GggeOG.

78. Anita Kumar, "Foreign Governments are Finding Ways to do Favors for Trump's Business," McClatchy DC Bureau, Jan. 2, 2018, http://bit.ly/2CagVbc.

79. See Global Witness, "Narco-a-Lago: Money Laundering at the Trump Ocean Club Panama" (Nov. 2017), http://bit.ly/2sNcyzb; Ron Fein, "Free Speech For People Calls for Investigation of Trump Ocean Club Panama," Free Speech For People, Dec. 21, 2017, https://freespeechforpeople.org/free-speech-people-calls-investigation-trump-ocean-club-panama/.

80. Juan Zamorano and Stephen Braun, "Trump's Company Asked Panama's President for Help in Hotel Dispute," *Bloomberg*, April 9, 2018, https://bloom.bg/2G27fRd.

81. Kumar, "Foreign Governments are Finding Ways to do Favors for Trump's Business," McClatchy DC Bureau.

82. "Trump Indonesia project is latest stop on China's Belt and Road," *South China Morning Post*, May 11, 2018, https://sc.mp/2rCpF5x.

83. See Heather Long, "Just about everything is odd about Trump's support of Chinese firm ZTE," *The Washington Post*, May 15, 2018, https://wapo.st/2rNWhKE; Ken Dilanian, "Top intelligence official says Chinese ZTE cellphones pose security risk to U.S.," NBC, May 15, 2018, https://nbcnews.to/2IpJ4Cg.

84. See S. V. Date, "Trump Orders Help For Chinese Phone-Maker After China Approves Money For Trump Project," *HuffPost*, May 14, 2018, http://bit.ly/2IoS7Dj.

85. See "Trump Golf Count, President Trump's Golf Outings," http://trumpgolfcount.com/displayoutings (last visited June 5, 2018).

86. Cristina Alesci and Curt Devine, "Secret Service paid Mar-a-Lago at least $63,000, documents show," CNN, Oct. 12, 2017, http://cnnmon.ie/2zj8yJc.

87. Jessica Estepa, "Secret Service spent $7,500 on golf carts during Trump's Thanksgiving Mar-a-Lago trip," *USA Today*, Nov. 29, 2017, https://usat.ly/2nf6DDn; Julia Fair, "Secret Service spent $137K on golf carts to protect Trump at New Jersey, Florida clubs," *USA Today*, Oct. 5, 2017, https://usat.ly/2yLvorF.

88. Cristina Alesci and Aaron Cooper, "Exclusive: DOD charged nearly

$140,000 at Trump branded properties," CNN, March 14, 2018, http://cnn.it/2Irgo83.

89. Drew Harwell and Amy Brittain, "Taxpayers billed $1,092 for an official's two-night stay at Trump's Mar-a-Lago club," *The Washington Post*, Sept. 15, 2017, http://wapo.st/2y3C9VB.

90. CREW, "Profiting from the Presidency".

91. Alesci and Cooper, "Exclusive: DOD charged nearly $140,000 at Trump branded properties," CNN.

92. *Id.*

93. CREW, "Profiting from the Presidency".

94. Jonathan O'Connell, "Football Team's Stay at Doral Resort Could Bolster Lawsuit Targeting Trump," *The Washington Post*, Jan. 8, 2018, http://wapo.st/2CI4Aug.

95. Martyn McLaughlin, "Donald Trump's Scottish resort paid by US taxpayers for 'VIP visit,'" *The Scotsman*, May 12, 2018, http://bit.ly/2IoUe5S.

96. Steven L. Schooner and Daniel I. Gordon, "GSA's Trump Hotel Lease Debacle," *Government Executive*, Nov. 28, 2016, http://bit.ly/2k4VNcG.

97. Letter from Hon. Elijah E. Cummings et al. to the Hon. Denise Turner Roth, Adm'r, Gen. Serv. Admin. (Nov. 30, 2016), http://bit.ly/2k56NqN.

98. Allan Smith, "Federal agency responds to letter from Democratic lawmakers claiming it said Trump must fully divest himself of his DC hotel," *Business Insider*, Dec. 14, 2016, http://read.bi/2k4WYZM.

99. Letter from Kevin Terry, Contracting Officer, Gen. Serv. Admin., to Donald J. Trump, Jr. (March 23, 2017), https://www.gsa.gov/cdnstatic/Contracting_Officer_Letter_March_23__2017_Redacted_Version.pdf.

100. See Patrick Madden, *It's Official: Trump's Son Takes Over Pennsylvania Avenue Hotel*, WAMU, Feb. 6, 2017, http://bit.ly/2lkv9S5.

101. Callum Paton, "Trump's Syria Strikes were 'After-Dinner Entertainment' at Mar-A-Lago," *Newsweek*, May 2, 2017, http://bit.ly/2sWcFf2.

102. Charles V. Bagli, "A Trump Empire Built on Inside Connections and $885 Million in Tax Breaks," *The New York Times*, Sept. 17, 2016, http://nyti.ms/2cXa6oi.

103. Steve Eder and Ben Protess, "Hotel Carrying New Trump Brand Secures $6 Million Tax Break," *The New York Times*, Feb. 21, 2018, http://nyti.ms/2HI UKvM.

104. Mike McIntire, "Donald Trump Settled a Real Estate Lawsuit, and a Criminal Case was Closed," *The New York Times*, April 5, 2016, https://nyti.ms/2rI941f.

105. Andrea Bernstein et al., "How Ivanka Trump and Donald Trump, Jr., Avoided a Criminal Indictment," *The New Yorker*, Oct. 4, 2017, https://goo.gl/vs5EZn.

106. *Id.*

107. First Amended Compl. at ¶ 358, *Palmer Gardens LLC v. Bayrock/Sapir Org. LLC*, No. 10-CV-5830 (S.D.N.Y. Sept. 13, 2010), Doc. No. 3.

108. Bernstein et al., "How Ivanka Trump and Donald Trump, Jr., Avoided a Criminal Indictment," *The New Yorker*.

109. *Id.*

110. McIntire, "Donald Trump Settled a Real Estate Lawsuit, and a Criminal Case was Closed," *The New York Times*.

111. Bernstein et al., "How Ivanka Trump and Donald Trump, Jr., Avoided a Criminal Indictment," *The New Yorker*.

112. Julia Harte, "Exclusive: A New York hotel deal shows how some public pension funds help to enrich Trump," Reuters, April 26, 2017, http://reut.rs/2pyu2QG.

113. See Oske Buckley, "A tumultuous time for Trump Soho: Free Speech For People leads the campaign to end illegal payments to Trump-owned businesses," Free Speech For People, Jan. 13, 2018, http://bit.ly/2rJcBwl; Julia Harte, "Campaign urges U.S. public pension funds to divest from owner of Trump hotel," Reuters, July 19, 2017, http://reut.rs/2vizeYK.

114. Hui-yong Yu and Caleb Melby, "Trump Organization Bought Out of Its Contract for Trump SoHo," *Bloomberg*, Nov. 23, 2017, https://goo.gl/8vo6rz; see also Shanna Cleveland, "Curbing Corruption One Step at a Time: Taking Trump out of Trump SoHo. A Victory for Divest Trump SoHo," Free Speech For People, Nov. 27, 2017, http://bit.ly/2LIga8U.

115. The Federalist No. 73, p. 440 (Alexander Hamilton) (Charles R. Kesler ed., 2003) (emphasis added).

116. David A. Fahrenthold and Jonathan O'Connell, "D.C., Maryland can proceed with lawsuit alleging Trump violated emoluments clauses," *The Washington Post*, March 28, 2018, https://wapo.st/2pLLT48.

117. Charles Doyle, Cong. Research Serv., *Impeachment Grounds: A Collection of Selected Materials* (Oct. 29, 1998), p. 5 (quoting 2 Richard Wooddesson, *Lectures on the Laws of England*, p. 601 (1st ed., 1792)); Radnofsky, *A Citizen's Guide to Impeachment*, p. 7.

118. James Madison, *July 20, 1787*, in *The Avalon Project: Madison Debates* (Yale Law Sch. Lillian Goldman Library ed., 2008), http://avalon.law.yale.edu/18th_century/debates_720.asp.

119. *Id.*

120. See, for example, John Ash, *New and Complete Dictionary of the English Language*, vol. 2 (London: Edward and Charles Dilly, 1775), available at http://bit.ly/2M7OaBe (defining "peculation" as "[t]he crime of robbing the public, an embezzlement of the public money"); Noah Webster, *A Compendious Dictionary of the English Language*, p. 219 (New Haven: Sidney's Press, 1806) (defining "peculation" as "embezzlement of the public money").

121. James Madison, *July 20, 1787*, in *The Avalon Project*.

122. Jonathan Elliot, *Debates in the Several State Conventions on the Adoption*

of the Federal Constitution vol. 3, *p.* 117 (Philadelphia: J. B. Lippincott & Co., 1891) (Virginia, June 7, 1788), http://bit.ly/2KTjVfU [hereinafter "Elliot's Debates"].

123. Elliot's Debates, vol. 3, p. 515 (Virginia, June 17, 1788) (emphasis added), http://bit.ly/2BHu37L.

124. The Federalist No. 65, p. 394 (Alexander Hamilton).

125. Elliot's Debates vol. 4., p. 126 (North Carolina, July 24, 1788), http://bit.ly/2BHO91G.

126. Lewis Deschler, *Precedents of the U.S. House of Representatives*, ch. 14 App.

127. William Brown, *House Practice: A Guide to the Rules, Precedents and Procedures of the House* (2011), ch. 27, § 4, p. 598.

128. *Id.* In 1974, the House Judiciary Committee also considered an article of impeachment against President Richard Nixon that, among various other charges, included a violation of the Domestic Emoluments Clause stemming from expenditures at Nixon's home and vacation home. In contrast to Trump's domestic emoluments, the amounts were relatively low (at most $92,000 over a four-year period), and they were not part of a pervasive pattern, as they had ended two years before impeachment hearings began. Furthermore, there was no evidence that Nixon knew that these expenditures were made from public funds. House Judiciary Committee, *Impeachment of Richard M. Nixon, President of the United States*, H.R. Rep. No. 93-1305, 120 Cong. Rec. 29,220 (1974), http://bit.ly/HR93-1305, pp. 220–21. These factors help explain why the Committee did not approve this article, and distinguish Nixon's relatively minor domestic emoluments from Trump's far more serious violations.

129. See Adam Liptak, "Lonely Scholar With Unusual Ideas' Defends Trump, Igniting Legal Storm," *The New York Times*, Sept. 25, 2017, https://nyti.ms/2rHoAaE.

130. See Eisen et al., *The Emoluments Clause*, Brookings Governance Studies; John S. Mikhail, "The Definition of 'Emolument' in English Language and Legal Dictionaries, 1523–1806" (working paper, 2017), https://ssrn.com/abstract=2995693.

131. See Norman L. Eisen and Richard W. Painter, "Trump Could Be in Violation of the Constitution His First Day in Office," *The Atlantic*, Dec. 7, 2016, http://theatln.tc/2ioApY4; see also Richard W. Painter et al., "Emoluments: Trump's Coming Ethics Trouble," *The Atlantic*, Jan. 18, 2017, http://theatln.tc/2jwtwNr.

CHAPTER 2

1. For more details on what is already known as of this date, see House Permanent Select Comm. on Intelligence, *Report on Russian Active Measures*, https://intelligence.house.gov/uploadedfiles/final_russia_investigation_report.pdf (March 22, 2018) ["House Intelligence Com-

mittee Majority Report"]; Minority Members of the House Permanent Select Comm. on Intelligence, *Minority Views to the Majority-produced "Report on Russian Active Measures, March 22, 2018,"* https://docs.house.gov/meetings/IG/IG00/20180322/108023/HRPT-115-2.pdf (Mar. 26, 2018) ["House Intelligence Committee Minority Report"]; Philip Bump, "A (so far) complete timeline of the investigation into Trump and Russia," *The Washington Post*, April 24, 2018, http://wapo.st/2E3jHQg; *Complaint DNC v. Russian Fed.*, No. 18-CV-03501 (S.D.N.Y. filed Apr. 20, 2018), Doc. No. 1.

2. For more up-to-date summaries, see the Moscow Project, http://www.the moscowproject.org (last visited June 5, 2018).

3. The Federalist No. 85, p. 521 (Alexander Hamilton). The classic study of the framers' "obsession with corruption" is Zephyr Teachout, "The Anti-Corruption Principle," 94 Cornell L. Rev., p. 341 (2009); see also Matt A. Vega, "The First Amendment Lost in Translation: Preventing Foreign Influence in U.S. Elections After *Citizens United v. FEC*," 44 Loy. L.A. L. Rev., pp. 951, 960 (2011).

4. James Madison, *July 20, 1787*, in *The Avalon Project*.

5. *Id.*

6. See Jared P. Cole and Todd Garvey, Cong. Research Serv., *Impeachment and Removal* 1, pp. 15–16 (Oct. 29, 2015), https://fas.org/sgp/crs/misc/R44260.pdf.

7. The Federalist No. 68, p. 411 (Alexander Hamilton).

8. Dir. of Nat'l Intelligence, "Assessing Russian Activities and Intentions in Recent US Elections" (2017), http://www.dni.gov/files/documents/ICA_2017_01.pdf; Senate Intelligence Committee, "Russian Targeting of Election Infrastructure During the 2016 Election: Summary of Initial Findings and Recommendations," May 8, 2018, http://bit.ly/SenIntel Summ5818; Karoun Demirjian, "Russia favored Trump in 2016, Senate panel says, breaking with House GOP," *The Washington Post*, May 16, 2018, https://wapo.st/2L4EpDq; see also Max Bergmann et al., "A Case Study in Collusion: The Hack and Release of Emails," The Moscow Project, May 16, 2018, https://themoscowproject.org/?p=3016.

9. Indictment, *United States v. Internet Research Agency LLC*, No. 18-CR-00032, D.D.C. (Feb. 16, 2018), Doc. No. 1, available at https://www.justice.gov/file/1035477/download. Relatedly, the Federal Election Commission has been considering this matter since Free Speech For People and the Campaign for Accountability filed a complaint against the Russian government for campaign finance law violations in December 2016. See *Free Speech For People v. Gov't of the Russian Fed.*, Matter Under Review No. 7207 (Fed. Election Comm'n filed Dec. 16, 2016), http://bit.ly/FSFPRussiaCpltDec2016.

10. Nick Penzenstadler et al., "We read every one of the 3,517 Facebook ads bought by Russians. Here's what we found," *USA Today*, May 11, 2018, https://usat.ly/2rAW4tm.

11. Natasha Bertrand, "'Help world peace and make a lot of money': Here's the letter of intent to build a Trump Tower Moscow," *Business Insider*, Sept. 8, 2017, http://read.bi/2vKtQND.

12. Anthony Cormier and Jason Leopold, "Trump Moscow: The Definitive Story Of How Trump's Team Worked The Russian Deal During The Campaign," BuzzFeed, May 17, 2018, https://bzfd.it/2IH2KSf.

13. Abigail Tracy, "'We Can Engineer It': Trump Associate Bragged About Using Deal with Putin to 'Engineer' Election," *Vanity Fair*, Aug. 28, 2017, http://bit.ly/2IGTqx.I.

14. Statement of the Offense, *United States v. George Papadopoulos*, No. 17-CR-00182 (D.D.C. Oct. 3, 2017), Doc. No. 19.

15. *Id.* ¶ 9; House Intelligence Committee Minority Report, *supra* note 1 in this chapter, p. 19.

16. Statement of the Offense, *United States v. George Papadopoulos*, No. 17-CR -00182 (D.D.C. Oct. 3, 2017), Doc. No. 19, ¶¶ 9–19.

17. See House Intelligence Committee Majority Report, *supra* note 1 in this chapter, p. 95 n. 192.

18. *Id.*, p. 48.

19. Adam Entous et al., "Sessions discussed Trump campaign-related matters with Russian ambassador, U.S. intelligence intercepts show," *The Washington Post*, July 21, 2017, http://wapo.st/2tnTokd.

20. Mark Landler and Eric Lichtblau, "Jeff Sessions Recuses Himself From Russia Inquiry," *The New York Times*, March 2, 2017, https://nyti.ms/2mwkEfi.

21. See Mike Levine, "Special counsel files 32-count indictment against former Trump campaign officials," ABC News, Feb. 22, 2018, http://abcn.ws/2H FyTFI.

22. Matt Apuzzo et al., "Code Name Crossfire Hurricane: The Secret Origins of the Trump Investigation," *The New York Times*, May 16, 2018, https://nyti.ms/2GpbIgM.

23. Robert Costa et al., "Secret FBI source for Russia investigation met with three Trump advisers during campaign," *The Washington Post*, May 18, 2018, https://wapo.st/2k6Y5Kx; Asha Rangappa, "The FBI didn't use an informant to go after Trump. They used one to protect him.," *The Washington Post*, May 18, 2018, https://wapo.st/2rSykBa.

24. Priscilla Alvarez and Elaine Godfrey, "Donald Trump Jr.'s Email Exchange With Rob Goldstone," *The Atlantic*, June 11, 2017, https://theatln.tc/2rHokeK; House Intelligence Committee Minority Report, *supra* note 1 in this chapter, pp. 24–30.

25. *Id.*

26. House Intelligence Committee Minority Report, *supra* note 1 in this chapter, p. 26.

27. *Id.*

28. *Id.*; Philip Bump, "What happened and when: The timeline leading up

to Donald Trump Jr.'s fateful meeting," *The Washington Post*, July 11, 2017, https://wapo.st/2v8dWMq.

29. K. K. Rebecca Lai and Alicia Parlapiano, "What We Know About Donald Trump Jr.'s Russia Meeting," *The New York Times*, July 18, 2017, https://nyti.ms/2L1xLhe.

30. See Sophie Tatum, "Putin Critic: Veselnitskaya 'an agent of the Russian government,'" CNN, April 27, 2018, https://cnn.it/2rHLYaY.

31. House Intelligence Committee Minority Report, *supra* note 1 in this chapter, p. 28.

32. *Id.*, p. 27.

33. Donald J. Trump (@realDonaldTrump), Twitter (June 9, 2016, 1:40 PM), https://twitter.com/realDonaldTrump/status/741007091947556864. Where Trump's tweets are quoted in this book, we have reproduced them without correcting for spelling, grammar, or punctuation.

34. Guccifer 2.0, "Dossier on Hillary Clinton from DNC" (June 21, 2016), https://guccifer2.wordpress.com/2016/06/21/hillary-clinton/

35. Guccifer 2.0, "Trumpocalypse and Other DNC Plans for July" (July 6, 2016), https://guccifer2.wordpress.com/2016/07/06/trumpocalypse/.

36. WikiLeaks, "The Podesta E-mails" (Oct. 7, 2016), https://wikileaks.org/podesta-emails/.

37. Julia Ioffe, "The Secret Correspondence Between Donald Trump Jr. and WikiLeaks," *The Atlantic*, Nov. 13, 2017, https://theatln.tc/2GfQPER; Andrew Kaczynski et al., "Trump advisor Roger Stone repeatedly claimed to know of forthcoming Wikileaks dumps," CNN, March 20, 2017, https://cnn.it/2GhSSIF.

38. Donald J. Trump (@realDonaldTrump), Twitter (Oct. 12, 2016, 9:46 a.m.), https://twitter.com/realdonaldtrump/status/786201435486781440.

39. House Intelligence Committee Majority Report, *supra* note 1 in this chapter, p. 72.

40. House Intelligence Committee Minority Report, *supra* note 1 in this chapter, p. 32.

41. See Andrew Kaczynski et al., "Trump advisor Roger Stone repeatedly claimed to know of forthcoming Wikileaks dumps," CNN, March 20, 2017, https://cnn.it/2GhSSIF.

42. Chuck Todd et al., "How Trump took advantage of Russian interference: Amplifying Wikileaks," NBC News, Feb. 19, 2018, https://nbcnews.to/2GjxtyB.

43. Ivan Levingston, "Trump: I hope Russia finds 'the 30,000 emails that are missing,'" CNBC, July 27, 2016, https://cnb.cx/2GiefJQ

44. Ken Dilanian et al., "FBI warned Trump in 2016 Russians would try to infiltrate his campaign," NBC, Dec. 18, 2017, https://nbcnews.to/2rHIKV4.

45. Mark Mazzetti et al., "Trump Jr. and Other Aides Met With Gulf Emissary Offering Help to Win Election," *The New York Times*, May 19, 2018, https://nyti.ms/2IV6EpU.

46. *Id.*

47. John Kelly and Steve Reilly, "Trump team issued at least 20 denials of contacts with Russia," *USA Today*, March 2, 2017, http://usat.ly/2mxcm6v.

48. *Id.*

49. Jo Becker et al., "Trump Team Met With Lawyer Linked to Kremlin During Campaign," *The New York Times*, July 8, 2017, https://nyti .ms/2uWPOMw;

50. Dara Lind, "Donald Trump Jr.'s ever-shifting excuses on Russia: a clear timeline," *Vox*, July 11, 2017, http://bit.ly/2rOopg3.

51. See Jacob Pramuk, "Here's Donald Trump Jr.'s full statement on his meeting with a Russian lawyer," CNBC, July 9, 2017, http://cnb.cx /2wowmA7.

52. Lori Robertson and Robert Farley, "Donald Trump Jr.'s Evolving Statements," Fact Check, July 13, 2017, https://bit.ly/2kQBNgm.

53. *Id.*

54. Jo Becker et al., "Trump's Son Met With Russian Lawyer After Being Promised Damaging Information on Clinton," *The New York Times*, July 9, 2017, https://nyti.ms/2rOI6VV.

55. Lori Robertson and Robert Farley, "Donald Trump Jr.'s Evolving Statements," Fact Check, July 13, 2017, https://bit.ly/2kQBNgm.

56. "The Trump Lawyers' Confidential Memo to Mueller, Explained," *The New York Times*, June 2, 2018, https://nyti.ms/2xEnmpa; Ashley Parker et al., "Trump dictated son's misleading statement on meeting with Russian lawyer," *The Washington Post*, July 31, 2017, http://wapo .st/2vh7dmA.

57. House Intelligence Committee Minority Report, *supra* note 1 in this chapter, p. 32.

58. See House Judiciary Committee, *Impeachment of Richard M. Nixon, President of the United States,* H.R. Rep. No. 93-1305, 120 Cong. Rec. 29,220 (1974), http://bit.ly/HR93-1305; see also Black, *Impeachment: A Handbook,* pp. 46–47; Jane Chong, "To Impeach a President: Applying the Authoritative Guide from Charles Black," *Lawfare*, July 20, 2017, https: //www.lawfareblog.com/impeach-president-applying-authoritative -guide-charles-black.

59. Black, *Impeachment*, p. 45.

60. See Bruce D. Brown, "Alien Donors: The Participation of Non-Citizens in the U.S. Campaign Finance System," 15 Yale L. and Pol'y Rev. 503, 510 n.37 (1996).

61. *Id.* at 511.

62. 52 U.S.C. §§ 30121(a)(1)(A), (C); 11 C.F.R. §§ 110.20(b), (f).

63. 52 U.S.C. § 30121(a)(2); 11 C.F.R. § 110.20(g). The statute defines "foreign national" to include not only foreign governments and their agents, but *any* foreign citizens who are not lawful permanent residents of the United States.

64. *Bluman v. Fed. Election Comm'n*, 800 F. Supp. 2d 281 (D.D.C. 2011) (3-judge court), aff'd mem., 565 U.S. 1104 (2012).

65. Richard Wolf and Gregory Korte, "Trump adds five names to list of potential Supreme Court justices," *USA Today*, Nov. 17, 2017, https://usat.ly/2irFhVX.

66. *Bluman*, 800 F. Supp. 2d, pp. 287–88 (quotation marks and citation omitted).

67. *Id.*, p. 285. 52 U.S.C. § 30109(d)(1)(A); see Ciara Torres-Spelliscy, "The Justice Department Is Now on the Campaign Finance Beat," Brennan Ctr. for Justice, Oct. 12, 2015, http://bit.ly/2x4DZKa.

68. 11 C.F.R. §§ 110.20(h)(1)-(2). See Bob Bauer, "Campaign Finance Law: When 'Collusion' Becomes a Crime: Part II," JustSecurity, June 7, 2017, https://www.justsecurity.org/41795/campaign-finance-law-collusion-crime-part-ii/.

69. 11 C.F.R. §§ 109.20, 109.21(b)(1)-(2).

70. U.S. Department of Justice, "Campaign Manager Sentenced to 24 Months for Coordinated Campaign Contributions and False Statements," June 12, 2015, http://bit.ly/2GhDzQb.

71. See Bob Bauer, "Considering the Legal Defenses of the Trump Jr. Meeting," JustSecurity, July 14, 2017, https://www.justsecurity.org/43111/legal-defenses-trump-jr-meeting/.

72. 52 U.S.C. § 30121(a)(2).

73. Bob Bauer, "Campaign Finance Law: When 'Collusion' with a Foreign Government Becomes a Crime," JustSecurity, June 2, 2017, https://www.justsecurity.org/41593/hiding-plain-sight-federal-campaign-finance-law-trump-campaign-collusion-russia-trump/.

74. 11 C.F.R. §§ 110.20(a)(4), (7); see also Bauer, *supra* note 73 in this chapter.

75. 18 U.S.C. § 371.

76. *Id.*

77. See generally Charles Doyle, "Federal Conspiracy Law: A Brief Overview," Cong. Research Serv., Jan. 20, 2016, https://fas.org/sgp/crs/misc/R41223.pdf.

78. 18 U.S.C. § 2(a); see also U.S. Department of Justice, U.S. Attorneys' Manual, Crim. Res. Manual § 2474, https://www.justice.gov/usam/criminal-resource-manual-2474-elements-aiding-and-abetting; Bob Bauer, "When Collusion with Russia Becomes a Crime: Part III—'Aiding and Abetting,'" JustSecurity, June 21, 2017, https://www.justsecurity.org/42387/collusion-russia-crime-part-iii-aiding-abetting/.

79. 18 U.S.C. § 371.

80. *Hammerschmidt v. United States*, 265 U.S. 182, 188 (1924).

81. See Emma Kohse and Benjamin Wittes, "About That Russia Indictment: Robert Mueller's Legal Theory and Where It Takes Him Next," Lawfare, March 7, 2018 (discussing cases of conspiracy to defraud the Federal Election Commission), http://bit.ly/2sEwuVF.

82. Indictment, *United States v. Internet Research Agency LLC*, No. 18-CR-00032 (D.D.C. Feb. 16, 2018), Doc. No. 1, available at https://www.justice.gov/file/1035477/download.

83. 18 U.S.C. § 3.

84. 18 U.S.C. § 4.

85. Jane Chong, "To Impeach a President: Applying the Authoritative Guide from Charles Black," *Lawfare*, July 20, 2017, https://www.lawfareblog.com/impeach-president-applying-authoritative-guide-charles-black; Black, *Impeachment: A Handbook*, pp. 46–47.

86. Annals of Congress, vol. 1, p. 387 (May 19,1789) (Washington: Gales and Seaton, 1834), available at https://bit.ly/2HrX48U.

87. Black, *Impeachment: A Handbook*, pp. 46–47 (emphasis in original).

88. See House Judiciary Committee, *Impeachment of Richard M. Nixon, President of the United States,* H.R. Rep. No. 93-1305, 120 Cong. Rec. 29,220 (1974), http://bit.ly/HR93-1305.

89. The federal government has criticized Russia and sometimes acted against Russian interests; it is Trump *himself* who almost never does.

90. U.S. Const. art. III, § 3, cl. 1.

91. For the case that Russia is not an "enemy" under the Treason Clause, see Steve Vladeck, "We Have Met the Enemy, and He Is . . .?," JustSecurity, March 21, 2017, https://www.justsecurity.org/39244/met-enemy-is/; Carlton F. W. Larson, "Five myths about treason," *The Washington Post,* Feb. 17, 2017, http://wapo.st/2moizUg; see also *United States v. Drummond,* 354 F.2d 132, 152 (2d Cir. 1965) (at height of Cold War, Department of Justice argued that "the Soviet Union is not an 'enemy' within the meaning of the Treason Clause"); *United States v. Rosenberg,* 195 F.2d 583, 609 (2d Cir. 1952) (rejecting claim by Rosenbergs, who were charged with espionage not treason, that they should have been charged with treason, and noting unanswered question of whether Soviet Union was an "enemy"); *United States v. McWilliams,* 54 F. Supp. 791, 793 (D.D.C. 1944) (in prosecution of Nazi sympathizers for conspiring to cause mutiny among armed forces from 1933 to 1940, concluding that offense could not be treason because "Germany did not become a statutory enemy until December 1941").

92. See Radnofsky, *A Citizen's Guide to Impeachment,* pp. 43–45.

93. Asher C. Hinds, *Precedents of the House of Representatives,* vol. 3, §2390, p. 811 (1907); see Radnofsky, *A Citizen's Guide to Impeachment,* pp. 43–44 and n.197.

94. The Federalist No. 85 (Alexander Hamilton), p. 521.

95. Black, *Impeachment,* p. 22.

96. James Madison, *July 20, 1787,* in *The Avalon Project.*

CHAPTER 3

1. Ali Vitali, "Trump's Tweets 'Official Statements,' Spicer Says," NBC, June 6, 2017, https://nbcnews.to/2GlT2yp.

2. *Knight First Amendment Inst. v. Trump*, No. 17-CV-5205 (S.D.N.Y. May 23, 2018), 2018 WL 2327290.

3. In addition to live testimony from former Federal Bureau of Investigation Director James Comey, former Acting Attorney General Sally Yates, Director of National Intelligence Dan Coats, and National Security Agency Director Admiral Michael Rogers, Comey's testimony also includes a prepared written statement submitted to the Senate Intelligence Committee on June 7, 2017. James B. Comey, Statement for the Record of Senate Select Committee on Intelligence (June 8, 2017), http://bit.ly/ComeyStmt6817.

4. Chris Cillizza, "The most stunning lines from Trump's 'Fox and Friends' interview," CNN, April 27, 2018, https://cnn.it/2IbBxmo.

5. See also Berke, Bookbinder, and Eisen, "Presidential Obstruction of Justice," *Brookings Governance Studies*.

6. Matt Apuzzo and Emmarie Huetteman, "Sally Yates Tells Senators She Warned Trump About Michael Flynn," *The New York Times*, May 8, 2017, http://nyti.ms/2soCoB7. On December 1, 2017, Flynn pleaded guilty to making false statements to the FBI regarding interactions with the Russian government, in violation of 18 U.S.C. § 1001. See Dan Mangan, "Read: Michael Flynn's plea agreement and how he lied to FBI," CNBC, Dec. 1, 2017, http://cnb.cx/2AKZdoE; *United States v. Flynn*, No. 17-CR-00232-RC (filed D.D.C. Nov. 30, 2017).

7. Office of the Press Secretary, Press Briefing by Press Secretary Sean Spicer, The White House, Feb. 14, 2017, http://www.presidency.ucsb.edu/ws/in dex.php?pid=123342.

8. James B. Comey, *Statement for the Record of Senate Select Committee on Intelligence* (June 8, 2017), http://bit.ly/ComeyStmt6817 (emphases added).

9. See Memorandum from James Comey, Director, FBI, to Andrew McCabe, James Baker, and James Rybicki, at 1 (Jan. 7, 2017) (on file with CNN), https://cnn.it/2Fv9axj.

10. See Memorandum from James Comey, Director, FBI, to Andrew McCabe, James Baker, and James Rybicki, at 3 (Jan. 28, 2017) (on file with CNN), https://cnn.it/2Fz9x9Y.

11. See Memorandum from James Comey, Director, FBI, to Andrew McCabe, James Baker, and James Rybicki, at 3 (Feb. 8, 2017) (on file with CNN), https://cnn.it/2FylVa9.

12. Vernon Silver, "Flight records illuminate mystery of Trump's Moscow nights," *Bloomberg*, April 23, 2018, https://bloom.bg/2rQGToi.

13. Aaron Blake, "Trump's unwieldy 'Fox and Friends' interview, annotated," *The Washington Post*, April 26, 2018, https://wapo.st/2HzNli5.

14. Donald J. Trump (@realDonaldTrump), Twitter (Dec. 2, 2017, 9:14 a.m.), https://twitter.com/realDonaldTrump/status/937007006526959618.

15. James B. Comey, *Statement for the Record of Senate Select Committee on Intelligence*.

16. James B. Comey, *Statement for the Record of Senate Select Committee on Intelligence* (emphases added).

17. Michael D. Shear and Adam Goldman, "Michael Flynn Pleads Guilty to Lying to the F.B.I. and Will Cooperate With Russia Inquiry," *The New York Times*, Dec. 1, 2017, https://nyti.ms/2keM7BI; Dan Mangan, "Read: Michael Flynn's plea agreement and how he lied to FBI," CNBC, Dec. 1, 2017, http://cnb.cx/2AKZdoE; Plea Agreement, *United States v. Flynn*, No. 17-CR -00232-RC (D.D.C. Dec. 1, 2017), Doc. No. 3, available at https://www.justice.gov/file/1015121/download.

18. The president's insistence that Flynn was a "good guy" also contributes to this point. "Providing a positive assessment of the subject of an investigation to a key decision-maker can also support a finding of obstruction." Berke, Bookbinder, and Eisen, "Presidential Obstruction of Justice," *Brookings Governance Studies*; see *United States v. Torquato*, 316 F. Supp. 846, 848 (W.D. Pa. 1970) (defendants obstructed justice under 18 U.S.C. § 1503 by asking intermediaries to tell a juror that an ally was a "good man who needed help").

19. Adam Entous et al., "Sessions met with Russian envoy twice last year, encounters he later did not disclose," *The Washington Post*, March 1, 2017, http://wapo.st/2mb6M95.

20. Michael S. Schmidt, "Obstruction Inquiry Shows Trump's Struggle to Keep Grip on Russia Investigation," *The New York Times*, Jan. 4, 2018, https://nytims/2EWB9qz.

21. Office of Public Affairs, U.S. Department of Justice, Attorney General Sessions Statement on Recusal (March 2, 2017), https://www.justice.gov/opa/pr/attorney-general-sessions-statement-recusal.

22. Michael S. Schmidt and Julie Hirschfeld Davis, "Trump Asked Sessions to Retain Control of Russia Inquiry After His Recusal," *The New York Times*, May 29, 2018, https://nyti.ms/2xrXxsc.

23. Michael S. Schmidt, "Obstruction Inquiry Shows Trump's Struggle to Keep Grip on Russia Investigation," *The New York Times*.

24. Michael S. Schmidt and Michael D. Shear, "Trump Says Russia Inquiry Makes U.S. 'Look Very Bad,'" *The New York Times*, Dec. 28, 2017, https://nyti.ms/2pTktN6.

25. Peter Baker et al., "Citing Recusal, Trump Says He Wouldn't Have Hired Sessions," *The New York Times*, July 19, 2017, https://nyti.ms/2uEfRLA.

26. Devlin Barrett et al., "The standoff between Trump and Sessions escalates," *The Washington Post*, July 25, 2017, http://wapo.st/2h15YST.

27. Donald J. Trump (@realDonaldTrump), Twitter (June 5, 2018, 4:31 a.m.), https://twitter.com/realDonaldTrump/status/1003962584352030720.

28. House Judiciary Committee, *Impeachment of Richard M. Nixon, President of the United States*, H.R. Rep. No. 93-1305, 120 Cong. Rec. 29,220 (1974), http://bit.ly/HR93-1305.

29. Michael S. Schmidt, "Comey, Unsettled by Trump, Is Said to Have

Wanted Him Kept at a Distance," *The New York Times*, May 18, 2017, http://nyti.ms/2s00ZZS.

30. James B. Comey, *Statement for the Record of Senate Select Committee on Intelligence*.

31. See notes 84–88 in Chapter 2.

32. Adam Entous and Ellen Nakashima, "Trump asked intelligence chiefs to push back against FBI collusion probe after Comey revealed its existence," *The Washington Post*, May 22, 2017, http://wapo.st/2ruKr9n.

33. Adam Entous, "Top intelligence official told associates Trump asked him if he could intervene with Comey on FBI Russia probe,' *The Washington Post*, June 6, 2017, http://wapo.st/2se4JnX.

34. *Id.*

35. Adam Entous and Ellen Nakashima, "Trump asked intelligence chiefs to push back against FBI collusion probe after Comey revealed its existence," *The Washington Post*.

36. In testimony to the Senate Intelligence Committee, Coats and Rogers gave carefully worded answers that they had never been "pressured" or "directed" to do anything illegal or inappropriate, but refused to answer direct questions about whether they had been "asked" to do such things. See Hearing before the Senate Select Comm. on Intelligence, Foreign Intelligence Surveillance Act, June 7, 2017, C-SPAN, http://c-spanvideo.org/xaa6d/; Nolan D. McCaskill, "Key moments from intel chiefs' testimony on Trump and Russia," *Politico*, June 7, 2017, http://politi.co/2rLQMen.

37. *The Smoking Gun Tape*, Watergate.info, http://watergate.info/1972/06/23/the-smoking-gun-tape.html.

38. James B. Comey, *Statement for the Record of Senate Select Committee on Intelligence* (emphasis added).

39. Michael Isikoff, "As investigators circled Flynn, he got a message from Trump: Stay strong," Yahoo News, May 18, 2017, https://yhoo.it/2iJNiZQ; cf. *United States v. Strode*, 552 F.3d 630, 634–35 (7th Cir. 2009) (affirming sentencing enhancement for obstruction of justice where defendant asked codefendants to "stay strong").

40. See Michael S. Schmidt and Maggie Haberman, "Mueller Has Early Draft of Trump Letter Giving Reasons for Firing Comey," *The New York Times*, Sept. 1, 2017, https://nyti.ms/2wYeSYw.

41. Kevin Johnson, "Here's what Deputy AG Rod Rosenstein told Congress about James Comey's firing," *USA Today*, May 19, 2017, https://usat.ly/2rzPXns.

42. Matt Apuzzo et al., "Trump Told Russians That Firing 'Nut Job' Comey Eased Pressure From Investigation," *The New York Times*, May 19, 2017, http://nyti.ms/2sY5b6n.

43. *Watch Lester Holt's Extended Interview With President Trump*, NBC News, May 11, 2017, http://nbcnews.to/2soiLJq; "Partial transcript: NBC News

interview with Donald Trump," CNN, May 11, 2017 (emphasis added), http://cnn.it/2pDDa2S.

44. "Full text: James Comey testimony transcript on Trump and Russia," *Politico*, June 8, 2017, http://politi.co/2lYCeFK.

45. Donald J. Trump (@realDonaldTrump), Twitter (May 31, 2018, 5:11 a.m.), https://twitter.com/realDonaldTrump/status/1002160516733853696.

46. Kevin Breuninger, "Rudy Giuliani: President Trump fired James Comey because he wouldn't say he wasn't a target of the Russia investigation," CNBC, May 3, 2018, https://cnb.cx/2jpQZRa. The next day, Giuliani issued a written statement to "clarify" his remarks, in which he simply asserted that "the President's dismissal of former Director Comey—an inferior executive officer—was clearly within his Article II power." "Full text: Rudy Giuliani issues statement clarifying his earlier remarks," *Politico*, May 4, 2018, https://politi.co/2HTPIAw.

47. See Norman Eisen and Noah Bookbinder, "We filed a complaint about Trump's ethics. Giuliani made it possible.," *The Washington Post*, May 4, 2018, https://wapo.st/2jqpgj2.

48. See Acting Attorney General Rod J. Rosenstein, Appointment of Special Counsel to Investigate Russian Interference with the 2016 Presidential Election and Related Matters, U.S. Department of Justice Order No. 3915-2017, May 17, 2017, https://www.justice.gov/opa/press-release/file/967231/download.

49. Donald J. Trump (@realDonaldTrump), Twitter (May 12, 2017, 5:26 a.m.), https://twitter.com/realDonaldTrump/status/863007411132649473.

50. Jonathan Martin et al., "Trump Pressed Top Republicans to End Senate Russia Inquiry," *The New York Times*, Nov. 30, 2017, https://nyti.ms/2BBmb04.

51. *Id.*

52. *Id.*

53. *Id.*

54. *Id.*

55. Michael S. Schmidt et al., "Trump's Lawyer Raised Prospect of Pardons for Flynn and Manafort," *The New York Times*, March 28, 2018, https://nyti.ms/2GB5QFe.

56. *Id.*

57. House Judiciary Committee, *Impeachment of Richard M. Nixon, President of the United States,* H.R. Rep. No. 93-1305, 120 Cong. Rec. 29,220 (1974), http://bit.ly/HR93-1305., pp. 2–3, 75–80.

58. For more on the point that follows, see John W. Dean and Ron Fein, "Nixon Lawyer: Donald Trump Abused Pardon Power When He Freed Joe Arpaio," *Newsweek*, Oct. 3, 2017, http://ti.me/2xNZyOf.

59. See Fed. R. Crim. P. 42; U.S. Department of Justice, U.S. Attorneys' Manual, Crim. Res. Manual § 780, http://bit.ly/2IlNjyy.

60. See Peter Baker, "Trump Pardons Scooter Libby in a Case That

Mirrors His Own," *The New York Times*, April 13, 2018, https://nyti
.ms/2GX9sTo.

61. Peter Baker, "Trump Wields Pardon Pen to Confront Justice System,"
The New York Times, May 31, 2018, https://nyti.ms/2xqBS3w; Philip
Rucker et al., "Trump pardons conservative pundit Dinesh D'Souza,
suggests others also could receive clemency," *The Washington Post*, May
31, 2018, https://wapo.st/2H6Go8g.

62. Donald J. Trump (@realDonaldTrump), Twitter (June 4, 2018, 5:35 a.m.),
https://twitter.com/realDonaldTrump/status/1003616210922147841.

63. Office of Legal Counsel, U.S. Department of Justice, Presidential or
Legislative Pardon of the President 370, Aug. 5, 1974, https://www
.justice.gov/file/20856/download; see also Laurence Tribe et al., "No,
Trump can't pardon himself. The Constitution tells us so.," *The Washington Post*, July 21, 2017, http://wapo.st/2gQVsxJ.

64. Maggie Haberman and Michael S. Schmidt, "Trump Ordered Mueller Fired, but Backed Off When White House Counsel Threatened to
Quit," *The New York Times*, Jan. 25, 2018, https://nyti.ms/2I8ShyA.

65. *Id.*

66. Maggie Haberman and Michael S. Schmidt, "Trump Sought to Fire
Mueller in December," *The New York Times*, April 10, 2018, https://nyti
.ms/2G4T5Pc.

67. *Id.*

68. Michael S. Schmidt and Michael D. Shear, "Trump Says Russia Inquiry
Makes U.S. 'Look Very Bad,'" *The New York Times*.

69. Michael S. Schmidt and Maggie Haberman, "Trump Asked Key Witnesses About Matters They Discussed With Special Counsel," *The New
York Times*, March 7, 2018, https://nyti.ms/2Dc2gvS.

70. *Id.*

71. "President Trump talks North Korea, Iran, Comey, Cohen, Dr. Ronny
Jackson and Kanye West in 'Fox and Friends' interview," Fox News,
April 26, 2018 (emphasis added), https://fxn.ws/2IFlRrF.

72. *Id.*

73. Adam Serwer, "How Trump Built an Obstruction of Justice Case Against
Himself," *The Atlantic*, Jan. 26, 2018, https://theatln.tc/2LnTBvy.

74. Mike Levine, "Exclusive: Fired FBI official authorized criminal probe
of Sessions, sources say," ABC News, March 21, 2018, http://abcn
.ws/2puXIwt.

75. As Comey later testified, he contemporaneously told three senior FBI
officials about his problematic conversations with Trump; McCabe was
one of the three.

76. See House Intelligence Committee Minority Report, *supra* note 1,
Chapter 2, p. 71; see also James B. Comey, *Statement for the Record of
Senate Select Committee on Intelligence* (June 8, 2017), http://bit.ly/Comey
Stmt6817.

77. Quinta Jurecic and Benjamin Wittes, "What We Know, and Don't Know, About the Firing of Andrew McCabe," Lawfare, March 17, 2018, http://law fareblog.com/what-we-know-and-dont-know-about-firing-andrew-mccabe.

78. Devlin Barrett, "Clinton ally aided campaign of FBI official's wife," *The Wall Street Journal*, Oct. 24, 2016, https://on.wsj.com/2KqVcA5.

79. D'Angelo Gore, "Trump Wrong About Campaign Donations," Fact-Check, July 26, 2017, https://www.factcheck.org/2017/07/trump-wrong-campaign-donations/.

80. *Id.*

81. Donald J. Trump (@realDonaldTrump), Twitter (July 25, 2017, 3:21 a.m.), https://twitter.com/realDonaldTrump/status/889792764363276288.

82. Donald J. Trump (@realDonaldTrump), Twitter (July 26, 2017, 6:48 a.m.), https://twitter.com/realDonaldTrump/status/890207082926022656; Donald J. Trump (@realDonaldTrump), Twitter (July 26, 2017, 6:52 a.m.), https://twitter.com/realDonaldTrump/status/890208319566229504.

83. Donald J. Trump (@realDonaldTrump), Twitter (Dec. 23, 2017, 12:27 p.m.), https://twitter.com/realDonaldTrump/status/944665687292817415.

84. Donald J. Trump (@realDonaldTrump), Twitter (Dec. 23, 2017, 12:30 p.m.), https://twitter.com/realDonaldTrump/status/944666448185692166.

85. See U.S. Department of Justice, Office of the Inspector General, *A Report of Investigation of Certain Allegations Relating to Former FBI Deputy Director Andrew McCabe* (Feb. 2018), https://oig.justice.gov/reports/2018/020180413.pdf; see also Sabrina McCubbin, "Summary: Office of Inspector General Report on Andrew McCabe's Firing and Response by McCabe's Lawyer," Lawfare, April 14, 2018, https://www.lawfareblog.com/summary-office-inspector-general-report-andrew-mccabes-firing-and-response-mccabes-lawyer.

86. *Id.*, p. 5.

87. *Id.*

88. Donald J. Trump (@realDonaldTrump), Twitter (March 16, 2018, 9:08 p.m.), https://twitter.com/realDonaldTrump/status/974859881827258369.

89. Donald J. Trump (@realDonaldTrump), Twitter (March 17, 2018, 10:34 a.m.), https://twitter.com/realDonaldTrump/status/975062797162811394.

90. "AP source says McCabe kept notes on Trump," Associated Press, March 17, 2018, https://bit.ly/2LZxsUo.

91. Donald J. Trump (@realDonaldTrump), Twitter (March 18, 2018, 5:22 a.m.), https://twitter.com/realDonaldTrump/status/975346628113596417.

92. Donald J. Trump (@realDonaldTrump), Twitter (April 13, 2018, 12:36 p.m.), https://twitter.com/realDonaldTrump/status/984877999718895616.

93. Donald J. Trump (@realDonaldTrump), Twitter (March 17, 2018, 5:12 p.m.), https://twitter.com/realDonaldTrump/status/975163071361683456.

94. Donald J. Trump (@realDonaldTrump), Twitter (Feb. 2, 2018, 3:33 a.m.), https://twitter.com/realDonaldTrump/status/959389424806191104.

95. Donald J. Trump (@realDonaldTrump), Twitter (March 17, 2018, 10:11

a.m.), https://twitter.com/realDonaldTrump/status/975057131136274432.

96. Donald J. Trump (@realDonaldTrump), Twitter (Feb. 28, 2018, 6:34 a.m.), https://twitter.com/realDonaldTrump/status/968856971075051521.

97. Donald J. Trump (@realDonaldTrump), Twitter (May 23, 2018, 3:54 a.m.), https://twitter.com/realDonaldTrump/status/999242039723163648.

98. Donald J. Trump (@realDonaldTrump), Twitter (April 7, 2018, 1:52 p.m.), https://twitter.com/realDonaldTrump/status/982722926305832960.

99. Donald J. Trump (@realDonaldTrump), Twitter (April 7, 2018, 2:00 p.m.), https://twitter.com/realDonaldTrump/status/982724858743328777.

100. Donald J. Trump (@realDonaldTrump), Twitter (May 2, 2018, 7:45 a.m.), https://twitter.com/realDonaldTrump/status/991690248399794176.

101. Matt Apuzzo et al., "Code Name Crossfire Hurricane: The Secret Origins of the Trump Investigation," *The New York Times*, May 16, 2018, https://nyti.ms/2GpbIgM.

102. *Id.*; see also Robert Costa et al., "Secret FBI source for Russia investigation met with three Trump advisers during campaign," *The Washington Post*, May 18, 2018, https://wapo.st/2k6Y5Kx; Robert Costa et al., "Who is Stefan A. Halper, the FBI source who assisted the Russia investigation?," *The Washington Post*, May 21, 2018, https://wapo.st/2khUNE9.

103. Asha Rangappa, "The FBI didn't use an informant to go after Trump. They used one to protect him.," *The Washington Post*, May 18, 2018, https://wapo.st/2rSykBa.

104. Donald J. Trump (@realDonaldTrump), Twitter (May 18, 2018, 6:50 a.m.), https://twitter.com/realDonaldTrump/status/997474432443707393.

105. Donald J. Trump (@realDonaldTrump), Twitter May 19, 2018, 2:27 p.m.), https://twitter.com/realDonaldTrump/status/997951982467014656 (May 20, 2018).

106. Donald J. Trump (@realDonaldTrump), Twitter (May 20, 2018, 10:37 a.m.), https://twitter.com/realDonaldTrump/status/998256454590193665.

107. Kevin Breuninger, "Experts: Rosenstein may have made the best move by quickly agreeing to Trump's demand for an investigation," CNBC, May 21, 2018, https://cnb.cx/2LjqZTX.

108. Kevin Johnson and Gregory Korte, "In extraordinary meeting, Trump gets involved in congressional oversight of Russia probe," *USA Today*, May 21, 2018, https://usat.ly/2rZrUjR.

109. Matthew Kahn, "Document: White House Statement on Wray, Rosenstein, Coats Meeting About FBI Informant," Lawfare, May 21, 2018, http://bit.ly/2IGJMXM.

110. Jeremy Herb et al., "White House lawyer attends start of Justice Dept. briefings," CNN, May 24, 2018, https://cnn.it/2GNpYjF.

111. 4 William Blackstone, *Commentaries on the Laws of England* *129 (emphases in original); see also McDowell, 67 Geo. Wash. L. Rev., pp. 640–41.

112. The Declaration of Independence para. 10 (U.S. 1776). The context there was different—the complaint was that the king had vetoed laws that would allow the colonists to establish their own courts, and had

thus left them dependent on often hostile royal courts—but the basic point is that the framers saw the king's obstruction as a serious charge in a bill of particulars justifying independence.

113. House Judiciary Committee, *Impeachment of Richard M. Nixon, President of the United States*, H.R. Rep. No. 93-1305, 120 Cong. Rec. 29,220 (1974), http://bit.ly/HR93-1305.

114. *Id.*

115. President Richard M. Nixon, The President's News Conference, March 6, 1974, http://www.presidency.ucsb.edu/ws/?pid=4377.

116. *Impeaching William Jefferson Clinton, President of the United States, for High Crimes and Misdemeanors*, H. Rep. No. 105-830 at *4–5 (105th Cong., Dec. 16, 1998), https://www.congress.gov/105/crpt/hrpt830/CRPT-105hrpt830.pdf.

117. See *Impeachment of Judge Samuel B. Kent*, H. Res. 520 (111th Cong. Jun. 24, 2009), https://www.congress.gov/111/bills/hres520/BILLS-111hres520rds.pdf.

118. See 18 U.S.C. §§ 1501–1521.

119. These include 18 U.S.C. §§ 1001, 1503, 1505, and 1512; see also Daniel J. Hemel and Eric A. Posner, *Presidential Obstruction of Justice*, 108 Cal. L. Rev. (forthcoming 2018), *27–29, https://papers.ssrn.com/sol3/papers.cfm?abstract_id=3004876; Berke, Bookbinder, and Eisen, "Presidential Obstruction of Justice," *Brookings Governance Studies*, Oct. 10, 2017, http://brook.gs/2jadWLb.

120. See, for example, Jared P. Cole and Todd Garvey, Cong. Research Serv., *Impeachment and Removal*, pp. 8–9 (Oct. 29, 2015), https://fas.org/sgp/crs/misc/R44260.pdf; House Judiciary Committee, *Constitutional Grounds for Presidential Impeachment*, pp. 21–25 (93d Cong., Feb. 1974), http://bit.ly/CGPI1974, pp. 21–25.

121. Steve Vladeck, "Trump still could have obstructed justice—even if he didn't break the law," *The Washington Post*, June 16, 2017, https://wapo.st/2rwYiwO.

122. See Berke, Bookbinder, and Eisen, "Presidential Obstruction of Justice," *Brookings Governance Studies*, pp. 35, 52–56 (discussing the "proceeding" requirement under different obstruction statutes), p. 61 (discussing whether an FBI investigation qualifies as a "proceeding"); see also *Marinello v. United States*, 138 S. Ct. 1101, 1110 (2018) (holding that a similar obstruction provision in the Internal Revenue Code may be triggered by a "reasonably foreseeable" proceeding); Jed Shugerman, "An Admission of Obstruction," *Slate*, June 3, 2018, https://slate.me/2M3GpMz.

123. See Berke, Bookbinder, and Eisen, "Presidential Obstruction of Justice," *Brookings Governance Studies*, p. 35.

124. *United States v. Cueto*, 151 F.3d 620, 630–31 (7th Cir. 1998).

125. For example, *United States v. Fasolino*, 586 F.2d 939, 941 (2d Cir. 1978); see Berke, Bookbinder, and Eisen, "Presidential Obstruction of Justice,"

Brookings Governance Studies, pp. 64–65 (discussing cases and arguing for "motivated by an improper purpose" interpretation).

126. Laurence H. Tribe, "Why Impeachment Must Remain A Priority," Take Care, May 23, 2017, http://takecareblog.com/blog/why -impeachment-must-remain-a-priority; see also 18 U.S.C. §§ 1503, 1505, 1512(c).

127. See 18 U.S.C. § 1001; see also U.S. Department of Justice, U.S. Attorneys' Manual, Crim. Res. Manual § 916, https://www.justice.gov/usam /criminal-resource-manual-916-false-statements-federal-investigator.

128. See, for example, Ben Schreckinger, "Trump's false claims to Comey about Moscow stay could aid Mueller," *Politico*, April 23, 2018, https: //politi.co/2qTlQtc.

129. House Judiciary Committee, *Impeachment of Richard M. Nixon, President of the United States*, H.R. Rep. No. 93-1305, 120 Cong. Rec. 29,220 (1974), http://bit.ly/HR93-1305.p. 2.

130. Daniel J. Hemel and Eric A. Posner, *Presidential Obstruction of Justice*, 108 Cal. L. Rev. (forthcoming 2018), *27–29, https://papers.ssrn.com/ sol3/papers.cfm?abstract_id=3004876.

131. Annals of Congress, vol. 1, p. 517 (June 17, 1789), available at https://bit .ly/2sNQPHj. For a discussion of this entire debate, see House Judiciary Committee, *Constitutional Grounds for Presidential Impeachment*, pp. 21–25 (93d Cong., Feb. 1974), http://bit.ly/CGPI1974, pp. 15–16.

CHAPTER 4

1. Memorandum from James Comey, Director, FBI, to Andrew McCabe, James Baker, and James Rybicki, at 11 (Feb. 14, 2017) (on file with CNN), https://cnn.it/2xrfcA6.

2. *Id.*

3. Federal law prohibits government officials from disclosing certain limited categories of "defense information" and "classified information," as well as specific prohibitions on disclosing information such as the identities of covert agents. Susan Hennessey and Helen Klein Murillo, "The Law of Leaks," Lawfare, Feb. 15, 2017, https://www.lawfareblog .com/law-leaks (quoting 18 U.S.C. §§ 793, 794, 798; 50 U.S.C. § 3121). But most of what Trump calls "leaks" do not fall into those categories; they are simply embarrassing disclosures of private conversations in the White House. So while a president could fire an aide for talking to the press about these private conversations, in many cases, the aide will have committed no crime.

4. See *Bartnicki v. Vopper*, 532 U.S. 514, 535 (2001).

5. Memorandum from James Comey, Director, FBI, to Andrew McCabe, James Baker, and James Rybicki, at 11 (Feb. 14, 2017) (on file with CNN), https://cnn.it/2xrfcA6, p. 11.

6. Donald J. Trump (@realDonaldTrump), Twitter (July 24,

2017, 5:49 a.m.), https://twitter.com/realDonaldTrump/status /889467610332528641. Sometime during the summer of 2017, Trump also reportedly asked a senator to open an investigation into Hillary Clinton. Jonathan Martin et al., "Trump Pressed Top Republicans to End Senate Russia Inquiry," *The New York Times*, Nov. 30, 2017, https://nyti.ms/2BBmb04.

7. "Listen: President Donald Trump to Larry O'Connor: I'm Very Unhappy the Justice Department Isn't Going After Hillary Clinton," WMAL, http://bit.ly/2IHQFw4; Philip Rucker, "Trump pressures Justice Department to investigate 'Crooked Hillary,'" *The Washington Post*, Nov. 3, 2017, http://wapo.st/2ztjNlH.

8. Donald J. Trump (@realDonaldTrump), Twitter (Nov. 3, 2017, 3:57 a.m.), https://twitter.com/realDonaldTrump/status/926403023861141504; Donald J. Trump (@realDonaldTrump), Twitter (Nov. 3, 2017, 4:03 a.m.), https://twitter.com/realDonaldTrump/status/926404584456773632; Donald J. Trump (@realDonaldTrump), Twitter (Nov. 3, 2017, 4:11 a.m.), https://twitter.com/realDonaldTrump/status/926406490763784194; Donald J. Trump (@realDonaldTrump), Twitter (Nov. 3, 2017, 4:55 a.m.), https://twitter.com/realDonaldTrump/status/926417546038923264; Philip Rucker et al., "Trump pardons conservative pundit Dinesh D'Souza, suggests others also could receive clemency," *The Washington Post*, May 31, 2018, https://wapo.st/2H6G08g.

9. Zeke Miller, "Trump says he's 'disappointed' with Justice Department, won't rule out firing Sessions," PBS, Nov. 3, 2017, https://to.pbs .org/2IaM55h.

10. Michael S. Schmidt and Maggie Haberman, "Justice Dept. to Weigh Inquiry Into Clinton Foundation," *The New York Times*, Nov. 13, 2017, https://nyti.ms/2jlAcBI.

11. Donald J. Trump (@realDonaldTrump), Twitter (Dec. 2, 2017, 6:13 p.m.), https://twitter.com/realDonaldTrump/status/937142713211813889.

12. Donald J. Trump (@realDonaldTrump), Twitter (Jan 2. 2018, 4:48 a.m.), https://twitter.com/realDonaldTrump/status/948174033882927104.

13. Donald J. Trump (@realDonaldTrump), Twitter (Feb. 21, 2018, 6:40 a.m.), https://twitter.com/realDonaldTrump/status/966321700588711936.

14. Donald J. Trump (@realDonaldTrump), Twitter (April 15, 2018, 4:57 a.m.), https://twitter.com/realDonaldTrump/status/985487209510948864.

15. Donald J. Trump (@realDonaldTrump), Twitter (May 14, 2018, 1:46 p.m.), https://twitter.com/realDonaldTrump/status/996129630913482755.

16. Donald J. Trump (@realDonaldTrump), Twitter (May 18, 2018, 6:38 a.m.), https://twitter.com/realDonaldTrump/status/997471413266247681.

17. Donald J. Trump (@realDonaldTrump), Twitter (June 7, 2018, 7:07 a.m.), https://twitter.com/realDonaldTrump/status/1004726490058182656.

18. Rebecca Ballhaus, "Trump Accuses FBI Agent of 'Treason,'" *The Wall Street Journal*, Jan. 11, 2018, https://on.wsj.com/2G58Cyd.

19. Ali Vitali, "Trump: Democrats' muted State of the Union reaction

'treasonous,'" NBC News, Feb. 5, 2018, https://nbcnews.to/2jOu2a8.

20. "President Trump talks North Korea, Iran, Comey, Cohen, Dr. Ronny Jackson and Kanye West in 'Fox and Friends' interview," Fox News, April 26, 2018, https://fxn.ws/2IFlRrF.

21. Aaron Rupar (@atrupar), Twitter (April 28, 2018, 4:50 p.m.) (embedded video), https://twitter.com/atrupar/status/990377655706030080.

22. Alex Horton, "Trump's 'traitor' rhetoric looms over Bowe Bergdahl's sentencing," *The Washington Post*, Oct. 23, 2017, http://wapo.st/2yHJgo6.

23. See Dakin Andone et al., "Bowe Bergdahl gets dishonorable discharge, avoids prison time," CNN, Nov. 4, 2017, http://cnn.it/2hCgluD.

24. Donald J. Trump (@realDonaldTrump), Twitter (Nov. 3, 2017, 9:54 a.m.), https://twitter.com/realDonaldTrump/status/926492915626663939.

25. Adam Edelman, "Trump says athletes who kneel during anthem 'maybe shouldn't be in the country,'" NBC News, May 24, 2018, https://nbcnews.to/2IM5utt.

26. Robert H. Jackson, Atty. Gen., U.S. Department of Justice, *The Federal Prosecutor*, Address to the Second Annual Conference of United States Attorneys (April 1, 1940), https://www.justice.gov/sites/default/files/ag/legacy/2011/09/16/04-01-1940.pdf.

27. Black, *Impeachment*, p. 42.

28. 10 U.S.C. § 837(a); see Steve Vladeck, "President Trump's Careless Rhetoric, Unlawful Command Influence, and the Bergdahl Court-Martial," JustSecurity, April 5, 2017, https://www.justsecurity.org/39541/president-trump-bowe-bergdahl-unlawful-command-influence/.

29. *Wright v. United States*, 732 F.2d 1048, 1056 (2d Cir. 1984) (Friendly, J.); see also *Young v. United States ex rel. Vuitton et Fils S.A.*, 481 U.S. 787, 807 (1987).

30. See Protect Democracy, "No 'Absolute Right' to Control DOJ: Constitutional Limits on White House Interference with Law Enforcement Matters," March 2018, http://bit.ly/2IIimoj; Jack Goldsmith, *Independence and Accountability at the Department of Justice*, Lawfare, Jan. 30, 2018, http://bit.ly/2LsE9ih.

31. See House Judiciary Committee, *Constitutional Grounds for Presidential Impeachment*, p. 20.

32. *Id.*

33. See House Judiciary Committee, *Impeachment of Richard M. Nixon, President of the United States*, H.R. Rep. No. 93-1305, 120 Cong. Rec. 29,220 (1974), http://bit.ly/HR93-1305.

34. See Frank Bowman, "President Trump committed another impeachable offense on Friday," *Slate*, Nov. 3, 2017, http://slate.me/2j6gXw5.

35. *Id.*

36. *Id.*

37. *Id.* (emphases in original).

1. See, for example, Jacey Fortin, "A Guide to Joe Arpaio, the Longtime Sheriff Who Escaped Strife," *The New York Times*, Aug. 27, 2017, https://nyti.ms/2vzWwbh; Hilary Hanson and Sam Levine, "Local newspaper tears into former Sheriff Joe Arpaio in savage Twitter thread," *Huffington Post*, Aug. 26, 2017, http://bit.ly/2icbHXw (summarizing Arpaio's history).

2. See Letter from Thomas E. Perez, Asst. Atty. Gen., U.S. Department of Justice, to Bill Montgomery, Cty. Atty., Maricopa Cty. (Dec. 15, 2011), https://www.justice.gov/sites/default/files/crt/legacy/2011/12/15/mcso_findletter_12-15-11.pdf.

3. *Ortega-Melendres v. Arpaio*, 836 F. Supp. 2d 959 (D. Ariz. 2011), aff'd sub nom. *Melendres v. Arpaio*, 695 F.3d 990 (9th Cir. 2012).

4. *Melendres v. Arpaio*, 989 F. Supp. 2d 822 (D. Ariz. 2013), aff'd in part, vacated in part on other grounds, 784 F.3d 1254 (9th Cir. 2015).

5. See Findings of Fact, *Melendres v. Arpaio*, No. CV-07-2513-PHX (D. Ariz. May 13, 2016), Doc. No. 1677; see also *Melendres v. Arpaio*, No. CV-07-2513-PHX, 2016 WL 3996453, at *1 (D. Ariz. July 26, 2016), appeal dismissed sub nom. *Melendres v. Maricopa Cty.*, No. 16-16663, 2017 WL 4315029 (9th Cir. Aug. 3, 2017).

6. *United States v. Arpaio*, No. CR-16-01012-001, 2017 WL 3268180, at *7 (D. Ariz. July 31, 2017), available at http://bit.ly/2k5SgQB.

7. Tom LoBianco and Jeff Zeleny, "Trump asked Sessions to consider dropping Arpaio prosecution, official says," CNN, Aug. 27, 2017, http://cnn.it/2iy3vjM.

8. Gregg Jarrett, "Trump 'seriously considering' a pardon for ex-Sheriff Joe Arpaio," Fox News, Aug. 14, 2017, http://fxn.ws/2uDfRwz.

9. Max Walker and Josh Frigerio, "Sheriff Joe Arpaio pardon: President Trump hints 'he'll be fine,'" ABC 15 News, Aug. 23, 2017, http://bit.ly/2k3M6k8.

10. The White House, President Trump Pardons Sheriff Joe Arpaio, Aug. 25, 2017, https://www.whitehouse.gov/the-press-office/2017/08/25/president-trump-pardons-sheriff-joe-arpaio.

11. Donald J. Trump (@realDonaldTrump), Twitter (Aug. 25, 2017, 7:00 p.m.), https://twitter.com/realdonaldtrump/status/901263061511794688.

12. U.S. Const. art. II, § 2, cl. 1.

13. 3 Elliot's Debates (June 18, 1788), http://bit.ly/2k64RDH.

14. *Id.*

15. *Ex parte Grossman*, 267 U.S. 87, 121 (1925).

16. Black, *Impeachment*, p. 34.

17. U.S. Department of Justice, U.S. Attorneys' Manual § 9-140.112 (Standards for Considering Pardon Petitions), https://www.justice.gov/usam/usam-9-140000-pardon-attorney#9-140.112. These are the criteria for pardon applications submitted through the Department of

Justice's Pardon Attorney, which account for the vast majority of presidential pardons, although the president may also pardon individuals who have not applied through that process.

18. Mark Joseph Stern, "Trump's Arpaio pardon is a bad sign for Mueller's investigation," *Slate*, Aug. 26, 2017, http://slate.me/2iaSsop.

19. Noah Feldman, "Arpaio Pardon Would Show Contempt for Constitution," *Bloomberg*, Aug. 26, 2017, https://bloom.bg/2yXFIBH.

20. See Br. for Martin Redish, Free Speech For People and Coalition to Preserve, Protect and Defend as Amici Curiae, *United States v. Arpaio*, No. 16 CR-01012, (D. Ariz. Sept. 11, 2017), appeal filed, No. 17-10448 (9th Cir. Oct. 19, 2017), Doc. No. 228-1, available at http://bit.ly/2k2bZkl; Martin H. Redish, "A Pardon for Arpaio Would Put Trump in Uncharted Territory," *The New York Times*, Aug. 24, 2017, http://nyti.ms/2xOAELz. Thanks to Dennis Aftergut for helping to develop these points.

21. For more on the point that follows, see Laurence H. Tribe and Ron Fein, "Trump's pardon of Arpaio can—and should—be overturned," *The Washington Post*, Sept. 18, 2017, http://wapo.st/2fvcQVp.

22. See *Meredith v. Fair*, 305 F.2d 343, 346–48 (5th Cir. 1962).

23. See *Meredith v. Fair*, 313 F.2d 532, 533 (5th Cir. 1962).

24. See *United States v. Barnett*, 330 F.2d 369, 376 (5th Cir. 1963).

25. See, for example, "Brown at 60: The Southern Manifesto and 'Massive Resistance' to Brown," NAACP Legal Defense Fund, http://www.naacpldf.org/brown-at-60-southern-manifesto-and-massive-resistance-brown (last visited June 5, 2018).

26. Nicholas deB. Katzenbach, *Some of It Was Fun: Working with RFK and LBJ*, p. 72 (New York: W.W. Norton & Co., 2008).

27. *Williams v. Rhodes*, 393 U.S. 23, 29 (1968).

28. *Inst. of Cetacean Research v. Sea Shepherd Conservation Soc'y*, 774 F.3d 935, 951–52 (9th Cir. 2014).

29. Violating a court order is *itself* an impeachable offense. In 2010, the House of Representatives included it among the articles of impeachment against Judge Thomas Porteous, and the Senate convicted him on that article. See Radnofsky, *A Citizen's Guide to Impeachment*, p. 82 and n.318.

30. It is true that, in the 1925 case of *Ex parte Grossman*, the Supreme Court recognized the president's power to pardon an individual for a contempt conviction arising from his flouting an injunction to stop selling liquor in the Prohibition era. 267 U.S. at 115, 120. But Arpaio's case is distinguishable. As noted above, Arpaio's case involves a pardon issued (1) for criminal contempt (2) for violating an injunction (3) issued to a government official (4) to cease a systemic practice of violating (5) individuals' constitutional rights. By contrast, the presidential pardon in *Grossman* involved only the first two elements. The due process issues stem from the last three elements, which were not at issue in *Grossman*.

31. *Cf.* Black, *Impeachment*, p. 34 ("Suppose a president were to announce

and follow a policy of granting full pardons, in advance of indictment or trial, to all federal agents or police who killed anybody in line of duty, in the District of Columbia, whatever the circumstances and however unnecessary the killing . . . [C]ould anybody doubt that such conduct would be impeachable?").

32. See *United States v. Arpaio*, No. 17-10448 (9th Cir. filed Oct. 20, 2017).

CHAPTER 6

1. Philip Bump, "Trump's speech encouraging police to be "rough," annotated," *The Washington Post*, July 28, 2017, https://wapo.st/2x85h2t.

2. Cleve R. Wootson Jr. and Mark Berman, "U.S. police chiefs blast Trump for endorsing 'police brutality,'" *The Washington Post*, July 30, 2017, http://wapo.st/2kbuOli.

3. See, for example, Sari Horwitz et al., "Sessions orders Justice Department to review all police reform agreements," *The Washington Post*, April 3, 2017, http://wapo.st/2nRko7Z.

4. Jenna Johnson and John Wagner, "Trump condemns Charlottesville violence but doesn't single out white nationalists," *The Washington Post*, Aug. 12, 2017, http://wapo.st/2fCneov (video).

5. Meghan Keneally, "Trump lashes out at 'alt-left' in Charlottesville, says 'fine people on both sides,'" ABC News, Aug. 15, 2017, http://abcn.ws/2vGcEcV.

6. Andrew deGrandpre, "Trump laments 'poor' Jeffrey Lord, the CNN analyst fired for tweeting a Nazi salute," *The Washington Post*, Aug. 22, 2017, http://wapo.st/2xrmsap.

7. Donald J. Trump (@realDonaldTrump), Twitter (Aug. 17, 2017, 11:45 a.m.), https://twitter.com/realDonaldTrump/status/898254409511129088.

8. Jenna Johnson and Jose A. DelReal, "Trump tells story about killing terrorists with bullets dipped in pigs' blood, though there's no proof of it," *The Washington Post*, Feb. 20, 2016, http://wapo.st/1OkWQMy.

9. See 18 U.S.C. § 2441(d)(1)(D).

10. U.S. Const. art. II, § 2, cl. 1.

11. By analogy, under the Uniform Code of Military Justice, a person who "counsels" or "commands" an offense is considered a "principal" subject to punishment as if he had committed the offense himself. 10 U.S.C. § 877(1).

12. Eileen Sullivan and Dan Bilefsky, "Trump Shares Inflammatory Anti-Muslim Videos, and Britain's Leader Condemns Them," *The New York Times*, Nov. 29, 2017, https://nyti.ms/2ByPyHZ.

13. *Id.*

14. *Id.*

15. See *Int'l Refugee Assistance Project v. Trump*, 883 F.3d 233, 250–52, 266 and n.15 (4th Cir. 2018), as amended (Feb. 28, 2018) (summarizing history).

16. U.S. Const. art. II, § 2.

17. U.S. Const. art. IV, § 4.

18. U.S. Const. amend. XIV, § 1. The Fourteenth Amendment applies to states; the same principle applies to the federal government through the Fifth Amendment. See *Bolling v. Sharpe*, 347 U.S. 497, 498–99 (1954).

19. *Loving v. Virginia*, 388 U.S. 1, 12 (1967) (overturning Virginia's statute banning interracial marriage).

20. Tribe and Matz, *To End a Presidency*, p. 65.

21. Maureen B. Costello, Southern Poverty Law Center, "The Trump Effect: The Impact of the 2016 Presidential Election on Our Nation's Schools," p. 4 (Nov. 28, 2016), https://bit.ly/2JfMUye.

22. Christopher N. Morrison et al., "Assaults on Days of Campaign Rallies During the 2016 US Presidential Election," 29 Epidemiology pp. 490, 492 (July 2018), http://bit.ly/2xHK2Vr. The study found no change in assault rates on days when the same cities held campaign rallies for Trump's principal opponent, Hillary Clinton.

23. Brian Levin and John David Reitzel, Center for the Study of Hate and Extremism, "Report to the Nation: Hate Crime Rise in U.S. Cities and U.S. Counties in Time of Division and Foreign Interference," pp. 3–4 (May 2018), http://bit.ly/2JlendN.

24. Janice Williams, "Hate crimes against Muslims are on the rise in the U.S.," *Newsweek*, July 17, 2017, http://bit.ly/2xJVkbH.

25. See Dan Barry and John Eligon, "'Trump, Trump, Trump!' How a President's Name Became a Racial Jeer," *The New York Times*, Dec. 16, 2017, https://nyti.ms/2kzNg3j.

CHAPTER 7

1. Donald J. Trump (@realDonaldTrump), Twitter (Aug. 1, 2017, 4:29 a.m.), https://twitter.com/realDonaldTrump/status/895970429734/11298.

2. Donald J. Trump (@realDonaldTrump), Twitter (Sep. 19, 2017, 10:22 a.m.), https://twitter.com/realDonaldTrump/status/910192375267561472; Ali Vitali, "Trump Threatens to 'Totally Destroy' North Korea in First U.N. Speech," NBC News, Sept. 19, 2017, https://nbcnews.to/2GCTrg7.

3. Donald J. Trump (@realDonaldTrump), Twitter (Sep. 23, 2017, 8:08 p.m.), https://twitter.com/realDonaldTrump/status/911789314169823232.

4. Donald J. Trump (@realDonaldTrump), Twitter (Oct. 1, 2017, 12:01 p.m.), https://twitter.com/realDonaldTrump/status/914565910798782465.

5. Donald J. Trump (@realDonaldTrump), Twitter (Oct. 1, 2017, 7:30 a.m.), https://twitter.com/realDonaldTrump/status/914497877543735296.

6. Karen DeYoung and John Wagner, "Trump threatens 'fire and fury' in response to North Korean threats," *The Washington Post*, Aug. 8, 2017, http://wapo.st/2hFWk8L.

7. Donald J. Trump (@realDonaldTrump), Twitter (Oct. 7, 2017, 12:45 p.m.),

https://twitter.com/realDonaldTrump/status/916751271960436737.

8. Zachary Cohen et al., "New missile test shows North Korea capable of hitting all of US mainland," CNN, Nov. 30, 2017, http://cnn.it/2icotVU.

9. Donald J. Trump (@realDonaldTrump), Twitter (Jan. 2, 2018, 4:49 p.m.), https://twitter.com/realDonaldTrump/status/948355557022420992.

10. Carol E. Lee et al., "Tillerson's Fury at Trump Required an Intervention from Pence," NBC News, Oct. 4, 2017, http://nbcnews.to/2AyNEcu; "Ruhle: My sources say Tillerson called Trump a 'F-ing moron,'" MSNBC, Oct. 4, 2017, http://on.msnbc.com/2BHiRYV; Graham Lanktree, "Did Rex Tillerson Call Trump a Moron," Newsweek, Oct. 4, 2017, https://goo.gl/xq6VT2; Paul Waldman, "Tillerson won't say whether he thinks Trump is a 'moron.' But he's not quitting," The Washington Post, Oct. 4, 2017, http://wapo.st/2BGQmdN; Eliza Rehlman, "Trump rages at NBC for report that said Tillerson called him a 'moron' after he wanted a dramatic increase in nuclear arsenal," Business Insider, Oct. 11, 2017, http://read.bi/2yf6eVy.

11. Joseph Bernstein, "Sources: McMaster Mocked Trump's Intelligence at a Private Dinner," Buzzfeed, Nov. 20, 2017, http://bzfd.it/2idHOGu.

12. Id.

13. Carol E. Lee et al., "Kelly says Trump is an idiot, mocks his policy ignorance, say officials," NBC News, May 1, 2018, https://nbcnews.to/2FAReBt.

14. Jonathan Martin, "Read Excerpts From Senator Bob Corker's Interview With The Times," The New York Times, Oct. 9, 2017, https://nyti.ms/2yUsYHz.

15. "Read Trump's Letter to Kim Canceling North Korea Summit Meeting," The New York Times, May 24, 2018, https://nyti.ms/2LtjY3c. The exact reasons for the summit's stop-start nature are complex, but apparently a key contributing factor was Trump's refusal to learn basic information about North Korea's capabilities and positions. As former White House aides told reporters, "Trump has resisted the kind of detailed briefings about enrichment capabilities, plutonium reprocessing, nuclear weapons production and missile programs that Mr. Obama and President George W. Bush regularly sat through." David E. Sanger, "Trump Grappling With Risks of Proceeding With North Korea Meeting," The New York Times, May 20, 2018, https://nyti.ms/2IE0gTi.

16. Gillian Edevane, "Who is Matthew Pottinger? Audio of White House official debunks Trump 'phony sources' smear against New York Times," Newsweek, May 26, 2018, http://bit.ly/2xmSIAl; Michael D. Shear, "Trump Falsely Says Times Made Up Source in Report on Korea Summit Meeting," The New York Times, May 26, 2018, https://nyti.ms/2xgdloV.

17. Karen DeYoung and John Wagner, "Trump and Kim declare summit a

big success, but they diverge on the details," *The Washington Post*, June 13, 2018, https://wapo.st/2t5r1GP.

18. Donald J. Trump (@realDonaldTrump), Twitter (April 11, 2018, 3:57 a.m.), https://twitter.com/realDonaldTrump/status/984022625440747520.

19. U.S. Const. art. II, § 2, cl. 1. The original public meaning indicates that the founders had a narrow view of this power. See, for example, Leon Friedman and Burt Neuborne, "The Framers, on War Powers," *The New York Times*, Nov. 27, 1990, https://nyti.ms/2BBixKX.

20. See Manual for Courts-Martial, United States ¶ 100a, pp. IV–144 (2016 ed.), http://bit.ly/2hpWku9.

21. *United States v. Herrmann*, 76 M.J. 304, 305 (C.A.A.F. 2017), reconsideration denied (C.A.A.F. July 13, 2017), and cert. denied, 138 S. Ct. 487 (2017).

22. *Id.* at 306.

23. Black, *Impeachment*, p. 35.

24. U.S. Const. amend. XXV § 4.

25. See James Madison, *September 8, 1787*, in *The Avalon Project* (emphasis added). As later noted by Representative William Lawrence of Ohio, English practice had even allowed impeachment of officials on the grounds they were "too *ignorant* to perform their duties." William Lawrence, "The Law of Impeachment," 15 Am. Law Reg. pp. 641, 653 (1867) (emphasis in original), http://bit.ly/2IGRu89. While excessive ignorance *alone* would probably not be accepted as an impeachable offense in the United States, this history forms an important backdrop for the framers' discussion of incapacity.

26. *Id.* (emphasis added).

27. *Id.* (emphasis added).

28. See House Judiciary Committee, *Constitutional Grounds for Presidential Impeachment*, pp. 42–43.

CHAPTER 8

1. Jonathan Peters, "Trump Twitter spreadsheet tracks 'a perpetual campaign against the press,'" *Colum. Journalism Rev.*, Dec. 21, 2017, http://bit.ly/2I 8uzyk.

2. Stephen Collinson, "On Day Two, Trump prayed, met the CIA, and attacked the press," CNN, Jan. 21, 2017, http://cnn.it/2j6zq9l.

3. "President Trump ranted for 77 minutes in Phoenix. Here's what he said," *TIME*, Aug. 23, 2017, http://ti.me/2wnGsOt. This was the same rally at which he asked rhetorically, "was Sheriff Joe convicted for doing his job?"

4. "President Trump talks North Korea, Iran, Comey, Cohen, Dr. Ronny Jackson and Kanye West in 'Fox and Friends' interview," Fox News, April 26, 2018, https://fxn.ws/2IFlRrF.

5. Ali Vitali, "Trump's Tweets 'Official Statements,' Spicer Says," NBC, June 6, 2017, https://nbcnews.to/2GlT2yp.

6. Donald J. Trump (@realDonaldTrump), Twitter (Feb. 15, 2017, 3:40 a.m.), https://twitter.com/realdonaldtrump/status/831830548565852160.

7. Donald J. Trump (@realDonaldTrump), Twitter (Feb. 17, 2017, 1:48 p.m.), https://twitter.com/realDonaldTrump/status/832708293516632065.

8. Donald J. Trump (@realDonaldTrump), Twitter (Nov. 25, 2017, 2:37 p.m.), https://twitter.com/realDonaldTrump/status/934551607596986368.

9. Donald J. Trump (@realDonaldTrump), Twitter (Nov. 27, 2017, 6:04 a.m.), https://twitter.com/realDonaldTrump/status/935147410472480769.

10. Donald J. Trump (@realDonaldTrump), Twitter (Dec. 30, 2017, 2:36 p.m.), https://twitter.com/realDonaldTrump/status/947235015343202304.

11. Donald J. Trump (@realDonaldTrump), Twitter (Jan. 2, 2018, 5:05 p.m.), https://twitter.com/realDonaldTrump/status/948359545767841792.

12. Donald J. Trump (@realDonaldTrump), Twitter (Feb. 11, 2018, 10:21 a.m.), https://twitter.com/realDonaldTrump/status/962753552824365056.

13. Donald J. Trump (@realDonaldTrump), Twitter (April 3, 2018, 3:34 a.m.), https://twitter.com/realDonaldTrump/status/981117684489379840.

14. Donald J. Trump (@realDonaldTrump), Twitter (April 8, 2018, 4:58 a.m.), https://twitter.com/realDonaldTrump/status/982950739441004544.

15. Donald J. Trump (@realDonaldTrump), Twitter (April 20, 2018, 1:25 p.m.), https://twitter.com/realDonaldTrump/status/987426984195174405.

16. Donald J. Trump (@realDonaldTrump), Twitter (April 21, 2018, 6:10 a.m.), https://twitter.com/realDonaldTrump/status/987679848284999680.

17. Donald J. Trump (@realDonaldTrump), Twitter (April 30, 2018, 3:49 p.m.), https://twitter.com/realDonaldTrump/status/991087278515769345.

18. Donald J. Trump (@realDonaldTrump), Twitter (May 4, 2018, 3:45 a.m.), https://twitter.com/realDonaldTrump/status/992354530510721025.

19. Donald J. Trump (@realDonaldTrump), Twitter (May 9, 2018, 4:38 a.m.), https://twitter.com/realDonaldTrump/status/994179864436596736.

20. Noah Bierman and Brian Bennett, "Trump threatens networks, saying it's 'disgusting the way the press is able to write whatever they want,'" Los Angeles Times, Oct. 11, 2017, http://lat.ms/2AudGxC.

21. Memorandum from James Comey, Director, FBI, to Andrew McCabe, James Baker, and James Rybicki, at 11 (Feb. 14, 2017) (on file with CNN), https://cnn.it/2xrfcA6,.

22. Donald J. Trump (@realDonaldTrump), Twitter (Dec. 7, 2015, 7:08 a.m.), https://twitter.com/realDonaldTrump/status/673881733415178240.

23. Damian Paletta and Josh Dawsey, "Trump personally pushed postmaster general to double rates on Amazon, other firms," The Washington Post, May 18, 2018, https://wapo.st/2k81HMr.

24. Donald J. Trump (@realDonaldTrump), Twitter (July 22, 2017, 3:33 a.m.), https://twitter.com/realDonaldTrump/status/888708453560184832.

25. Donald J. Trump (@realDonaldTrump), Twitter (July 24, 2017, 7:23 p.m.), https://twitter.com/realDonaldTrump/status/889672374458646528.

26. Donald J. Trump (@realDonaldTrump), Twitter (July 24, 2017, 7:28 p.m.), https://twitter.com/realDonaldTrump/status/889673743873843200.

27. Donald J. Trump (@realDonaldTrump), Twitter (July 24, 2017, 7:36 p.m.), https://twitter.com/realDonaldTrump/status/889675644396867584.

28. Donald J. Trump (@realDonaldTrump), Twitter (Dec. 29, 2017, 5:04 a.m.), https://twitter.com/realDonaldTrump/status/946728546633953285.

29. Donald J. Trump (@realDonaldTrump), Twitter (March 31, 2018, 5:45 a.m.), https://twitter.com/realDonaldTrump/status/980063581592047617; Donald J. Trump (@realDonaldTrump), Twitter (March 31, 2018, 5:52 a.m.), https://twitter.com/realDonaldTrump/status/980065419632566272.

30. Donald J. Trump (@realDonaldTrump), Twitter (April 3, 6:55 a.m.), https://twitter.com/realDonaldTrump/status/981168344924536832.

31. Paletta and Dawsey, "Trump personally pushed postmaster general to double rates on Amazon, other firms," *The Washington Post*.

32. *Id*.

33. Donald J. Trump (@realDonaldTrump), Twitter (Oct. 11, 2017, 6:45 a.m.), https://twitter.com/realDonaldTrump/status/918110279367643137.

34. Donald J. Trump (@realDonaldTrump), Twitter Oct. 11, 2017, 6:55 a.m.), https://twitter.com/realDonaldTrump/status/918112884630093825.

35. Donald J. Trump (@realDonaldTrump), Twitter (Oct. 11, 2017, 5:09 p.m.), https://twitter.com/realDonaldTrump/status/918267396493922304.

36. Donald J. Trump (@realDonaldTrump), Twitter (Nov. 29, 2017, 4:16 a.m.), https://twitter.com/realDonaldTrump/status/935844881825763328.

37. Donald J. Trump (@realDonaldTrump), Twitter (Dec. 9, 2017, 5:02 a.m.), https://twitter.com/realDonaldTrump/status/939480342779580416.

38. *Id*.

39. Donald J. Trump (@realDonaldTrump), Twitter (Dec. 9, 2017, 3:14 p.m.), https://twitter.com/realDonaldTrump/status/939634404267380736.

40. CNN, "Sanders: ESPN host's tweet a 'fireable offense,'" Sept. 13, 2017, https://cnn.it/2jOl8tf.

41. Donald J. Trump (@realDonaldTrump), Twitter (March 30, 2017, 7:27 a.m.), https://twitter.com/realDonaldTrump/status/847455180912181249.

42. Jackie Wattles, "Trump's chief of staff: 'We've looked at' changing libel laws," CNN, April 30, 2017, http://cnnmon.ie/2qildKS.

43. Callum Borchers, "White House blocks CNN, *New York Times* from press briefing hours after Trump slams media," *The Washington Post*, Feb. 24, 2017, http://wapo.st/2lE6R2t.

44. Julie Hirschfeld Davis, "Trump Bars U.S. Press, but Not Russia's, at Meeting With Russian Officials," May 10, 2017, https://nyti.ms/2pz45Ms.

45. Matt Apuzzo et al., "Trump Told Russians That Firing 'Nut Job' Comey Eased Pressure From Investigation," *The New York Times*, May 19, 2017, http://nyti.ms/2sY5b6n.

46. Brian Stelter, "With cameras banned, CNN sends sketch artist to White House briefing," CNN, June 24, 2017, http://cnnmon.ie/2sog8sd.

47. Michael M. Grynbaum, "The Network Against the Leader of the Free World," *The New York Times*, July 5, 2017, https://nyti.ms/2uMeLtY.

48. Zoe Tillman, "The Justice Department Deleted Language About Press Freedom And Racial Gerrymandering From Its Internal Manual," Buzzfeed, April 29, 2018, https://bzfd.it/2jm2QQ8.

49. Reporters Comm. for the Freedom of the Press, *Press Freedoms in the United States 2017* (March 2018), http://bit.ly/RCFP2017.

50. *Id.* p. 13.

51. Paul Farhi, "Press advocates see Trump's words behind physical attacks on journalists," *The Washington Post*, May 25, 2017, http://wapo.st/2qoJDy4.

52. Donald J. Trump (@realDonaldTrump), Twitter (July 2, 2017, 6:21 a.m.), https://twitter.com/realDonaldTrump/status/881503147168071680.

53. Joel Simon and Alexandra Ellerbeck, "With press freedom under attack worldwide, US is setting wrong example," Comm. to Protect Journalists, May 2, 2017, https://cpj.org/x/6c96.

54. Ahmed Abu Zeid, Spokesman, Ministry of Foreign Affairs, Egypt (@MfaEgypt), Twitter (Nov. 26, 2017, 1:34 p.m.), https://twitter.com/MfaEgypt/status/934898253006626819.

55. Patrick Wintour, "'Fake news': Libya seizes on Trump tweet to discredit CNN slavery report," *The Guardian*, Nov. 28, 2017, https://www.theguardian.com/world/2017/nov/28/libya-slave-trade-cnn-report-trump-fake-news; see also Michael M. Grynbaum, "Trump and Russia Seem to Find Common Foe: The American Press," *The New York Times*, Nov. 27, 2017, https://nyti.ms/2ibLUi2.

56. U.S. Const. amend. I.

57. 403 U.S. 713, 717 (1971).

58. Pres. John F. Kennedy, *The President and the Press*, April 27, 1961, http://www.presidency.ucsb.edu/ws/?pid=8093.

59. Pres. George W. Bush, *President's Statement on World Press Freedom Day*, May 3, 2007, http://bit.ly/2JfccMF.

60. *Id.*

61. Donald J. Trump (@realDonaldTrump), Twitter (May 9, 2018, 4:38 a.m.), https://twitter.com/realDonaldTrump/status/994179864436596736.

62. *Bantam Books, Inc. v. Sullivan*, 372 U.S. 58, 67 (1963). The discussion in this section draws heavily from Frank D. Lomonte and Linda Riedemann Norbut, "'Failing New York Times' v. Trump: Is There a First Amendment Claim for Official Condemnation by Tweet?," 33 Comms. Law. 1 (Winter 2018), http://bit.ly/W2018CL.

63. *Okwedy v. Molinari*, 333 F.3d 339, 344 (2d Cir. 2003) (per curiam).

64. *Id.*, p. 344; Lomonte and Norbut, *supra* note 62 in this chapter, pp. 22 to 23.

65. Lomonte and Norbut, *supra* note 62 in this chapter, p. 25.

66. *Id.*

67. House Judiciary Committee, *Constitutional Grounds for Presidential Impeachment*, pp. 21–25 (93d Cong., Feb. 1974), http://bit.ly/CGPI1974, p. 20.

68. *Backpage.com, LLC v. Dart*, 807 F.3d 229, 231 (7th Cir. 2015).

CHAPTER 9

1. See Callum Borchers and Kevin Uhrmacher, "How the Trump team's Stormy Daniels story shifted again and again," *The Washington Post*, May 4, 2018, https://wapo.st/2x2g5im; Michael Rothfeld and Joe Palazzolo, "Trump Lawyer Arranged $130,000 Payment for Adult-Film Star's Silence," *Wall Street Journal*, Jan. 12, 2018, https://on.wsj.com/2ICOZ2K.

2. Louis Nelson, "Giuliani: What if Daniels allegations came out during 2016 election?," *Politico*, May 3, 2018, https://politi.co/2GgsLl4.

3. See Borchers and Uhrmacher, "How the Trump team's Stormy Daniels story shifted again and again," *The Washington Post*. Ms. Clifford has also alleged that she was physically threatened, apparently by Trump associates, to stay silent about the affair. See "Stormy Daniels Describes Her Alleged Affair with Donald Trump," CBS News, March 28, 2018, https://cbsn.ws/2x2ogbJ. Her attorney has suggested that at least some of the threats were issued after Trump took office. Depending on the facts, this might constitute extortion. And even if Trump did not specifically use federal personnel, any explicit or implicit threat from the president or his business associates carries that implication.

4. 52 U.S.C. §§ 30101(8)(A)(i) (defining "contribution"), (9)(A)(i) (defining "expenditure"). For a thoughtful analysis of some of the legal issues, see Thomas Frampton, "The Coming Storm? Hush Money and the Federal Election Campaign Act," Harv. L. Rev. Blog, Jan. 29, 2018, http://bit.ly/2Ik1AaR.

5. See 52 U.S.C. §§ 30101(8)(A) (defining "contribution"), 30101(9)(A) (defining "expenditure"), 30104(b) (requiring reporting), 30116(a)(1)(A) (limiting contributions).

6. John Wagner, "Trump acknowledges his lawyer was reimbursed after payment to Stormy Daniels," *The Washington Post*, May 3, 2018, https://wapo.st/2KxaH9V.

7. Robert Costa, "Transcript: Giuliani interview with *The Washington Post*," *The Washington Post*, May 3, 2018, https://wapo.st/2HMAHQQ.

8. See U.S. Office of Gov't Ethics, OGE Form 278e, May 15, 2018, https://oge.box.com/v/Trump2018Annual278.

9. See 5 U.S.C. app. §§ 101, 102, 104; 18 U.S.C. § 1001.

10. Letter from David J. Apol, Acting Dir., Office of Gov't Ethics, to Rod J. Rosenstein, Deputy Atty. Gen., Department of Justice (May 16, 2018), https://oge.box.com/v/OGELettertoDOJ.

11. *Id.*

12. Walter Shaub (@waltshaub), Twitter (May 16, 2018, 10:40 AM), https://twitter.com/waltshaub/status/996807561402863616.

13. See, for example, Rosalind S. Helderman et al., "Cohen's $600,000 deal with AT&T specified he would advise on Time Warner merger, internal company records show," *The Washington Post*, May 10, 2018, https://wapo.st/2KQpA7f.

14. Josh Boswell and Ryan Parry, "Michael Cohen asked for 'millions of dollars' to 'pass to Trumps,'" *Daily Mail*, May 15, 2018, https://dailym.ai/2Gk94J6.

15. 18 U.S.C. § 201(b). This statute also prohibits a "gratuity," which is similar but slightly different from a bribe. *Id.* § 201(c). For a discussion of the differences, see U.S. Department of Justice, U.S. Attorneys' Manual, Crim. Res. Manual § 2043, https://www.justice.gov/usam/criminal-resource-manual-2043-comparison-elements-crimes-bribery-and-gratuities.

16. 18 U.S.C. § 1951.

17. 18 U.S.C. § 371.

18. Andrew E. Kramer, "Ukraine, Seeking U.S. Missiles, Halted Cooperation With Mueller Investigation," *The New York Times*, May 2, 2018, https://nyti.ms/2KwaP9p.

19. Jonathan Chait, "Did Trump Bribe Ukraine to Stop Cooperating With Mueller?," *N.Y. Mag.*, May 2, 2018, https://nym.ag/2GsJjGE.

CHAPTER 10

1. See Acting Attorney General Rod J. Rosenstein, Appointment of Special Counsel to Investigate Russian Interference with the 2016 Presidential Election and Related Matters, U.S. Department of Justice Order No. 3915-2017, May 17, 2017, https://www.justice.gov/opa/press-release/file/967231/download; 28 C.F.R. § 600.4(a).

2. Laurence H. Tribe, "Why Impeachment Must Remain A Priority," Take Care, May 23, 2017, http://takecareblog.com/blog/why-impeachment-must-remain-a-priority. In past impeachments, Congress has not required any culpable state of mind. For example, in the impeachment trial of Judge West H. Humphries, a federal judge who joined the Confederacy during the Civil War and helped make war against the United States, the question of his motive or intent was neither raised in the articles of impeachment nor discussed at the Senate trial. See Radnofsky, *A Citizen's Guide to Impeachment*, p. 44.

3. For example, Professor Laurence Tribe and Joshua Matz suggest that a major reason that Congress did not pursue impeachment against President Reagan for the Iran-Contra Affair was that, once the affair was exposed, Reagan "cooperated with investigators . . . and signaled openness to enhanced oversight of covert actions." Tribe and Matz, *To End a Presidency*, p. 74. Trump, by contrast, openly and unrepentantly flaunts his brazen defiance of the limits of the law and the Constitution.

4. See James Madison, *September 8, 1787*, in *The Avalon Project*.

5. H.R. Res. 705, 115th Cong., available at https://www.congress.gov /bill/115th-congress/house-resolution/705.

6. See Tribe and Matz, *To End a Presidency*, pp. 142–44.

7. See Andrew Kohut, "How the Watergate crisis eroded public support for Richard Nixon," Pew Res. Ctr., Aug. 8, 2014, http://pewrsr.ch /V7nvbQ.

8. See, for example, Public Policy Polling, *Voters Like High School Gun Protesters; Don't Like NRA*, March 27, 2018, http://bit.ly/2IFuJle (46 percent support impeachment); Quinnipiac Poll, *Trump Is Intelligent, But Not Fit Or Level-Headed, U.S. Voters Tell Quinnipiac University National Poll*, Jan. 10, 2018, http://bit.ly/2IDjsSx (45 percent support impeachment); Public Policy Polling, *Voters Think Trump Should Resign Over Harassment Allegations*, Dec. 14, 2017, http://bit.ly/2IHLix2 (51 percent support impeachment; 53 percent believe he should resign).

9. The Declaration of Independence, para. 30 (U.S. 1776).

AFTERWORD

1. Letters, "Using Impeachment Fears to Energize the G.O.P.," *The New York Times*, April 11, 2018, https://nyti.ms/2HsUG3B.

ACKNOWLEDGMENTS

This book grew out of a shorter white paper on the legal grounds for impeachment hearings that was presented at the National Press Club on December 6, 2017, for which we are grateful to Professor Catherine J. Ross of George Washington University Law School, Professor Jennifer Taub of Vermont Law School, and Professor Steven Shiffrin of Cornell Law School, all of whom provided valuable insights into the legal grounds for impeachment. For review of this book, we are further grateful to Professor Ross, Professor Taub, Montana Supreme Court Justice (ret.) James C. Nelson, and Barbara Ann Radnofsky for their insights; and to Tom Bacon, Jonah Fein, Robert Joynt, Joanna Kamhi, Daniel Kane, and Aspen Webster for assistance with research and the manuscript. Our thanks as well to Steve Cobble, who first proposed to us that we expand our white paper into a book, and to John Nichols, for his powerful foreword and his key support. Finally, thank you to our publishers at Melville House for collaborating with us in making this book a reality.

ABOUT THE AUTHORS

Ron Fein, legal director of Free Speech For People, is a constitutional lawyer who previously served as assistant regional counsel in the U.S. Environmental Protection Agency, where he received the National Gold Medal for Exceptional Service. He appears regularly on television and in the op-ed pages of *The Washington Post*, commenting on constitutional matters.

John Bonifaz is the co-founder and president of Free Speech For People. He previously served as the executive director and general counsel of the National Voting Rights Institute, and as the legal director of Voter Action, a national election integrity organization. A distinguished attorney, he has been at the forefront of key voting rights battles across the country for more than two decades, and is a winner of a MacArthur Foundation Fellowship Award.

Ben Clements is the chair of the Board of Directors of Free Speech For People and chair of its legal committee. He is also a founding partner of the Boston law firm Clements & Pineault, LLP. His clients have included the state and federal governments, candidates for state and federal office, senior public officials, large corporations, and small businesses. He is a former federal prosecutor and former chief legal counsel to Massachusetts Governor Deval Patrick.

ABOUT THE FOREWORD AUTHOR

John Nichols is the national affairs correspondent for *The Nation* and associate editor of *The Capital Times*, the daily newspaper in Madison, Wisconsin, as well as a contributing writer for *The Progressive* and *In These Times*. He is the author or co-author of numerous books, including *The Genius of Impeachment* and *The Death and Life of American Journalism*, and is a regular television commentator on political matters.